Contemporary Britain

Contemporary Britain: A Survey with Texts is a wide-ranging collection of primary sources on the concerns of people living in Britain today. Covering many important aspects of British life, from national image and identity to social behaviour and 'moral panics', *Contemporary Britain* provides an accurate picture of life in the United Kingdom at the beginning of the 21st century. It offers sources and commentary on:

- Britain's role in world affairs
- British national identity
- constitutional reform within Britain
- social institutions, including the NHS
- political parties
- morality and religion

Accessible and invaluable, *Contemporary Britain: A Survey with Texts* is an essential companion to anyone studying current British civilization.

John Oakland is Senior Lecturer in English at the Norwegian University of Science and Technology. He is author of *A Dictionary of British Institutions: A Student's Guide* (Routledge, 1993), *British Civilization* (Routledge, 4th edition, 1998) and *American Civilization* (Routledge, 2nd edition, 1997) with David Mauk.

Contemporary Britain

A survey with texts

John Oakland

London and New York

First published 2001
by Routledge
11 New Fetter Lane, London EC4P 4EE

Simultaneously published in the USA and Canada
by Routledge
29 West 35th Street, New York, NY 10001

Routledge is an imprint of the Taylor & Francis Group

© 2001 John Oakland for selection and editorial content;
individual articles to their authors

Designed and typeset in Sabon and Helvetica
by Florence Production Ltd, Stoodleigh, Devon
Printed and bound in Great Britain by
TJ International Ltd, Padstow, Cornwall

British Library Cataloguing in Publication Data
A catalogue record for this book is available from the British Library

Library of Congress Cataloging in Publication Data
   Contemporary Britain: a survey with texts / edited by John Oakland.
      p. cm.
      Includes bibliographical references and index.
      1. Great Britain—History—Elizabeth II, 1952- 2. Great Britain—History—
   Elizabeth II, 1952—Sources. I. Oakland, John.
   DA592 .C614 2001
   941.085—dc21   00–045732

ISBN 0–415–15037-X (hbk)
ISBN 0–415–15038–8 (pbk)

Contents

Preface

This book contains texts and commentaries that illustrate central debates about the contemporary nature and possible future direction of British society. They cover political and constitutional structures, national images and identities, the economy, international perspectives and domestic social conditions. They often reveal strongly opposed opinions on these matters and many address policies stemming from the election of a Labour government in May 1997.

The book is intended mainly for overseas students of English who are following British Studies or Civilization courses, although students in other subject areas may find it useful. It can be used in conjunction with textbooks that give more factual and historical information on Britain. But the book can also be read in its own right, since sufficient interlocking commentaries and notes are provided in which to place the texts. Essay topics, questions on terminology and suggestions for further reading are included at the end of each chapter and are intended to serve as a study context.

The selected texts are *about* Britain and are written by commentators concerned with various aspects of British life. But they have to be 'unpacked' and evaluated (particularly in terms of tone and argument), ideally in the form of group discussion exercises. In this process, it is hoped that students will not only develop a critical understanding of the texts in themselves, but also of what British (and other) people think about the country. Students should appreciate the variety of opinions offered in these pages (both text and commentary) and be suspicious of simple answers to complex questions. They should be aware that Britain is a diverse society with many, often conflicting, parts, institutions and values. Change can occur rapidly as well as slowly. But the arguments and perspectives in the chapters address issues that are problematic and still in flux.

A book of this type is necessarily indebted to a wide range of sources for its facts, ideas and statistics, to which acknowledgement is gratefully made (see further reading and chapter notes). Particular thanks go to *Britain: An Official Handbook* (the current edition of which contains the latest information); *British Social Attitudes*; Market and Opinion Research International (MORI); regular surveys by *The Times* and *The Sunday Times*; and Mintel, Gallup, NOP and ICM opinion polls.

Acknowledgements

Acknowledgement is made for permission to use the following material within the book:

The Rt. Hon. Paddy Ashdown MP for his article of 30 January 1994 (author copyright); the Rt. Hon. Tony Blair MP for 'Britain is on a roll, whatever popstars say' 29 March 1998, 'Why Britain needs a new welfare state' 15 January 1998, 'Why schools must do better' 7 July 1997 and 'Teenage mums are all our business' 8 September 1998 (author copyright); The Rt. Hon. David Blunkett MP for 'Time's up for schools that fail' 20 May 1997 (author copyright); Lord Melvyn Bragg for 'The bit of politics that led Ben Elton astray' 20 April 1998 (author copyright); The Centre for Policy Studies, London, for permission to reproduce the article by David Selbourne 'Our moral wasteland' 30 December 1998; by kind permission of the *Daily Mail*, 'This insidious urge to reshape Britain' 23 June 1998, 'Weakening the ties of a United Kingdom' 2 July 1999, 'Blair is driving us out of the NHS' 6 July 1999; The Rt. Hon. David Davis MP for 'Blair's brave new Britain is a catastrophe' 5 August 1999 (author copyright); © *The Economist*, London 'An Italian in London' 8 January 1994, 'The strangest Tory ever sold' 2 May 1998, 'Ideology: beyond left and right' 2 May 1998, 'Reclaiming Britain's constitution' 14 October 1995, 'Democracy's second age' 14 September 1996, 'A federal Britain' 27 March 1999, 'Why Britain needs a Bill of Rights' 21 October 1995, 'The army: over-stretched and over there' 17 July 1999, 'Darling's anniversary' 31 July 1999, 'Labour's crusade' 25 September 1999, ' The Health Service at 50' 4 July 1998, 'Education, education, education' 10 April 1999; Larry Elliott for 'The wrong continent' 12 July 1998 (author copyright); the Rt. Hon. William Hague MP for 'Europe? Oh, don't mention it, Mr Blair' 9 June 1999 (author copyright); reproduced by permission of Hodder and Stoughton Limited, an extract from *The Essential Anatomy of Britain: Democracy in Crisis* by Anthony Sampson (1992) pp. ix-xi; Lord Howe of Aberavon, CH, QC for 'This House is built on solid ground' 2 August 1999 (author copyright); *The Independent* for permission to reproduce 'Do we need Europe?' by John Lichfield 20 May 1996; Lord Irvine of Lairg for 'Devolution is not a revolution' 10 February 1996 (author copyright); Simon Jenkins for 'Party of freedom has shackled us all to the state' 8 October 1998 (author copyright); The Rt. Hon. Charles Kennedy MP for 'A sickness at the heart of our nation' 11 August 1999 (author copyright); John Lloyd for 'Nudging between Row and Kowtow' 24 April 1998 (author copyright); *The London Review of Books* and Ross McKibbin for permission to reproduce 'Third Way, Old Hat' from *The London Review of* Books, volume 20, number 17, 3 September 1998; Lord Mackay of Clashfern for 'A house devolved against itself' 7 February 1996 (author copyright); Macmillan Press Ltd for permission to reproduce the extract from *Britain in Decline* by Andrew Gamble (1994) pp. xiii-xxi; News International (*The Times, The Sunday Times* and *The Sun*) for permission to reproduce 'Large bottoms rule, okay?' by Robert Harris in *The Sunday Times* 3 March 1996 © Times Newspapers Limited, 1996, 'Cool it' by Philip Norman in *The Sunday Times* 5 April 1998 © Times Newspapers Limited, 1998, 'Going soft? Britain is still a nation of hard-headed people' by David Smith in *The Sunday Times* 19 April 1998 © Times Newspapers Limited, 1998, 'British unity in diversity' by Mary Ann Sieghart in *The Times* 22 April 1995 © Times Newspapers Limited, 1995, 'Disunited we stand' by Brian Deer in *The Sunday Times* 5 February 1995 © Times Newspapers Limited, 1995, 'Hooked on hatred of the English' by Fergus Kelly in *The Sunday Times* 3 March 1996 © Times Newspapers Limited, 1996, 'Scotland rouses the beast of English nationalism' by Andrew Neil in *The Sunday Times* 28 April 1996 © Times Newspapers Limited, 1996, 'Confident Celts put England in shade' by Mark Henderson in *The Times* 1 February 1999 © Times Newspapers Limited, 1999, 'Mods and Rockers' in *The Times* 6 July 1998 © Times Newspapers Limited, 1998, 'Hague pledges to remake Tories' by Philip Webster in *The Times* 20 January 1999 © Times Newspapers Limited, 1999, 'Turn left for No. 10' by Simon Jenkins in *The Times* 27 January 1999 © Simon Jenkins/Times Newspapers Limited, 1999, 'Kennedy's dilemma' in *The Times* 10 August 1999 © Times Newspapers Limited, 1999, 'Need to know' in *The Times* 25 May 1999, 'A dysfunctional family?' by Magnus Linklater in *The Times* 23 October 1997 © Magnus Linklater/Times Newspapers Limited, 1997, 'An unhealthy state' in *The Sunday Times* 11 July 1999 © Times Newspapers Limited, 1999, 'Higher education - a fraud or worth every penny?' by John O'Leary in *The Times* 20 August 1999 © Times Newspapers Limited, 1999, 'Drug-taking Britain is "worst in Europe"' by Victoria Fletcher and Ian Brodie in *The Times* 12 January 1999 © Times Newspapers Limited, 1999, 'Bolt-down Britain' by Tim Rayment in *The Sunday Times* 7 January 1996 © Times Newspapers Limited, 1996, 'Pupils taught marriage is "just one option" for family life' by Judith O'Reilly in *The Sunday Times* 10 January 1999 © Times Newspapers Limited, 1999, 'O go all ye faithful' by Rebecca Fowler in *The Sunday Times* 5 December 1993 © Times Newspapers Limited, 1993, 'All God's children' by Rebecca Fowler in *The Sunday Times* 7 November 1993 © Times Newspapers Limited, 1993, 'Is Britain really a nation of racists?' by Stephen Bevan and Nicholas Rufford in *The Sunday Times* 28 February 1999 © Times Newspapers Limited,1999; © *New Statesman*, 1998, 'The making of cruel Britannia' by John Lloyd 26 June 1998; *Newsweek*, 6 July 1998, © 1998 Newsweek, Inc. 'Rebranding rationale', 'Nothing cool about being coarse' and 'A tale of two nations' all rights reserved. Reprinted by permission; The New York Times Syndicate for permission to reproduce '"Cool Britannia" looks more like Fool Britannia' from *The International Herald Tribune* 15 April 1998; Matthew Parris for 'Mongrels not Angles' 21 November 1998 (author copyright); The Rt. Hon. the Lord Patten PC for his article of 30 January 1994 (author copyright); Melanie Phillips for 'We should shut down the race industry' 20 December 1998 (author copyright); Lord Rees-Mogg for permission to reproduce 'NATO is still our sword and shield' 2 February 1998 (author copyright); The Rt. Hon. The Lord Richard PC QC for 'The secret enemies of democracy' 18 August 1999 (author copyright); Routledge Limited for permission to reproduce extracts from *Understanding Post-War British Society* by James Obelkevich and Peter Catterall (1994) pp. 1-8; The Rt. Hon. Jack Straw MP for 'True peers are made not born' 25 April 1996 (author copyright); *The Sun* for reader comment 'A big con' 28 March 1998; Peter Taylor for permission to reproduce 'Unpeeling the Orange' from *The Daily Mail* 2 July 1999.

Contemporary Britain: the context

The texts in this chapter were written in the 1990s and place British society in the context of recent history. They are grouped under headings that indicate significant debates, developments and attitudes in British life over the late twentieth century (Decline, The Establishment, Centralization and democracy, and Models of British society).

Public opinion polls sometimes portray Britain as a society full of alleged weaknesses and worrying concerns. Politicians and commentators also often seem interested in presenting the country as a 'problem' (or a series of 'problems') and suggesting their own 'remedies', usually under the guise of 'modernization'. But Britain is a generally equable society and most of its people seem to operate on established personal and social norms, conscious of both tradition and change. It is not a static country (in spite of the 'conservative' and 'quaint' images often attributed to it) and is subject to periods of transition, which inevitably involve a tension between past and present.

However, since at least the 1960s, many critics have focused on 'the state of Britain' and have portrayed a country in decline on moral, social, political and economic grounds. In their view, the society continues to be unsure about itself and its identity, both nationally and internationally.

Some observers have maintained that Britain needs fundamental structural reforms and attitudinal change in virtually every area of national life in order to remedy decline and embrace 'modernization'. Other commentators have argued that evolutionary or gradualist change on pragmatic lines is required, which, as they see it, would be characteristic of British historical development. Nevertheless, on both sides, questions are asked about Britain's future direction, its institutions, its place in Europe and the world and its status as a United Kingdom.

The debates have often focused on macro or large-scale issues such as the weaknesses of the economic system, political and constitutional inadequacies, imperial decline, the alleged non-competitive nature of British society and the performance (or lack of it) of national institutions. Some texts in this chapter illustrate the economic arguments for decline and some stress cultural, institutional and democratic weaknesses. But others describe the vitality and variety of entrepreneurial activity and individual behaviour in British life, which are often expressed outside strict organizational or institutional restraints.

In terms of ordinary Britons' reactions to their society, certain issues, such as health, education and crime, continue to be of great concern and there is frequently a gap between what politicians propose and what the mass of the people find important or acceptable. In January 2000, the public opinion poll organization MORI[1] reported those issues that the British public considered to be most important for them:

Healthcare	(71 per cent)
Education	(55)
Law and order	(49)
Unemployment	(36)
Pensions	(31)
Taxation	(30)
Managing the economy	(28)
Public transport	(26)

Europe	(24)
Environment	(21)
Housing	(18)
Defence	(13)
Animal welfare	(9)
Northern Ireland	(8)
Constitution/devolution	(7)
Trade unions	(4)

Respondents regarded the responses of political parties to the first five items as significant in helping them to decide which party they might support at the next general election (possibly in May 2001). These issues emphasize the everyday importance of public services, jobs and financial security for many people. But the public did not rank so highly those areas that the Labour government and commentators also considered to be central to British life, such as the trade unions, defence, Northern Ireland and the constitution/**devolution**.

The MORI poll was echoed in some respects (but differed in others) by a February 2000 Mintel opinion poll[2] dealing with British lifestyles. Matters like owning one's own house (64 per cent), having a car (53), life insurance (40) and a personal pension (40) were important parts of individuals' lives, as were consumer and leisure activities. These emphases suggest a return to material preoccupations and spending rather than an emphasis on saving after the difficult economic climate of the early 1990s. But other concerns, such as the National Health Service (37), keeping in close touch with one's family (35) and state education (14), were also important.

The British public still depends upon and expects state spending on what it considers to be essential social or public services, in spite of recent emphases by both Conservative and Labour governments upon more personal responsibility and taking control of one's own life. Polls in 1999 and 2000 suggested that Britons feel that the Labour government has not delivered on its 1997 election promises in these areas. But the above personal lifestyle items indicate that people are also able to operate on individual levels of choice (see text 8) and see the need to prepare for their future requirements, especially at a time when public services are under strain.

As background to the texts, the recent history of Britain can be divided into three periods: one, the continuous rule by Conservative governments from 1979–97 (under the Prime Ministerships of Margaret Thatcher 1979–90 and John Major 1990–97); two, a very severe economic recession (1988–92), which adversely affected the British people and the Conservative government; and, three, the victory of the Labour Party (under the leadership of Tony Blair) over the unpopular Conservatives in the general election of May 1997.

devolution
Devolution is the transfer of some political powers from the central government in Westminster to Assemblies in Wales (1999) and Northern Ireland (2000) and a Parliament in Scotland (1999). It also includes the election of a mayor and Assembly (2000) to run London.

Thatcherism
The government policies associated with the Conservative Prime Minister Margaret Thatcher (1979–90).

Victorian values
A vague term, but usually centred on allegedly traditional values generated by the individual and the family structure: thrift, temperance, good housekeeping, patriotism, duty, hard work, self-reliance, practical Christianity and family values.

back to basics
An attempt to bring about a return to traditional values in education, social work and attitudes to crime; to reinforce traditional values of decency and civic community.

The early Conservative period was characterized by what became known as **Thatcherism**. Although opinions differ about the nature and success of Thatcherism (see text 5), the term was associated with policies such as free-market economics, the attempt to cut taxation and public spending and the encouragement of so-called **Victorian values**. There was an emphasis on entrepreneurial activity, personal responsibility, meritocracy and the creation of an enterprise culture (as opposed to a dependency culture in which people depended on the state to provide their needs). John Major largely continued Thatcherite economic programmes and vainly tried to introduce a '**back-to-basics**' value system. The present Labour government, while still following broadly Conservative economic policies, has since 1997 attempted to 'modernize' Britain and present a creative, dynamic image of the country to the world. This exercise has been widely criticized on grounds of definition and implementation (see Chapter 2).

■ ■ ■

Decline

The relative reduction of Britain's former world role, which arguably continues to influence the national mentality to varying degrees, has to be considered in a historical context. The first text addresses Britain's national and international 'decline' in the twentieth century. It explains this downturn not only on economic grounds and a related loss of world status, but also in terms of political and attitude weakness. It examines Britain's position in the world economic system (globalization) rather than solely its performance as a self-contained nation. It is often argued that globalization and a necessary interdependence inevitably affect every national economy and nation states allegedly must come to terms with this fact of life, although there are nationalist and other reactions to such influences (see text 2 in Chapter 3). The Conservative government had to confront Britain's reduced condition, both domestically and internationally, in 1979.

1 *Britain in Decline*
Andrew Gamble
(London: Macmillan, 4th edition, 1994) abridged

Britain has now been in decline for a hundred years . . . Two processes stand out – the absolute decline in the power and status of the British imperial state, and the relative decline of the British economy with its long-standing failure to match the rates of expansion of its rivals.

The starting point of Britain's decline was the position of unrivalled dominance it had achieved during the nineteenth century. By 1900 Britain controlled over one-fifth of the world's land surface and ruled one-quarter of the world's population. Its land forces remained small but its navy was still maintained at a level where it would be superior to the two next most powerful navies combined. The foundations of this empire had been the commercial and strategic policies pursued by the British state for 250 years. Its consolidation and further extension in the nineteenth century had been the result of the industrial and technological lead Britain established by being the first major economy to industrialize. The height of Britain's industrial domination of the world was reached in the middle decades of the nineteenth century. At that time one-third of the world's output of manufactured goods came from Britain. Britain produced half the world's coal and iron, half the world's cotton goods, almost half its steel. From this position Britain conducted one-quarter of the world's trade and built up a massive commercial and financial predominance. Even in 1900 Britain still accounted for one-third of the world's exports of manufactures, and the registered tonnage of British shipping was more than the tonnage of the rest of the world combined. London was the unchallenged commercial and financial centre of the new capitalist world economy. The international monetary system was centred upon the gold standard and the pound sterling . . .

By the last decade of the twentieth century a very different picture presented itself. The British Empire had disappeared . . . Britain retained some of the trappings of a great power. It still had a **nuclear arsenal**, substantial and well-equipped armed forces, and a permanent seat on the UN Security Council. But it was no longer the kind of global power it had been in the first half of the century, and its proud tradition of sovereign independence was increasingly circumscribed by the new realities and requirements of interdependence. The security and economic relationships forged with the United States and Western Europe after 1945 were indications of how limited British **sovereignty** had become.

The British economy was incomparably richer and more productive in 1990 than in 1900 but it was no longer the world leader or the powerhouse of the world economy. It remained one of the richest economies in the world, but its position and performance relative to other countries in the leading group had substantially weakened. On a range of indicators Britain had slipped behind and despite several determined attempts showed no signs of being able to catch up.

The slope of Britain's descent has not been constant. There have been periods of recovery, even of advance and success, [but] the efforts of [the] governing class have failed to arrest . . . decline . . .

nuclear arsenal
Britain's independent nuclear deterrent mainly based on four new submarines armed with Trident missiles.

sovereignty
The legal and practical ability to operate unilaterally as an independent nation state.

balance of payments
A trade gap or deficit in the balance of payments is created when imports exceed exports.

... the decline in world power and the relative decline in economic perform-ance are inextricably linked. They are part of the same process ...

One of the most persistent aspects of the discourse on decline is the belief in a 'British disease', a malady whose causes lie deep in British psychology and British culture. A popular diagnosis of this 'disease' in the 1960s and 1970s was that the country was living beyond its means. The British consumed too much and worked too little ...

What made such assertions plausible were repeated economic crises – over the **balance of payments**, public expenditure, and pay. The nation it was said was importing more than it exported, the government was spending more than it raised in taxes, and the workers were demanding the distribution of a bigger cake than the one they were producing. The consequences of such behaviour were placing Britain's future prosperity and its traditional freedoms in danger.

The favourite political scapegoat for the British disease used to be the trade unions. Their behaviour was most frequently cited as the reason why Britain's payments would not balance, why public expenditure was out of control ... and why inflation was accelerating ...

When Margaret Thatcher left office in 1990 trade unions had been weakened by a decade of high unemployment and anti-union legislation. The Government claimed the change in the climate of industrial relations as one of their greatest successes. Management had regained the power to manage. But the symptoms of the British disease appeared little affected. The public finances and the balance of payments were once again out of control and heading for record deficits. Inflation was rising sharply and the economy was moving back into recession ...

... Some [writers] have attempted to explain Britain's post-war failure in terms of the cyclical patterns at work in the history of all great empires [eg Rome, Venice, Spain] ... As in other small states which have created empires the qualities and attitudes which assisted Britain to rise and expand were discarded or neglected by the later generations which inherited the imperial position. They developed instead tastes, needs, and activities which were sustainable only so long as Britain retained its economic and military leadership, yet which tended to undermine the basis of that strength. Britain's rise to world power was followed by the development of a pervasive 'anti-enterprise' culture and a social conservatism at all levels, particularly in education and business management, which persistently blocked successful modernisation and adaptation.

[Other critics maintain that the] real source of Britain's decline is traced to the attitudes and the behaviour of political élites.[3] [Such views were cited by]

Thatcherite ministers as evidence that Britain required a radical change in the climate of ideas, a cultural revolution to rebuild a vibrant capitalist economy . . .

[Critics such as] Corelli Barnett[4] argued that the euphoria of victory [in 1945] allowed . . . failings [such as poor management, **overmanning**, **restrictive practices**, low investment and low productivity] to be ignored. Post-war reconstruction was fatally flawed by being directed on the one hand to the building of a universal welfare state, a New Jerusalem . . . and on the other hand to the preservation of Britain's world role. Both New Jerusalem and the world role assumed a strong economy which no longer existed. Their spending programmes were therefore erected on very shaky foundations.

. . . The cultural thesis [of decline] often presents an exaggerated and misleading picture of the British economy and its performance, but [critics of this thesis] are sometimes in danger of asserting the contrary – that there has been no decline at all, and that all the problems dealt with as problems of decline are no more than normal problems of change and adjustment . . .

Understanding British decline . . . requires analysis of the complex interplay between the decline in British power and the decline in British competitiveness. What was different about Britain's Empire compared with the great empires of the past was that it became inextricably linked with a global process of capital accumulation which resulted in the creation of an interdependent world economy and a rate of growth of population and material wealth far surpassing any levels previously achieved in human history.

Britain's expansion may have been launched upon foundations that were similar to those of many previous empires, but it reached its zenith and was consolidated under very different ones. When earlier empires that arose from a self-sufficient agricultural base collapsed, the imperial state was forced back to this base, once decline had reached a certain point. That possibility disappeared for Britain during the nineteenth century. At a certain stage of its development Britain abandoned such foundations, merging its future irrevocably with the wider world economy.

All discussion of British decline must start from Britain's relationship to the world economy that was the means of Britain's rise, which was transformed in the course of that rise, and to which Britain remains tied. What has to be explained is why the most dynamic and expansionist nation in modern European history, the organizer of the largest world empire, the pioneer of industrialization, and the country renowned above all others for continuity of its institutions and the political skill of its ruling class, should have lost out . . . in competition with Germany, France, and Japan. The eclipse of British

overmanning
More workers in the workforce than are necessary to do a job.

restrictive practices
Trade unions using techniques and methods of working that hinder productivity.

shakeout
The closing down or streamlining of businesses, particularly in heavy industry and manufacturing (deindustrialization) as the economy became increasingly composed of the service and information technology sector.

military power by the United States and Russia was widely forecast as early as the 1840s because of the much greater human and physical resources they could command. What was not anticipated was the relative inability of the British *economy* to maintain its dynamism and compete with its rivals.

A central problem for British [commentators] in the twentieth century has been why the British economy proved so weak and why political attempts to overcome this weakness were not successful . . . [A]lthough Britain had clearly lost its economic leadership to the United States by 1914, and had fallen behind other competitors in the 1950s and 1960s the response [to decline] was a very long time in coming.

One explanation is that for most of the period of its decline the British state has proved able to negotiate a gradual descent. At no point did failing power threaten a major rupture in institutional continuity or an irreversible collapse of British prosperity. The decline in the world power of the British state occurred in stages. The continuing expansion of the British economy helped to compensate for that decline and to limit its impact. The British state used its considerable political, ideological, economic and financial resources, which had been accumulated during the period of British dominance of the world economy, to buy time, to stave off challenges and to delay adjustments. When crises shook the world economy, the British state and the British economy were strong enough to ride them out. But this success reduced the will to tackle many internal weaknesses which gradually became more significant as Britain's relative position deteriorated.

During the world economic downturn in the 1970s, the relative weakness of the British economy, tolerated for so long, became increasingly unsupportable, and brought growing political and social tensions. The world recession changed the political climate by threatening to turn relative decline into absolute decline . . .

In the 1970s Britain came to be widely perceived as a weak link among the leading economic powers. The worries about the balance of payments, inflation, and public spending were symptoms of wider anxieties about Britain's economic future, because of the apparently unstoppable tide of imports and the inability of so many sectors of British industry to compete. The extent of the **shakeout** which took place in the 1970s and 1980s prompted many people to ask how much further the contraction could go. What would be the end of it? A Britain with no industry at all? Unemployment and destitution of an unimaginable scale? Exports insufficient even to pay for the imports needed to feed the population . . .?

Many found it difficult to comprehend how a nation that was on the winning side in two world wars could lose the peace and succumb to the commercial challenge of rivals defeated on the battlefield. How could a nation that showed such unity in the Second World War, and was so long renowned for its traditions of civility and **consensus**, appear to be disunited and racked by conflict, envy, and cynicism in the 1960s and 1970s? Why was Britain, unable to achieve an economic miracle in the 1950s, still unable to achieve one in the 1960s when so many faults had been identified and so many remedies proposed, and when, for a time, all parties and all major interests subscribed to growth and a strategy for modernising the British economy?

■ ■ ■

The topic of British decline continues to be a source of conflicting academic debate (see further reading). Gamble's book (above) discusses whether the Thatcher years (1979–90) should be seen as the political response that restructured the economy and stabilized decline, or as merely the latest episode in a continuing downward spiral. It is often argued that economic inadequacies were in fact finally halted by Conservative governments and the adoption of new policies by all political parties. But problems, such as interest rates, inflation, industrial performance and productivity, investment, international crises, manufacturing weakness, unemployment, the balance of payments and boom and bust cycles, have always periodically affected the British economy, irrespective of which government is in power.

While the Conservative government under John Major suffered from a severe recession (1988–92), it recovered and the Labour government in 1997 inherited a relatively strong economy from the Conservatives. Britain today has the world's fourth largest economy (after the USA, Japan and Germany) and its performance (2000) is relatively healthy, with reasonably strong economic growth. But being a large economy does not mean that Britain is one of the leading richest or most competitive nations in **Gross Domestic Product** (GDP) terms.

The Labour government has successfully steered the economy since the 1997 general election and quickly **made the Bank of England independent**. Since then inflation has been under control and interest rates have been relatively low, although they have started to move up again. The government has also kept a tight grip on the public finances (public spending) while increasing indirect (or 'stealth') taxes; the economic expansion begun in 1992 under the Conservatives is now the longest in the post-war period; and employment (jobs) is at a record 27.5m. Unemployment was 1,098,000 in July 2000 (the lowest level since 1980) and the unemployment rate at 3.8 per cent was the lowest since 1975.

However, in 2000, worrying signs of a traditional kind appeared (see text 7 in Chapter 2): manufacturing industry was under pressure; car production was

consensus
Basic agreement among the main political parties after 1945 as to how British society and its economy were to be managed.

Gross Domestic Product
The total amount of money in Britain each year derived from earnings and investments of citizens, services and corporations.

made the Bank of England independent
This means that the Bank, rather than the government, now sets interest rates.

C.P. Snow
English writer and
novelist, 1905–80.

Westminster
The centre of British
political power,
containing Parliament
(the House of Lords
and the House of
Commons) in London.

Whitehall
The centre of the Civil
Service bureaucracy in
London.

William Cobbett
English political and
social writer,
1762–1835.

A.J.P. Taylor
English historian,
1906–90.

Henry Fairlie
British political
commentator, writer
and journalist 1924–89.

threatened (with the closure of plants and the laying off of workers); industrial productivity per worker was lower than in some competitor countries; a high-value pound on the international exchange market was creating problems for businessmen (particularly in the export of manufactured goods); there was a growing disparity between different sectors of the national economy and between rich and poor; earnings pressure in some fields (such as the financial sector) and consumer demand were increasing; the housing market was booming (now stabilized), particularly in the south-east of England; and there was a threat of higher interest rates to curb a possible rise in inflation. Economists argued that these features were signs of inherent instability in the British national economy.

■ ■ ■

The Establishment

Britain's relative decline and alleged lack of 'modernization' have often been attributed to 'the Establishment'. This is a vague and variously defined concept. It is often taken to be a ruling élite (or series of élites) in British society whose interlocking membership has traditionally centred on institutions such as the monarchy, the Church of England, the legal system, Parliament, the Civil Service (Whitehall), the older professions, the ancient universities and independent (private) schools. The next text argues that the Establishment and its influential power-centres negatively control policies in national life and are resistant to modernization.

2 *'Large bottoms rule, okay?'*
Robert Harris
(*The Sunday Times*, 3 March 1996) abridged

The great Cambridge mathematician G.H. Hardy nursed a passionate and life-long hatred for what he called 'the large-bottomed'. By 'large-bottomed' he meant, according to his friend, **C.P. Snow**, 'the confident, booming, imperialist, bourgeois English': the judges and the bishops, the rulers of **Westminster** and **Whitehall** – the group which **William Cobbett**, a century earlier, had denounced as 'The Thing', which **A.J.P. Taylor** and **Henry Fairlie** christened in the 1950s 'the Establishment'.

Hardy has been dead for nearly 50 years, but the large-bottomed, like the poor, are always with us. Occasionally we are told that Britain has a 'new

Establishment' centred on business, or advertising, or even, God preserve us, the media [see text 8 in Chapter 2]. Do not believe it. The same old gang [eg monarchy, Whitehall and Westminster] is still in place, making sure nothing much changes in this country . . . This is the way it is in Britain. The large-bottomed inquire into the large-bottomed, and the only thing you can be sure of is that when the process finishes, everyone's bottom will remain firmly in contact with a well-upholstered official seat.

In *The Sleep of Reason*, C.P. Snow wrote of 'the ten thousand people' who run this country, and who will always go on running it, whichever party is in power. I would guess that 10,000 is an overestimate, and that the true number is only half that. But whatever the size of the British Establishment, the lesson is . . . you cannot beat it.

Nothing will really alter in Britain as long as our rulers – our real rulers, rather than our apparent ones – are drawn from the same narrow gene pool . . . As long as it remains unchanged, everything remains unchanged, and nothing short of a revolution will shift it . . .

■   ■   ■

The deficiencies of British life have often been related to the mentality and behaviour of Establishment institutions. In the early 1990s, as Britain was emerging slowly from economic recession, a number of commentators (such as Martin Jacques) criticized 'the Establishment'; argued that the British people had increasingly lost confidence in the country's leadership; and maintained that Britain's institutions did not reflect the changing requirements of both Britain and the modern world.[5]

But Jacques also argued that the influence and authority of the old Establishment were in fact being eroded as British society changed radically and popular culture expanded. In this view, the old-style social frameworks of hierarchy and deference, which tended to preserve and characterize the Establishment, were being replaced as society itself became more diverse, pluralistic, fragmented and individualized. People were becoming more independent, self-possessed, inquiring and irreverent, and less tied to class structures, political party or gender. The values of this new Britain, particularly on economic and business levels, were said to be dynamic, meritocratic, entrepreneurial and forward-looking.

Jacques maintained that while much economic modernization reflected these values, any such change must also be accompanied by cultural and institutional modernization. The wider society had to embrace similarly new and 'modern' ideas of diversity, pluralism, efficiency and vision. While the old Establishment institutions allegedly did not possess these virtues, Jacques believed that the modernistic trends in British culture would continue to expand and that institutions must respond to such movements.

Yet at the same time as these developments were arguably taking place, it was felt, and continues to be strongly felt in some quarters, that there was still a desire by many Britons and their institutions to live in the past and to see Britain nostalgically in terms of traditional images rather than coming to grips with the present. The continuity and relative stability of British history over the centuries has allegedly made it difficult to face radical change. But the increasing criticism of old Establishment institutions suggested that historical tradition and images were becoming less significant for British people. Indeed, it is often argued, rightly or wrongly, that Britons (particularly the young) are now profoundly unhistorical or ahistorical.

It is sometimes felt that the views of cultural critics might have influenced the modernising ideas and vocabulary gradually adopted by the Labour Party and government in the late 1980s and the 1990s. Yet it is debatable, or at least arguable, whether such modernistic developments are in fact widespread in Britain on either economic or cultural levels (see texts in Chapter 2). It is also legitimate to consider whether the old Establishment has reinvented itself (mutated) under the pressure of events or whether it has indeed been replaced by new power-centres, which have many of the old Establishment's interlocking characteristics (see texts 5, 6 and 7). The next two texts are opposed responses to the criticism that 'the Establishment' and British institutions do not reflect the modern world or people's aspirations. They focus on political, historical and social perspectives.

3 *John Patten*
(former Conservative Secretary of State for Education)
(Author copyright, 30 January 1994) abridged

[Some critics, such as Martin Jacques, argue that Britain is] backward looking and nostalgic ... What I cannot stomach is the fundamental mistake in [their] interpretation of British history. [They] portray an old Britain with its certainties and a new Britain with a mass of uncertainties. So the culture of old Britain has given way, [they] argue, to doubt and a collapse of the 'Establishment'.

This view is false, even if it is fashionable. The history of these islands is one of continuity and change. Many features of contemporary British culture can be traced back hundreds of years, and the centrality of our parliamentary state to the 13th century. When the country has faced economic, social and political challenges, there have always been incremental reforms and various adjustments to structures and our way of life. That is pretty well illustrated from the **Reform Acts** to the **enfranchisement of women**; from the creation of the **welfare state** to membership of the **European Union**. The British instinct is to respond in a pragmatic way to particular challenges. That is consistent with our political culture.

Yes, there has been significant change. Yes, there will continue to be change. We have had to come to terms with the loss of an empire. We have had to think through the consequences of European Union and are still doing so. We are progressively more meritocratic than before.

Yet the remarkable thing is that there has been no fundamental collapse of our political culture. Our institutions have adapted to the needs of the time. Nor do we have closed institutions. We have open élites, with multiple routes to the top . . .

The '**Establishment**', always hard to define, mutates and adapts to new shapes and new players. Rather than the 'Establishment', [critics] should have in [their] sights our failure to have a true education culture post-1945 and the debilitating effects of mindless egalitarianism . . .

Critics . . . adopt a constricted time frame. They view the period from 1945 to 1970 as representing the settled 'norm' of the British constitution and our political culture. The reality is probably that those post-war decades were the exceptions not the rule . . .

4 *Paddy Ashdown*
(former leader of the Liberal Democrats)
(Author copyright, 30 January 1994) abridged

[Critics and Martin Jacques] . . . paint a picture of a [British] political system that is failing. [They are] right.

Britain since the war has been transformed from a society of hierarchy, deference and conformity to a multi-layered, multi-dimensional society that is less

Reform Acts
Acts of Parliament in the nineteenth century to increase the number of people (mainly male) granted the right to vote in elections.

enfranchisement of women
The gradual granting of the vote to women, finally achieved for all adult women in 1928.

welfare state
Essentially created by the Labour government from 1945, although the earlier Liberal government had already implemented many welfare reforms.

European Union
Britain joined the then European Economic Community (EEC) in 1973.

The Establishment
Some critics argue that the 'Blair project' of modernization, a progressive political centre and attempted consensus amounts to yet another form of the Establishment.

effective governance
Tony Blair admits that
his politics is an
attempt to dispense
with the traditional
confrontation of left and
right (see text 2 in
Chapter 5).

press
Newspapers and the
print media.

estates
Mainly public housing
estates, provided by
local councils. But can
include private housing
estates.

rule-bound and more heterogeneous. The 'set menu' society, defined by class and confined by social geography, has given way to an '*à la carte*' society of individualism, diversity and choice. Yet politics has not responded to these changes.

As society becomes more fluid, the collective identity on which the party system itself is predicated is rapidly disappearing. As society becomes more diverse, the left-right, two-party confrontational Westminster game seems evermore of an anachronistic hindrance to **effective governance**. This dangerous dislocation is almost everywhere in evidence.

The forces that shape our lives have become increasingly international, and choices have become increasingly individual. Yet in politics both trends have been ignored and power is concentrated at the level of the central nation-state.

Successful individuals and institutions are innovative, adventurous, flexible, experimental, professional, open and accountable. Yet politics (and especially the House of Commons) has become a conspiracy to resist any change in its own structure . . . Meanwhile, as deference has declined, a more independent public and **press** has become less docile in the face of economic and political failure.

National self-confidence has withered with the experience of relative economic decline and reduced international influence. Disrespect for the whole political class has grown as politicians have found it increasingly hard to deliver in office. Disillusionment with our politics has been fuelled by the failure of politicians to reinvigorate Britain's political system with the reform needed to make it more responsible to late-20th-century society.

Where politicians are succeeding today – and not only in Britain – they are doing so, especially at the local level, by empowering people to use their talents to the full.

Given the right environment and opportunities, most people would now rather do things for themselves than have them done for them. People run **estates**, set up businesses and generate wealth on their own initiative. They will organise crime-fighting initiatives, tackle pollution in their local environment . . . There is enormous energy lying untapped in our communities – the energy of Britain's greatest renewable resource, its people.

For the forward-looking politicians the task now is to map out the frontiers being discovered by individuals and communities as they seek to tackle the problems they face in their communities, and actively to support their efforts to help themselves. The task is to establish a new democratic settlement between

politics and people by dispersing power, **devolving** decision-making and responsibility, improving the quality of representation, enhancing influence over
taxation and spending, and increasing involvement in decision-making through
instruments of direct democracy. The task is to transform our political
institutions into open, enabling institutions that give people and communities
the power to change things themselves. The task is to use the power of government actively to support initiatives owned by the people, rooted in the community, and based on partnership and participation.

[The British] crisis of politics can be tackled. We do not need to despair. But
it requires leadership, radical new ideas, a commitment to put power into the
hands of local communities, and a new dynamism in the corridors of power
which simply is not there.

■ ■ ■

These responses reflect ideological positions about the nature of change in Britain.
Conservatives often take an evolutionary and pragmatic approach, which is allegedly
in keeping with the reality of British history. They argue that institutions change
slowly as they and people adapt to new situations. But Conservative governments
in fact have instituted radical alterations in recent years. The left-of-centre position
in opposition traditionally argued for more fundamental changes to the structure of
society and the system of government, although Labour governments have historically often been cautious in their approach when they have actually achieved power.
The Liberal Democrats favour radical reform and its devolved implementation at
local and regional levels. This involves giving centralized political power back to the
people and concentrating on local initiatives.

■ ■ ■

Centralization and democracy

Pressures for the devolution of centralized political power to regional levels have
resulted in an Assembly for Wales (1999), a Parliament for Scotland (1999), an
executive mayor and Assembly for London (2000) and an Assembly and Executive
in Northern Ireland (2000). But, despite these decentralizing reforms, it is alleged
that there has in fact been an increased centralization in British political and institutional life in the past 20 years, which covers many fields and is dangerous for
democracy. For example, local government below the regional level has lost many
of its traditional functions and money-raising authority to central government. It
could be argued that this centralizing trend has created new forms of 'the
Establishment' spread through interlocking elements such as central government,

devolving
Transferring decision-
making from a
centralized source to
local levels.

Leviathan
A mythical sea or river monster.

Downing Street
The official London residence of the British prime minister.

council houses
Public housing to rent, provided by local authorities.

popular culture, business and the media. The next text argues that political and financial centralization increased under Conservative governments (1979–97) and became particularly centred on the office of the Prime Minister, Whitehall and the Treasury (or government finance department).

5 'Party of freedom has shackled us all to the state'
Simon Jenkins[6]
(Author copyright, 8 October 1995) abridged

When the Conservatives took office in 1979, Margaret Thatcher pledged to end a politics that had 'enlarged the role of the state and diminished the role of the individual'. They would cut government and set the people free. But they have failed: after 16 years the **Leviathan** of the modern state has been streamlined and reinvigorated rather than shrunk.

To a large extent, Thatcherism is a myth. Thatcher's government and that of her successor, John Major, have consumed roughly the same proportion of the nation's wealth as did Labour – currently the same 43 per cent as in 1979. Within the state sector, the Conservatives have concentrated power on the central institutions of **Downing Street** as never before in peacetime. Indeed, their standardization of financial control comes close to completing the 'nationalization of welfare' initiated by Attlee's [Labour] government of 1945. The Tory state is now the most centralized in the western world.

This paradox is one of the ironies of 20th-century politics. We know the familiar catalogue. Thatcher defied the unions and set the private sector free. She sold a quarter of all **council houses** and half the state trading industries and services. She widened share ownership. New incentives have been brought to bear on many public services. Producer power has been curtailed and the consumer empowered.

All this is true, but it is only part of the truth. In studying the great reforms of the Thatcher–Major era, we find the role and power of central government have been extended, not reduced . . .

[For example, under the Conservatives, the police, universities, further education, hospitals, public housing] . . . were brought under central resource planning . . . [and are] now run by central government.

Nationalization is not just about ownership. It is about power. The usurping of control over a service, private or public, by the central state is 'nationalization', whether carried out by regulation or transfer of accountability or ownership. There has been no greater casualty of such a transfer than local government. In 1985 a quarter of all public spending was by local councils and more than a half of that was raised by local discretionary taxes. With the introduction of [central controls], this discretion has been superseded by a regime of Stalinist rigidity. Elected councils are now virtual sub-contractors for central government, supplying roads, schools, and homes to budgets approved in Whitehall.

. . . The patronage of the state is today more extensive than under any Stuart monarch, running everything from hospitals and schools to Stonehenge and music on the **South Bank**. The seizure by the **Treasury** from local councils of the revenues of their **business rates** in 1988 was, by my estimate, the biggest nationalization by any British government ever. Control over some £14 billion of revenue a year passed straight to the Treasury . . .

Under both Thatcher and Major, the privatization of some old industries concealed the nationalization of new ones . . . In each case a service formerly performed by the private or voluntary sector now operates under Treasury terms and conditions.

The golden years of Thatcherism were in truth brief ones. They commenced with the election victory of 1987 and continued with the privatizations of the early Major years. Yet even the Golden Years were primarily about divesting public ownership, not public control . . . The private sector might have regained these assets, but the government exercises effective control . . .

To understand this phenomenon we must understand that the ideology of Thatcherism was a late invention. There was no mention of privatization in the 1979 Tory manifesto – Thatcher herself had banned the word as too radical. What she avidly supported was centralization, because it appeared to help what was the true crusade of her early years: reduced public spending and thus lower taxes. Hence the lethal paradox: only by cutting public spending could state power be curbed, yet only by enhancing state power, so Thatcher thought, could spending be cut.

The 1980s were not really the decade of Thatcherism, they were the decade of Treasuryism. The cabinet wrestled to control the cost of the welfare state. This required control over any agency of the public sector that might show the slightest indiscipline . . . With the advent of . . . Whitehall control over local budgets, local spending [by local government] became central spending, determined by the Treasury in all but name. The same applied to health authorities, police authorities and nationalized industries.

South Bank
A complex of cultural buildings on the south bank of the river Thames in London.

Treasury
The British government department that is in charge of, and controls, national finances under the leadership of the Chancellor of the Exchequer.

business rates
A tax that commercial companies must pay on the value of their business premises.

sacred cow
Immune from interference.

written constitutions
Britain does not have a written constitution contained in any one document, as is the case in many countries. A written constitution describes the powers of central authorities, but also contains provision to rectify any abuse of that power.

overpowering executive
Central government.

presidential-style
Although 'presidential' has been applied to the Labour administration, there are restrictions and constraints (such as public opinion and the party apparatus) upon the Prime Minister's use of power, which make the argument somewhat dubious.

money subsidies and financial policies
Devolved self-government in Wales, Scotland and Northern Ireland is largely financed from, and therefore arguably controlled economically by, Westminster and Whitehall in London.

Yet this did not lead to some new sense of fiscal discipline . . . [T]he Tories have indulged in some of the most reckless spending splurges since the war. From defence (at first) to pensions, from housing to social security, from law and order to health, one area after another was declared a '**sacred cow**' and untouchable. As government ministers took more power they found they also took more blame . . . They spent more money to reduce the blame. The Treasury sought more power to curb the money, and found itself spending even more in consequence. I estimate that by 1992 successive attempts to curtail local government had cost the Tories 4p on the basic rate of income tax. This is the true cost of nationalization.

What is most ironic is that the agency of this nationalization should have been the Conservative party. This was once the party of provincial England, of pluralism, of institutional as well as personal autonomy. It was a mass party . . . It had a distaste for government as something socialist. In Thatcher, it even chose a leader who expressed that distaste vociferously.

But the Tory party has turned its back on this pluralism. As it dismantles local democracy, it has seen its activists evaporate . . . The cabinet's contempt for local government is not just inefficient, it is subversive of democracy. I began my research sceptical of what **written constitutions** could do to check an **overpowering executive** [see text 1 in Chapter 5]. I have changed my mind. If Margaret Thatcher could not restrain central government's instinctive lust for power, nobody else will. Written constitutions, warts and all, are the only hope.

■ ■ ■

Reform groups (such as Charter 88), academic critics and widespread media comment suggest that political centralization has continued.[7] Despite constitutional reforms and devolution in Wales, Scotland, Northern Ireland and London, it is argued that a '**presidential-style**' Labour government has developed since 1997, in which power is centralized in the Downing Street prime ministerial machine at the expense of democratic accountability through the House of Commons and Parliament.

Money subsidies and financial policies are tightly organized by the Treasury and the Chancellor of the Exchequer. Such centralizing and controlling tendencies have allegedly been encouraged by the example and power of the British media, by the employment of unelected political advisers in government and by the emergence of 'spin-doctors' (unelected government press secretaries who are concerned to put the most positive view – or spin – on government policies). These developments have led to criticisms of the Labour government machine, which are reflected in the next text.

6 ' "Cool Britannia" looks more like Fool Britannia'

Philip Bowring
(*The International Herald Tribune*, 15 April 1998) abridged

. . . The Blair obsession with image, with form over substance, adds to the media's sense of importance. Media manipulation and news management are natural goals of government. But Mr Blair and his right-hand men have taken it to new heights. Ministers have found themselves on the receiving end of policy directives from Mr Blair's press secretary . . .

There is a direct link between this media-driven system and the presidential style of government that Mr Blair has adopted.

Given Labour's **huge majority**, Parliament is more than ever a rubber stamp, and ministers are more than ever subservient to Downing Street. Personalized populism . . . driven by the tabloid media, is replacing both institutional power and grassroots participatory democracy.

The presidential trend might have some merit were it accompanied by an American-style separation of powers. But the lack of checks and balances has contributed to a string of sleazy episodes of influence peddling and jobs for the boys remarkable for a government so young. . . .

■　■　■

Other commentators argue that centralized and quasi-monopolistic power has also grown stronger in the media, the business world, commercial companies and the European Union. In this process, the consumer, the individual and democracy allegedly suffer, lose influence and voice and become powerless. In the next text, Anthony Sampson, who has anatomized British society for many years, itemizes those areas of British life that suffer from a 'democratic deficit' or lack of democratic input by the grass roots.

huge majority
An overall majority of
177 seats in the House
of Commons.

shareholders
Shareholders have bought shares in a company and are therefore the owners of that company. But they are largely at the mercy of those directors and managers who actually run the business on a daily basis.

influence of European institutions and pressures
The influence of the European Union in many aspects of British life has increased considerably. EU law is superior to British domestic law when there is a conflict between the two and EU directives are immediately applicable in Britain.

7   *The Essential Anatomy of Britain: Democracy in Crisis*

Anthony Sampson

(London: Hodder and Stoughton, 1992) abridged

[This book] . . . focuses . . . sharply on essential crisis points [in Britain]: particularly the weakening of democratic representation which accelerated during the eighties, which has affected nearly all the power-centres [of British life], and which is still more evident in the wider context of Britain-in-Europe. The democratic crisis shows itself also in commercial areas where decision-making has been taken over by a few groups and people, most visibly in the highly-centralized media which condition many people's attitudes to life. While businesses claim to offer the consumer greater choice, major decisions are taken by a tiny group of people, and **shareholders**' representation is now threatened as much as the voters' . . .

[The book] moves to the agglomerations, upheavals and scandals in finance and insurance, and the predicament of industrial managers and small businessmen in a country dominated by powerful corporations; concluding with the most influential wielders of concentrated power, the controllers of the media.

[The book] looks at the casualties of these trends during the eighties: first the workers, workless and homeless . . . then the local councils, provincial cities and regions which have all seen much of their former autonomy disappear towards London.

As the tour progresses, it becomes less of a tour of a self-contained island, more a tour of Britain-in-Europe; for the **influence of European institutions and pressures** is evident in almost every sphere . . .

[I try] to sum up my own concerns about the weakness of democracy in [a] thirty-year perspective. For I believe that Britain's anatomy now shows very serious deformities, which require urgent attention, and which can only be put right by much greater public protest and involvement – which are not yet much in evidence.

■   ■   ■

Models of British society

However, despite their apparent power, national institutions, the State, the government, 'the Establishment', business concerns and the European Union do not absolutely determine all areas of British life. Many British people operate at levels of popular culture and individualism, often in reaction to powerful institutions.

The next text is written from a sociological point of view, cautions against easy descriptions of Britain and stresses the inadequacies of various academic or ideological models of British society. It argues that while sociologists and historians may attempt to evaluate societies theoretically in terms of class, capitalism, hegemony and other factors, it is often better to try to understand how ordinary people actually organize and live their lives. In this view, British society is diverse and ever-changing and incapable of being summed up in any simple, fashionable formula or theory.

8 *Understanding Post-War British Society*
James Obelkevich and Peter Catterall
(London: Routledge, 1994) abridged

British society is a complicated affair, full of loose ends and bits that don't fit. This may be a good thing for the people who live in it, but it is a source of frustration for those who study it and try to understand it. Every attempt to sum it up in a simple formula – as a 'class society' or whatever – has proved to have so many exceptions and qualifications that it was more trouble than it was worth. The first thing to understand about British society is that there are no short-cuts, no master keys ... [A] few lessons ... [about models of British society might be suggested] ...

The first is about the role of ideology. A decade or two ago the ideology most in favour was Marxism ... In its time Marxism had a positive role to play. It reminded us that society was not a harmonious, integrated, organic unity; that poverty was a reality; and that class differences still mattered.

But Marxism got many things wrong. It was at a loss to account for the spread of affluence and the rise in living standards. Even on its chosen ground of class, it was unconvincing. Its master theme of class struggle could not be squared with what was actually happening in post-war Britain. It could not

false consciousness
The Marxist notion that
the working classes are
induced to believe by
ruling forces in society
that the capitalist
economic system is
natural, fair,
unavoidable and more
efficient than any
alternative.

hegemony
Antonio Gramsci
argued that 'false
consciousness' was a
trick perpetuated by
the ruling classes who
brainwashed the
proletariat into
accepting messages of
civil society that
resulted in the
hegemony (control or
manipulation) of the
ruling capitalist class
over society.

neo-liberal
The neo-liberal political
tradition upholds the
role of the free market
and sees much
government activity as
unnecessary, and even
a hindrance. Often
associated with
Thatcherite policies
from 1979.

come to terms with the middle classes – their growth, diversity and cultural fragmentation. And it was equally baffled by the working classes, who so often voted for the 'wrong' political party – the Conservatives – rather than for Labour. This lack of fit between Marxist notions of class consciousness and the actual voting behaviour of the working class was an embarrassment, and it could not be covered up by such devices as '**false consciousness**' or '**hegemony**'. The fact was that most workers were not socialists and did not want a socialist revolution; their political outlook was incapable of being explained in Marxist categories . . . If Marxism ever provided an adequate analysis of British society – which may be doubted – it does no longer.

Our problem is that while we can see the deficiencies of Marxism, we do not as yet have an alternative set of reference points to put in its place. One possibility is the **neo-liberal** and free market ideas that came back into fashion in the 1980s. They propose a very different model of social behaviour, based on individual aspirations and expectations, and they have had an impact upon economic and, increasingly, on social policy. But their effect on British sociology, so far, has been limited . . .

Today the most fashionable ideology is feminism. Like any ideology, it has strengths and weaknesses, and its effects on sociology have been mixed. Its great positive contribution has been to bring women, and gender, into the centre of sociological enquiry . . .

But feminism also has its less helpful side. Just as Marxism often degenerated into a series of crude leftist slogans known as vulgar Marxism, so feminism has its contemporary equivalent in what could be called vulgar feminism. Its reductionist catchphrases are all too familiar: 'patriarchy', women's 'common oppression', 'women's values', the family as a 'site of oppression', 'all men are rapists', 'feminism is the theory, lesbianism the practice', etc., etc. The result is a seductive but simplistic tale of evil, powerful men oppressing helpless, innocent women. Far from opening our eyes to hidden truths, this kind of sloganising only creates new myths, and prevents us from seeing women, and men, as they really are. The result is demonology, not sociology.

One of its most misleading assumptions is that women were nothing but victims. But there have been millions of exceptions, notably the working-class women who, far from being subordinate and put-upon, were the powerful, central and dominant figures in their families. Nor, contrary to the myth of 'common oppression', were all women equally disadvantaged: middle- and upper-class women were among the most privileged people in society and had vastly more in common with their husbands than with their working-class (or black) 'sisters', whom they shamelessly exploited when they employed them as domestic servants. No more convincing is the claim that women are excluded from power. **Margaret Thatcher** not only attained supreme power but wielded it more ruthlessly than any male prime minister in British history. And women today[8] hold the posts of **director of public prosecutions** and of director of **MI5** – at the heart of the state's security apparatus.

It is well known that since the end of the war the proportion of women in paid employment has increased dramatically. But the claim that *all* working women want to pursue 'careers', and are only held back by 'glass ceilings' imposed by men, is yet another myth. Undoubtedly such barriers existed and still exist, but historically working women have jobs rather than careers. The primary commitment for many women is often still not to work but to their traditional role in rearing a family – just as it was for their predecessors in the 1940s.

Another source of error has been the tendency to inflate the achievements of feminism, to assume that if women's condition improved, feminism deserves the credit. But the expansion of higher education, for example, which benefited women (especially those from the middle class) far more than it did men, came before, not after, the revival of feminism at the end of the 1960s. Feminism was not the cause of women's entry into university education: it was, if any-thing, one of its consequences. Similarly, the trend for married women to return to paid employment started early in the post-war period and owed nothing to feminism. Misleading too is the tendency to inflate the size of the feminist move-ment itself – to assume that all women are discontented with their lot and are in some sense feminist. In fact, most women have accepted their role in the family and in society and have not questioned or challenged it. Far from being instinctive feminists, most women have rejected the feminist movement and what they see as its dogmatism and arrogance . . .

Marxism and feminism can both provide powerful insights. But each also has its blind spots and its limitations. Just as Marxists had little to say to workers who preferred the *Sun* to *New Left Review*, so feminism makes a poor guide to the vast majority of women who are not feminist, who reject feminism, and who find *Woman* and *Best* more rewarding than *Spare Rib*. People have to be understood in their own terms: this cannot be done by imposing on them some alien ideological agenda – Marxist or feminist – from outside.

Some of these same criticisms apply to what is probably the dominant outlook in British sociology today, which is feminist and left of centre. It tends to be highly critical of British society, which it sees as swarming with inequalities and injustices. It seeks to expose the evils of racism and sexism, the disparity in power and in life-chances between rich and poor. It is appalled by the unfairness it sees in British society. Inevitably it is disappointed by the fact that these evils do not arouse more protest, more opposition. It asks why the

Margaret Thatcher
Britain's first woman
Prime Minister, 1979.

**director of public
prosecutions**
The DPP heads the
public prosecution
service in England,
Wales and Northern
Ireland, which prefers
charges against criminal
suspects.

MI5
Part of the Secret
Services organization,
traditionally concerned
with internal intelligence
matters within Britain.

Sun
Popular best-selling
tabloid daily
newspaper.

New Left Review
Intellectual left-wing
periodical.

Woman
Popular best-selling
women's weekly
magazine.

Best
Popular women's
magazine.

Spare Rib
Feminist, leftist
magazine.

dominant
Used in the sense of a culture composed of a dominant class or group, whose values determine what British society is, or is supposed to be.

radical
Used in the sense of alternative values and ideas opposed to the 'dominant culture'.

widening of the gap between rich and poor
This assumption is questioned by some critics who argue that more people became better off and that even the lowest paid increased their economic standing.

'oppressed' – workers, women, blacks and others – do not challenge the system, reform it, even overthrow it.

Such a question is certainly worth asking. There is a great deal of inequality in Britain, and exposing and highlighting it is one of sociology's essential duties. Yet few people, even its main victims, do much about it. One explanation is to blame the media. There would be more protest, it is often said, if only the media did not conceal injustice and distract attention from a corrupt system. But this does not take us very far. The media expose faults, failings and injustices in Britain every day of the week. The real answer is that faults, failings and injustices are only part of the picture. Britain cannot be understood merely as a collection of 'social problems', as an anthology of 'oppression', whether based on class, race, gender or whatever. Nor can it be understood in terms of 'struggle' – whether between '**dominant**' and '**radical**', middle class and working class, men and women, old and young, or whites and blacks. There is much more to British society than this simple tale of goodies and baddies.

Sociology, if it is to fill in the larger picture, needs to look at some of the more positive things that have happened in Britain during the last few decades. There is, above all, the huge improvement in standards of living. Despite the **widening of the gap between rich and poor** during the 1980s, most people are far better-off now than their predecessors were a generation ago. Working-class people today take for granted such things as domestic appliances and foreign holidays which then were in short supply, or unavailable, even to the well-off. There has also been a great deal of upward social mobility. Many young people from working-class families entered higher education and embarked on non-manual careers; even larger numbers started work in manual occupations and climbed into non-manual ones. Women too benefited from the expansion of higher education. Indeed, the number of women going to university increased much faster than the number of students from working-class backgrounds. British society has often been described, by sociologists and others, as rigid and class-ridden. But it has also shown a remarkable degree of openness and mobility. If Britain is divided into three classes, then of the men in the top or 'service' class – professionals, managers, proprietors and supervisors – those from manual, working-class origins actually outnumber those born in the service class itself. The majority of British men have either moved into a different class from the one in which they were born, or have married a woman from a different social class. Women's mobility is comparable. Class is a reality, but it is not set in stone. British society does not consist of fixed, monolithic classes, but of much more porous, heterogeneous groupings, in which the majority of people have personal or familial links across class lines.

No one could deny that Britain has its share of conflict. But just as significant is the fact of consensus and shared values. By the standards of many advanced societies, overt conflict, let alone violence, is surprisingly rare in Britain. As many foreign visitors and observers have noted, one of the most striking things about Britain – despite war, industrialisation and relative decline – is its sheer continuity, the absence of violent social and political disruption. In any international ranking of social stability, Britain, despite the increase in poverty, ranks near the top of the league table. Any study of British society that highlights the conflict presents a very distorted picture of the society as a whole. And with the fall in strikes and industrial disputes in recent years, it could be argued not only that conflict is *not* the most important feature of British society, but also that it is one that is in decline.

[One also has to consider the role of the state in Britain]. That role still includes the state's traditional primary duty of protecting the country from external threats and of preserving law and order … (The growth, and abuse, of the 'secret state', with its powers of surveillance, control and covert action, is one of the more worrying developments of the post-war period.)

But no one could ignore the fact that during this period the state's field of operations has expanded enormously, and now extends beyond its traditional role. Even in the Thatcher and post-Thatcher years, the state has carried on planning, directing, regulating, employing, subsidising. Indeed, it spends money – and collects taxes – on a vast scale. Public expenditure is the equivalent of about 40 per cent of gross domestic product. Well over half of this expenditure, moreover, is now devoted to the welfare state – to health, education, housing and so on. **Social security transfer payments** alone account for a third of government spending, the equivalent (though not counted as part of) over 10 per cent of GDP. Compared with its fairly restricted range of activities earlier in the century, the state now gives the impression of intervening in just about every corner of British life. It has become a central fact in post-war society.

The question, however, is whether it is *the* central fact. And here there are areas for scepticism. Of course, the state is ultimately responsible for the legal framework within which British society is supposed to operate; but that framework is itself a reflection of past social attitudes … And rarely is the law a detailed blueprint: rather, it sets limits to what people can do, and leaves a good deal of leeway within them. [T]here are also places where there is no consensus on what the law ought to be and where it is widely ignored. Where the law is out of touch with contemporary reality, people usually find ways round it.

We also need to be a little sceptical in evaluating the effectiveness of the state in its more specific areas of activity. The state may appear to have policies for everything, but that does not mean that those policies are always successful,

secret state
The intelligence services such as MI5 (domestic coverage) and MI6 (international operations).

Social security transfer payments
Payments such as Income Support for those in financial need.

Sainsbury's
A leading supermarket chain.

Tesco
A leading supermarket chain.

interest rates
From 1997, it is the Bank of England, not the government, that sets interest rates.

National Health Service
The free state service that provides medical services to all by doctors, hospitals and other health professionals.

tower blocks
High-rise blocks of flats in the public housing sector usually situated in inner city areas, some of which have now been demolished.

or that they are the only factor in the situation. In the area of food and diet, for example, the policies of the Ministry of Agriculture, Food and Fisheries certainly count for less than those of **Sainsbury's** and **Tesco** . . . Social policy often simply reacts to developments not of its making. And for consistent ineffectiveness and failure, it would be hard to match the record of governments in trying to manage the economy. Their policies have shown far more misses than hits, despite (or because of) the fact that they had plenty of expert advice from economists, and despite the fact that they controlled the main economic levers, such as **interest rates**.

The gap between what governments want and what they get can be seen in the biggest (and most expensive) policy area of all, the welfare state. The aims of its founders, after 1945, were nothing less than to liberate the people of Britain from ignorance, want, squalor, idleness and disease. Today even its most ardent champions would not claim that it has achieved those aims. While it has undoubtedly done much good, overall it has been something of a disappointment, falling well short of the high hopes expressed for it in the 1940s and 1950s. Although the nation's health has undoubtedly improved since the establishment of the **National Health Service**, the NHS cannot take all the credit for this, nor has it succeeded in eliminating serious disparities in illness and mortality between classes and regions. In housing, **tower blocks** are universally acknowledged as a human disaster.

But perhaps the most striking example of the failure of government has been the steady rise in crime. Crime has gone on increasing[9] throughout the postwar period, in periods both of high and of low unemployment, despite changes in policing, sentencing, and the party in office. Indeed, government policies have been blamed by critics of both left and right for contributing to the crime wave. Where the left argues that Thatcherite economic policies of the 1980s led to unemployment and crime, the right, meanwhile, has pointed an accusing finger at 'liberal' educational and social policies of the 1960s, which it claims have undermined respect for law and order. Both sides recognise that the effects of policy may be very different from those intended.

Society is not just a lump of clay to be given shape by the master hand of the policy-maker. Within it are interests and forces that have a life and will of their own and which, actively or passively, resist and deflect the might of the state, making its policies ineffective if not actually counterproductive. Social policy is only one influence among many on social conditions. If it is often the most publicly visible, it is only occasionally the most important. That does not stop reformers of all kinds from looking to the state to make the changes they seek. Compared with corporations and other institutions in British society, the state is more public, more accessible and easier to influence. But its frequent lack of success should be a lesson to us. The state is still the most direct and

obvious way of trying to change society. But it is not the best way of understanding society.

An obsession with the state and with policy has one further bad effect. It leads
to a preoccupation with causes and origins, to the neglect of results and
outcomes. To turn again to the question of food and diet, what matters in
the end is not the policies, whether of the government or of the supermarkets
or of the food industry, but what people actually eat and the role of food in
their lives. And to understand these things we need to talk to the people themselves. The proof of the pudding is not after all in pudding policy, or in the
pudding industry, but in the eating. In housing, similarly, what matters is not
just the government's housing policy, or the role of **building societies** and local
authorities, but how people actually use their houses and live in them. In the
end we need to study outcomes: not just what policies do to people but what
people do with policies.

A final lesson is the importance of history. Critics of British society have often
despaired of its apparently invincible conservatism – its immobility and resistance to change. But ... it has been far from static. Since 1945 it has been
through phases of austerity and prosperity, booms and slumps, of demographic
booms and bulges. There have been big changes, on the whole beneficial, in the
lives of women and of the working classes. Contrary to the theory of a fixed and
immutable Britain, these changes have not been limited to the surface of society
but have reached its deeper structures. And they are still taking place.

 ## Exercises

Write short essays on the following topics

1 Discuss the relevance of competing political, governmental, ideological and
   cultural forces to the notion of social change. How does society change?

2 What impressions of British society do you receive from the above texts?

3 Do you consider that Britain is still in decline? Or has it changed? If so,
   how?

4 Many of the texts refer to the 'individual' and 'individualism'. What do
   these words mean in a British context?

5 Critically examine the references to 'Thatcherism' in the texts and try to
   define what the term means.

6 What is meant by 'modernization'?

building societies
Financial organizations
that lend money (loans)
to people wishing to
buy domestic property.
The loan is paid back
with interest over time.

Explain and examine the following terms

institutions	the Establishment	culture
feminism	recession	'back-to-basics'
globalization	'British disease'	deficit
Whitehall	pragmatic	Liberal Democrats
manifesto	Cabinet	populism
tabloid	councils	'glass ceilings'
grass roots	hegemony	'spin doctors'
inflation	interest rates	centralization

Further reading

Abercrombie, Nicholas *et al.* (1994) *Contemporary British Society*, Cambridge: Polity Press.
Christopher, David (1999) *British Culture: An Introduction*, London: Routledge.
English, Richard and Kenny, Michael (eds) (1999) *Rethinking British Decline*, London: Macmillan.
Hutton, Will (1996) *The State We're In*, London: Vintage.
Johnson, Paul (ed.) (1994) *Twentieth-Century Britain: Economic, Social and Cultural Change*, London: Longman.
Marwick, Arthur (2000) *A History of the Modern British Isles 1914–1999*, Oxford: Blackwell Publishers.
Obelkevich, James and Catterall, Peter (eds) (1994) *Understanding Post-War British Society*, London: Routledge.

Notes

1. Market and Opinion Research International (MORI) (2000) for *The Times* London: 28 January.
2. *British Lifestyles*: Mintel (2000), *The Times* London: 9 February.
3. See M. Wiener (1981) *English Culture and the Decline of the Industrial Spirit, 1850–1980*, Cambridge: Cambridge University Press; and C. Barnett (1986) *The Audit of War*, London: Macmillan, and (1972) *The Collapse of British Power*, London: Methuen.
4. See note 3.
5. Martin Jacques (1994) 'The erosion of the Establishment', *The Sunday Times*, London: 16 January.
6. See also Simon Jenkins (1995) *Accountable to None: The Tory Nationalization of Britain*, London: Hamish Hamilton.
7. Tom Baldwin (2000) 'Charter 88 accuses Blair of dictatorship', *The Times* London: 21 June.
8. They do so no longer in these two cases.
9. Some critics argue on the contrary that crime has decreased. Much depends on the reliability and validity of crime statistics and how these are interpreted.

Chapter 2

Images of Britain

In contemporary debates, it is frequently argued that the British people are attempting, partly successfully and partly unsuccessfully, to come to terms with their positions in a rapidly changing domestic and international world. Within Britain, this process of adaptation allegedly produces tensions between the rich and the poor, between nostalgia (or traditionalism) and modernization and between acceptance of change and reaction to it.

John Galsworthy
English writer
1867–1933.

St James's Street
Central London.

Notting Hill
West London.

Labour in mourning
The Labour Party was
in opposition 1979–97
and its policies were
proving unattractive to
the electorate. It had
lost two successive
general elections in
1979 and 1983.

The texts in this chapter illustrate how Britain and its people are seen from home and abroad; how the country is responding to contemporary conditions; how politicians and opinion-moulders are seeking to bring about change; and, crucially, the nature of such change. As in Chapter 1, there are very opposed views on these topics and a central problem is to try to determine valid representative perspectives.

External images

The first three texts were written in the 1990s by an Italian correspondent, a British journalist (commenting on foreign perceptions of Britain) and an expatriate Englishman. Their views contrast quite considerably and it may arguably seem that some (particularly those dealing with the alleged growth of a hooligan, yobbish, loutish or coarse culture) cannot serve as a valid comment on a whole society. Less desirable characteristics are obviously present among Britons, but debate continues as to whether these are minority and unrepresentative elements among many other more positive ones. The first text describes Britain within the perspective of recent history.

1 'An Italian in London'
Beppe Severgnini
(*The Economist*, 8 January 1994) abridged

> When after months of travel, one returns to England,[1] he can taste, smell and feel the difference in the atmosphere, physical and moral – the curious damp, blunt, good-humoured, happy-go-lucky, old-established, slow-seeming formlessness of everything

So **John Galsworthy** saw his country – above all 'cosy' and glorying in its ability to muddle through. Foreigners see things rather differently. I have watched modern Britain not only from the comfortable heights of *The Economist*'s building in **St James's Street**, but also from the challenging lows of a basement flat in **Notting Hill**, and have travelled through most of the rest of the country. My views may irritate but that, at least in part, is my intention. Italians are not keen fans of cosiness.

In 1984, with Thatcherism in full bloom and **Labour in mourning**, I arrived in London as my newspaper's correspondent[2] and watched Margaret Thatcher try hard to change the nation. Britain's peculiar and – to any foreigner – highly visible class system was only one piece of tradition she tried (and failed) to reform. Even those who cannot stand her admit as much. What her opponents believe, though, is that her ruthless remedies were, at the end of the day, unnecessary. Many British people (and most of my friends) do not seem entirely convinced that the country was **going to the dogs** at the end of the 1970s, and believe (though they are loath to voice their feelings aloud) that being one of the oldest democracies of the world and having had the largest empire, the British are somewhat special. And special people will always find a way out, one way or another.

They are wrong. Thatcherism has been like a trumpet call blared in the ears of those who were asleep in a sinking ship: it is hardly surprising that the people who were woken up that way are ungrateful. Pre-Thatcherite Britain – the one I got to know as a student in the 1970s – was not a nation like other nations. It was more like a church, in which all institutions, from industries and trade unions to the judiciary and the police, from universities to the civil-service bureaucracy, were sacred and perennial. They were supposed to work well, but often they didn't.

Such ingrained conservatism could be a blessing if carefully monitored. Any sensible Italian envies the British love and respect for tradition. The trouble is that very often the British love of what is ancient and well-known turns into fear of what is new and unknown. The class system itself survives because it has always been there. People in Britain, apparently, do not want to experience the unsettling feeling associated with change.

It is not, therefore, surprising that Mrs Thatcher frightened so many. She wanted a quiet and contented nation to be restless and busy. She made a lot of mistakes, I believe: some were only a matter of tone and presentation, some of substance. But the refusal of the harsher side of Thatcherism is no excuse for resuming the bad old ways . . .

Britain does not need tranquillity – which would be immediately converted into genteel decay. It needs more shaking up. In spite of the recession [1988–92], a few things have improved. Money is no more a dirty word, and people gingerly ask you to pay up for whatever you do and wherever you do it . . . The north of England, where I have travelled extensively both in the mid-1980s and in 1993, has stopped moaning and has rolled up its sleeves, displaying some of the grit and determination that astounded the world 150 years ago.

There are other areas where I was glad to see that the country has picked up. Take race relations, where Britain can teach a thing or two to France and

going to the dogs
Declining rapidly.

privatization
Economic policy associated with the Conservative governments 1979–97: the selling of publicly owned enterprises to the private sector and private ownership, usually through the sale of shares in companies.

red phone boxes
Traditional phone boxes in the street, now largely replaced.

underclass
That group of poor, deprived, disadvantaged or alienated people who occupy the bottom rung of the class and wealth statistics.

service industry
The service sector is the largest segment of the national economy, dealing with, for example, leisure, financial and commercial services.

Germany,[3] or personal freedoms, which in Britain are still widely respected (there are signs that even the very British, and most amusing, obsession with secrecy is easing). Take the relatively straightforward tax system, which any Italian, burdened by 147 tributes, looks at with misty eyes. Consider **privatization**, which Britain has mastered more than any other country. Or look at the state of British industry. It still has a long way to go but, compared with the 1970s and early 1980s, is now lively, competitive and in rude health . . .

Gloom-artists

For some mysterious reason, though, most of my British friends seem to find all this irrelevant. They prefer to remember the country's past glory, rather than its worthy present. The British prefer to praise things when they are either dead or dying (from the House of Lords to **red phone boxes**). They love to talk about decline, and one is never sure what they mean by the word . . .

Of course, there are things that need sorting out . . . From overly bureaucratic police forces to an ageing judiciary, from juvenile crime to poor education, from feeble local government to a growing **underclass**. But I can easily name a hundred things that the British should be proud of, but aren't. These range from their commerce to their performing arts, from bits of their **service industry** to most of their press, from broadcasting to science, from their military to their truly unique, even mystifying, sense of humour.

Virtues unrewarded

The British are good at living next to each other, and at pulling together when need be. Government in Britain is better than almost anywhere else . . . the machinery of the British government is still reasonably efficient and clean. What John Gunther, an American journalist and traveller, wrote in the 1930s still rings true: 'the standard of public life in England is the highest in the world; honour and idealism play a part in politics that the suspicious foreigner finds it difficult to understand.'[4]

Political scandals in Britain are also few and far between. Most of the time they involve a young woman (some of the time a young man) and are almost touching in their display of forgiveable human fallibility. Italian scandals are nastier, more sordid and definitely more boring. They always revolve around the same commodity: money . . .[5]

The nation's foundations, in other words, are sound. Never mind the weak state of the monarchy or the Church of England (Britain would do better without either a monarchy or a state religion). British nationalism – when it is sober and is not paraded around football grounds – is healthy, an expression of

Britons' genuine affection for their country rather than an ugly or aggressive expression of contempt towards others [compare with texts 2 and 3, and texts on national identity in Chapter 3].

The British do not seem to have any inhibitions about being British:[6] the country's geography, undoubtedly, helps. So does history. Britain has no big chunk of its past it needs to forget – unlike Japan, Germany or Italy. As there is no British **Vichy** and no British Vietnam, Britain has also fewer hang-ups than either France or the United States. In 20th-century Britain there has been no scuttling around censoring monuments and covering memorials. The bits of history the British want to remove (from the **bombing of Dresden**, to some colonial heavy-handedness, to their treatment of the Irish), they do so painlessly, in a careless sort of way.

The British still display two other characteristics I noticed on my first visit in the 1970s: stoicism and thrift. They still put up with anything: rain, queues and bombs in London, and they do not need much, judging by the same plain decors of most British homes (and by the atrocious home-improvement offers in the Sunday newspapers' colour supplements, a source of amazement for every foreigner). **Walter Bagehot** wrote that the British have a redeeming feature: they are dull. It is an interesting observation. Just look what sort of state we Italians, who think we are clever, have produced.

And yet the British themselves seem unable to appreciate any of the achievements of modern Britain, and prefer to dwell on the embarrassments, mistakes and **cock-ups** (of which, to be fair, there is no shortage). It is a form of masochism which brings people to enjoy sporting defeats more than victories . . . Not once was I told how good British theatre or the **BBC World Service** still are, or how impressive **Marks and Spencer** and British Airways have become.

There are many more examples of the British failing to appreciate what they do well and concentrating instead on what they do badly. The nation whose supremacy in the 19th century spanned so many fields – 'with the notable exceptions of abstract philosophy, music, cuisine and lovemaking', as Luigi Barzini, my countryman, once noted – has managed to excel again. This time, though, its triumph is a sour one. The British have managed to turn grumbling into an art form, and are kilometres ahead of anyone else at it.

Europeans? Well, let's see

Whenever I am in Britain, the British are busy quarrelling about Europe. When I first came as a student, in the early 1970s, the country was arguing about its belated entry into the **Common Market**, where it should have been in the

Vichy
The French Vichy government under Marshall Pétain that collaborated (1940–44) with the Germans during the Second World War.

bombing of Dresden
Anglo-American mass bombing of Dresden, Germany at the end of the Second World War, February 1945.

Walter Bagehot
British writer (1826–77), author of *English Constitution* (1867).

cock-ups
Errors and incompetence.

BBC World Service
Worldwide radio station, broadcasting in English and other languages from Bush House, London.

Marks and Spencer
Well-known chain of quality national stores, which has suffered from a loss of sales and appeal in recent years.

Common Market
The name by which the earlier European Economic Community was known.

common agricultural policy
The policy by which agriculture in the European Union is directed and controlled.

Maastricht
The Maastricht Treaty of the European Union 1991.

Dunkirk spirit
The evacuation of British and other Allied troops from Dunkirk, northern France, in 1940 after the German advance had forced them to retreat.

1940s
The Second World War, 1939–45.

first place, using its skills and experience to lead the continent. When I came back to London as a journalist in the mid-1980s, Mrs Thatcher was fighting furiously about the **common agricultural policy** and Britain's contribution to the budget. On this visit it was Mr Major wrangling over **Maastricht**.

I found Britain's Maastricht debate both sad and hilarious. The Maastricht saga could have been avoided if someone had stood up and said loud and clear that there really was no choice. The British are right to be wary of yet another vast and vague continental design. But Maastricht had to be accepted, as Britain is either in Europe or in limbo. If it leaves, or takes a back seat, the country will gently decline, just as the Republic of Venice or Portugal have declined (they too were proud imperial powers based on commerce).

The fact that Britain is now firmly inside the European Union, of course, does not mean that the British are Europeans. When asked, they will say they are, as any Italian, Dutch or German would. But Britons always have to ponder before replying – unlike anyone else in Europe. Their answer will follow 'a long thoughtful pause in which all other continents are mentally evoked and regretfully discarded' (Barzini again). Now, admittedly, that 'long thoughtful pause' has become shorter, but it is still there.

This suits me fine. I think that in Europe there are no true Europeans, apart from a few over-enthusiastic expatriate Americans. On the continent (and on the islands off its coast) live the same number of British, French, Italians, and a few more Germans, and about 100m other people of different nationalities, as they did before the creation of the European Union. All this crowd have quite a few things in common, work well together and enjoy each others' company. This is more than enough to build a prosperous and peaceful Europe. I hope that all my British readers agree. They need not, therefore, evoke the **Dunkirk spirit** to resist European integration. To be alone against enemies in the **1940s** was heroic. To be alone among friends in the 1990s would be ludicrous.

■ ■ ■

Other foreign correspondents[7] at the end of the 1990s remarked on how in their view Britain was changing socially, with a very visible increase in wealth. They considered that it had become a more entrepreneurial, risk-taking society, which was less dependent on the state. Britain also seemed to have become a more cooperative European nation.

But, following research on how the British are seen abroad, the following text revealed another, more negative side to perceptions of the British. It also suggests that the English are seen differently from the Welsh, Scots and Irish and introduces the notion of national identities, which is discussed more fully in Chapter 3.

2 'The making of cruel Britannia'
John Lloyd
(*The New Statesman*, 26 June 1998) abridged

> We think we are civilized, warm-hearted people, but abroad,
> they think Britons of all classes are just naturally violent.

Britannia is perceived to be cruel abroad; a blow to a self-image based on a vision of warm hearts bobbing about benignly on a moderate intake of warm beer. As some foreigners see it, the country wallows in a left-over, upper-class imperial pride; others see it as a leading exporter of **yobs**.

For Britannia, at least now, read England. England, cut out from the rest of Britain by the unique British habit of separating itself into its component nations/regions in order to fail more often to win the **World Cup**, is seen to have the yobbiest culture in Europe. Or had, until Germany salvaged some of the shame of **Marseilles** by staging rampages of its own yobs. The other three of Britain's component parts are assuring everyone with even more indecent haste than normal that they are not English – especially the Scots who, **in France**, presently bask in the unaccustomed sun of gentleness and decorum.

It is the English whose upper classes provide the accent of evil in Hollywood movies and Disney cartoons. It is the English whom Paul Keating, the acerbic former premier of Australia, characterized in an interview this year as a mix of arrogance and comic **Blimpishness**. It was England which, in the words of one of its yobs arrested two weeks ago in Marseilles, 'used to own three-quarters of the f . . . ing world' and now must pay a long, slow fine for the privilege.

Foreigners do not think that English violence is a lower-class monopoly; nor do our own upper classes. As the Tory MP Alan Clark reminded us this week, most kinds of violence are permitted in **the Eton wall game** . . .

Drinking to stupor is part of it, sex another. English men of all classes regard abroad as a place to drink; some see it as a place to display their manhood to their peers by aggression to foreigners. Latin men – in South America and in

yobs
Persons given to violence, drunkenness and bad behaviour, both in private and public.

World Cup
In football.

Marseilles
Football World Cup 1998, France.

in France
Football World Cup, 1998. English football hooliganism and violence continued at the UEFA Cup Final in Copenhagen and the European Championships in Belgium/The Netherlands in 2000.

Blimpishness
Refers to a pompous and reactionary person.

Eton wall game
Played with a ball against a red brick wall in Eton College.

the Falklands
The military campaign against the Argentinian occupation of the Falkland Islands in the South Atlantic 1981–82.

the Gulf
The allied military campaign against Iraq, 1991.

Bulldog Drummond
Leading character in novels/thrillers by the English writer H.M. McNeile (Sapper) 1888–1937.

Richard Hannay
Leading character in novels by the Scottish writer John Buchan 1875–1940.

Europe – tend to show off to women. The British, and other northern European men, show off to men, and take sex, if at all, as an afterthought . . .

Wild strands [of behaviour] are what other countries all too often see of the British. We still export our criminals, though no longer to the colonies [but to the Spanish 'Costa del Crime' and Turkish Cyprus] . . . British paedophiles go abroad to find illegal sex more easily than they can in their own country.

When Britons get into trouble abroad, we tend to see them as innocents. Other countries see typically troublesome British behaviour and typically crass British arrogance – especially when the culprits are let off lightly . . .

As well as criminals . . . we also still export soldiers. Along with two other former imperial powers, the French and the Russians, we retain standing armies abroad – young men with little to do except routine duties in peaceful places. They are naturally bored and they amuse themselves with long drinking bouts . . .

The British army, one of the most efficient in the world, has become a cultural as well as a financial burden, adding to the negative perceptions of Britannia abroad. Armies have depended on male aggression, channelled and disciplined for war. That is still required at times – in **the Falklands, the Gulf** and, after a fashion, in Northern Ireland. But for much of the rest of the time it is a matter of managing boredom.

Meanwhile, male aggression is being privatized, and that is also being exported. Britain, with the US, is one of the two largest sites for private armies in the world . . .

. . . The British private armies – some ten of them headquartered in London, with an estimated 10,000 men, former British soldiers under arms and more on call – are not mere jumped-up security details. They are, according to Millius Palawiya, a Zimbabwean lawyer and writer, 'powerful enough to dislodge any government in Africa' – or, for that matter, protect and defend one. The men they employ are often drawn from élite units such as the Special Air Squadron, the Parachute Regiment and the Marines: men trained in deadly violence, who find it hard to lay it aside afterwards. The British admire themselves for this. The private soldiers are, after all, part of an old tradition. Behind them stands a century of English heroes – **Bulldog Drummond, Richard Hannay,** James Bond – who saved the world with carefully targeted violent acts. Abroad, it is seen as another example of the cruelty at Britannia's heart.

But the most potent image presently is that of the yob. That football hooliganism is intrinsically linked to nation and to the aggressive projection of nation was shown, even more clearly than now, in February 1995. That was when a group of young men, some of whom were members of the neo-Nazi Combat 18, incited a riot at Dublin's Lansdowne Road stadium during a game against England and hurled abuse, bottles and bricks at Irish fans. They were there in defence of Britain in general and **Ulster** in particular. Identifying the **Irish nation** with the IRA, they screamed their hatred of the Irish from the terraces.

There has been violence abroad continually for the past decade: during the 1988 World Cup finals in the Sardinian city of Cagliari, in the 1992 European Nations Cup finals in Sweden. The past two years have been worse; in 1996 Nottingham Forest fans beat up German police ... when their team lost away to Bayern Munich. After Germany beat England at Wembley, British fans rampaged through central London, hunting for foreign tourists and smashing foreign cars ...

Last year the World Cup qualifier in Rome between Italy and England was accompanied by prolonged clashes between the police and hooligans – clashes which were, incredibly, blamed by many in Britain on the Italian police, prompting *La Stampa* to write that 'hooliganism is not an Italian problem, it is an English problem . . .'[8]

The image of English nastiness may be an irritant to foreigners, but, in fairness, it should be acknowledged that it also serves a useful purpose. The historic anti-English grudge comes often from nations such as Australia and the US, both used as gulags to which Britain exported its criminals. This has helped to inscribe in those societies a demotic, anti-posh culture that loves to preserve snob-England in the aspic of their own self-image, presenting themselves as plain men and women, the plainer and more honest in contrast to England's sinuous élitism. England, for the Americans and Australians, is a fast and easy track to feeling democratic – as it is for the Scots.

The English really do have a problem with abroad. All countries do. Our version of it is a reluctance to fit medium-ranking status to past global pretensions. It is not a blind arrogance; increasingly, it is an uncertain one ...

But cruel cannot be easily banished by cool. The world needs the arrogant Englishman, the cruel despoiler of other cultures, the **thick** general raised on the Eton wall game who nods at massacres, the befuddled **Forster** heroine whose sexual repression is projected on the licentiousness of 'the natives'. It is part of the global collective treasure trove of stereotypes, and will not be given up. Cool does not play as well as cruel; it is our late millennial version of the **white man's burden**.

■ ■ ■

Ulster
Northern Ireland.

Irish nation
The Republic of Ireland (Eire).

thick
Stupid.

Forster
E.M. Forster (1879–1970), English novelist, some of whose novels such as *A Passage to India* and *Where Angels Fear to Tread*, explore the relationship between Britons and foreigners and have been made into films.

white man's burden
Africa, in the nineteenth century, was known as the white man's burden, which had to be civilized.

leather
Cricket ball.

willow
Cricket bat.

Quentin Tarantino
Film director known for
violent films such as
Pulp Fiction and
Reservoir Dogs.

Bob Geldof
Former pop singer and
organizer of the *Live
Aid* charity.

Harry Enfield
English television
comedian.

football fans
World Cup in France,
1998.

The next text suggests that negative social behaviour (loutishness and coarseness) is not only confined to Britons (or the English) abroad. It is also visible within Britain itself and affects both urban and rural areas throughout the country. It is arguably tied to changing social patterns, involves both the affluent and the underprivileged and has apparently become a permissible and acceptable activity.

3 'Nothing cool about being coarse'
Michael Elliott
(*Newsweek*, 6 July 1998) abridged

> Britain's global image: a nation of foul-mouthed drunks who hanker for a punch-up.

Midsummer's Day in England: brilliant sunshine, refracted into a thousand shades of green; a slow, heavy feel to the afternoon. And cricket: the clunk of **leather** on **willow**, white-clothed men (pretty equally divided among three races – this is New Britain, right?) gently ambling about in suburban London. Then a batsman is given out. He returns, disgusted, to the pavilion, where children are playing; and the air turns blue with as many of the derivatives of the word 'f . . .' as are grammatically possible, and a few that aren't. Goodbye, Jane Austen; hello, **Quentin Tarantino**.

Old Britain, New Britain: how about Coarse Britain? As a frequent visitor to my native land, I find that what often strikes me most powerfully is a yobbish culture, so pervasive that Britons themselves no longer seem to notice it. On prime-time TV the night after the cricket match, **Bob Geldof** casually used a four-letter word, and a popular comedy show starring **Harry Enfield** featured sketches of extraordinary crudity. Thinking that others must have been just as offended as I was, I scanned the papers the next morning; not a word.

Then there is the booze. You don't have to be one of the long-suffering French, forced to live with thousands of loutish **football fans**, to know that what one might call 'aggressive drinking' has become the quintessential leisure activity of the British male. In 1986, I wrote a book on London that predicted the demise of the pub – 'smelly and smoky, serving bad food in Victorian and Edwardian palaces' . . . I don't think I've ever written anything that has been proved more completely wrong. The pub has become the central temple of British culture. Worse . . . pub culture is no longer contained within an establishment's walls; it now spreads into the street outside, where the pint-swilling

British loudly discuss their two other modern obsessions. 'Culture,' writes Melanie Phillips in *The Observer*, 'has been reduced to football and sex.' Personally, I've been obsessive about football for roughly four decades, and I've got nothing particular against sex, either; but I know exactly what Phillips means when she says, 'Our wider culture glorifies lowest common denominator values.'

It's easy to pretend that Britain has always been like this; look at **Hogarth**'s prints of 18th-century London. But that's too easy. In large measure, the coarseness of modern British culture is genuinely new. In his terrific recent book *Classes and Cultures: England 1918–1951*, the Oxford academic Ross McKibbin muses on the tranquillity of the massive crowds that watched football between the wars. 'Most important,' writes McKibbin, 'the "culture" of football was still aligned to the ruling civic culture in which public violence was strongly deprecated.' So the question is: what happened to that old civic culture?

There are no easy answers. You could argue that the respectable middle class lost its self-confidence as the **counterculture** and economic decline fed on each other in the 1960s and 1970s. You could point to the wasting away of religion as a source of moral authority. You could blame (and many would) Margaret Thatcher, for forging a weird alliance between free-market economics and a macho, sexist streak in Britain, evident every day in the pages of *The Sun*, Thatcherism's loudest megaphone. My own, small, contribution to this debate is to note the way in which Britain has been transformed from a place where pleasure was an indoor activity to one where it increasingly takes place in the open air. For all I know, in the 1950s, the whole of the **East End** got **legless** every Saturday night. But the drunks didn't use to run their fumes and vomit in our faces. They do now.

You can date the birth of outdoor Britain precisely; the summer of 1980, when the refurbished fruit and vegetable market in **Covent Garden** was reopened as a collection of shops, bars and restaurants, opening into the piazza. At the time, this seemed like a triumph; just a few years before, the brutalists whose concrete slabs had wrecked half of inner London had plans to work their evil ways in Covent Garden. And indeed, when I spent a Sunday morning there recently, the market and the piazza were brimming with life . . . Then I turned the corner into Floral Street, keen to show my daughter the place where the fashion designer Paul Smith opened his first, tiny shop in the late 1970s. What *she* noticed was not Paul's shop, but that the street stank of Saturday night's urine.

Dismiss this, if you like, as the dyspeptic rantings of a middle-aged fogey. If Coarse Britain did nothing but offend people like me, it might be tolerable.

The Observer
British quality Sunday newspaper.

Hogarth
William Hogarth, English painter and engraver 1697–1764. Known for his low-life portraits of London.

counterculture
Youth and intellectual revolt against adult and established norms and values in the 1960s.

The Sun
British best-selling tabloid daily newspaper.

East End
Of London.

legless
Drunk.

Covent Garden
Central London.

G-7 industrial countries
The leading industrial nations, including Britain, which have occasional summit meetings to discuss world economic problems.

In fact, it has (or soon will have) an economic cost. In the global economy, nations and cities win and keep business very largely on the extent to which they can offer highly skilled workers a decent lifestyle, which is itself a function of perception and image. 'Rebranding' Britain, as Mark Leonard argues . . .[9] is not an intrinsically stupid objective. But the 'brand attributes' of Britain (and Britons) are not just, or mainly, those of a heritage theme park and honey for tea. They are, as the billions who have watched the World Cup now know, drink, bad language, and a penchant for a punch-up.

Britain simply can't afford that. It is not a heaven on earth. Of all the **G-7 industrial countries**, it is the only one where you can neither reliably get a tan in summer nor ski in winter. Britain's charms as a place to live and do business are not as obvious as those of Provence and Bavaria, never mind California or Sydney. In the 1960s and 1970s, I watched the image of Liverpool, my hometown, transformed from that of a great international port to that of a city with aggressively proletarian values and work-shy employees. Some rebranding; Liverpool has never recovered its former economic strength. If the cultural coarseness of Britain is allowed to continue unabated, that fate awaits the whole nation.

■ ■ ■

Internal images

The 'rebranding' and 'cool' in the last two texts refer to an attempt to modernize Britain by the Labour government since 1997. British politicians have always had their perceptions of what Britain is or should be and have tried to change the national image. During the 1980s and 1990s, the Labour Party in opposition was 'modernized' under its party leaders Neil Kinnock, John Smith and Tony Blair in order to appeal to the British people and regain political power.

'New Labour' won the 1997 general election and embarked on the 'modernization' of Britain itself. The slogan of 'Cool Britannia' was initially associated with this process, as Britain's profile was to be transformed for international consumption. But opinions differ on the success or otherwise of 'modernization' and on what it is actually intended to do or mean. The term also raises very conflicting views about what Britain and the British are like. The next text questions the validity of the 'Cool Britannia' campaign and suggests that it was an unnecessary marketing ploy, with little representative connection to the reality of most Britons' lives.

4 'Cool it'

Philip Norman
(*The Sunday Times*, 5 April 1998) abridged

The final names were announced last week for Panel 2000, the so-called Committee of Cool that will refashion, or 'rebrand', Britain's image abroad to the joint glory of the millennium and our New Labour government.

The 33-strong body . . . including media figures, sporting personalities, business people and diplomats, are the shock troops of Tony Blair's Cool Britannia crusade. It is they who will decide how to transform our international profile, as Blair desires, from ancient, stuffy and tradition-ridden, to modern, energetic, outward-looking and hip . . .

The cooling of Britain has been an obsession with the government since it assumed power . . . The obligation has been placed squarely on us all to make ourselves just as modern-minded, switched-on and cool as our leader.

During the past 11 months, Cool Britannia has ranked as high on the political agenda as **European Monetary Union**, the Northern Ireland peace process, the National Health Service or welfare reform. There has been talk of drastic cuts in 'archaic' ceremonial, such as the **state opening of Parliament**, and of turning the Queen into some homely, bicycling monarch on the Dutch model . . . Hip pop groups, hip sculptors, sports personalities, actors and soap opera stars have been invited to prime ministerial receptions and earnestly quizzed about the way they think the nation should move forward . . . Huge official energy, as well as almost £1 billion, has been dedicated to selling the millennium experience as a transcendent vision of New Labour's New Britain in action.

Blair himself denies ever having used the expression 'Cool Britannia' . . . But on the face of it, his logic seems sound enough. 'What I am bothered about is Britain's standing in the world, the strength of our economy and the prosperity of the British people,' he says. 'That is why I want Britain to be seen as a vibrant, modern place, for countries wrapped in nostalgia cannot build a strong future.'

To be fair, almost every incoming government of the past 50 years has sought to rebrand the country in some way or another. **Attlee** launched old Labour's welfare state in 1945 with a vision of 'a new Jerusalem'. **Churchill** in 1953

European Monetary Union
European Monetary Union (EMU) created the euro (the common European currency) in 1998, which became applicable in 11 European Union states on 1 January 1999. Britain did not join.

state opening of Parliament
Usually takes place every Autumn in the House of Lords.

Attlee
Clement Attlee, Labour Prime Minister 1945–51.

Churchill
Winston Churchill, Conservative Prime Minister 1951–55.

Harold Wilson
Harold Wilson, Labour
Prime Minister 1964–70
and 1974–6.

focus group
Political party
researchers use
representative groups
of people in order to
investigate particular
areas of interest to the
party, e.g. welfare
reform and education.
The information and
opinions gained from
focus groups is then
often fed into party
policy.

hijacked the Queen's coronation to link his last Tory administration with 'a new Elizabethan age'. **Harold Wilson** in 1964 produced his almost hallucinogenic picture of a new Britain 'forged in the white heat of the technological revolution' . . .

But for some, the question at issue is not whether Britain needs rebranding so much as the motives of the rebranders. Is New Labour trying to say that history only really began at the moment it took power? Francis Maude, the Tory culture spokesman, thinks so, for one: he has denounced Panel 2000 as 'not representative of the nation' and has castigated Cool Britannia as a cynical political ploy. 'There is no reason why the British people should wish to abandon their sense of identity for something cooked up in a Labour party **focus group**,' he said . . .

A government striving to make both us and itself 'cool', you might think, has perfectly caught the zeitgeist of late 1990s Britain. 'Cool', after all, is the ultimate accolade that can be bestowed by anyone between the age of 6 and 18 (along with 'awesome' and 'wicked'). Could there be a more up-to-date concept?

Well, yes actually. 'Cool', as a synonym for something nifty and enviable, dates back at least as far as the mid-19th century. Victorian schoolboy literature throngs with charismatic figures described as 'cool customers' or . . . 'as cool as a cucumber' . . . Popular music and its enthusiasts have been describing themselves as 'cool', to set themselves apart from, and above, the prosaic adult world, for the best part of half a century . . .

For today's young, cool begins and ends with wearing the right designer-labels, predominantly French, American or Italian. These still manage to maintain an aura of exclusivity despite appearing on garments often mass-produced by the million . . . Long gone is the subtle cachet of a garment's unmistakable look or inimitable cut . . .

What we see, in fact, is cool without style. Indeed, style is a quality that seems achingly absent from the rising generation that New Labour's style-strategists and focus groups so earnestly study . . .

The bottom line is that you can be cool without style, but if you're stylish, you can't help being cool. It is not a question of being young, and certainly not of having been born into the era of New Labour . . . Style is indefinable yet unmissable . . .

Despite our national identity crisis, style is still something Britain possesses in abundance, to the continuing admiration and envy of other races. Unfortunately, it is mostly to be found in the very areas that New Labour seeks to de-emphasize. What could be more stylish than a Georgian [house or shop] facade, a Gloucestershire cottage garden, a sweep of chalk cliffs above the **Solent**, a detachment of the Household Cavalry, a rowing eight out on the Thames?

What could be more inimitably stylish than a Rolls-Royce? . . . John Major's vision of village-green cricket, warm beer and spinsters cycling to evensong may have been as shamelessly **spin-doctored** as Cool Britannia, but it had a germ of truth, and it still resonates . . .

Everyone on Panel 2000 must know in his or her heart that this rebranding business is essentially a marketing man's conceit; that for summer after summer into the new millennium, tourists will continue to come to Britain for the same reasons they always have – royalty, Shakespeare, thatched cottages and the Beatles . . .

■ ■ ■

The celebrities, who had initially welcomed the victory of the Labour Party and who are arguably at the forefront of popular culture in contemporary Britain, soon reacted to its policies. The popular music paper *New Musical Express* published a special issue in 1998 in which bands and rock stars criticized Labour for its alleged 'betrayal' of young people in proposed welfare cuts. The 'Cool Britannia' slogan was increasingly ridiculed and criticized. But the 'modernization project' was still defended officially, as the next two texts illustrate. They comment on the perceived need to create an economically and socially prosperous Britain.

5 *'Rebranding rationale'*
Mark Leonard (a member of Panel 2000)
(*Newsweek*, 6 July 1998) abridged

One hundred and fifty years ago the German poet Heinrich Heine was asked where he would like to be at the end of the world. 'England,' he replied, 'because everything happens a hundred years later there.' Beneath Heine's humour lies a serious point. Ask a businessman in Ohio, a housewife in Gdansk or a rickshaw wallah in Delhi what they think of Britain and you will get a picture that is stuck in the past: a sort of heritage theme park with bad food,

Solent
A sea channel separating the Isle of Wight from mainland England.

spin-doctored
Governmment media spokespersons (spindoctors) who attempt to put the right or government-correct interpretation on public messages.

Savoy
Hotel in central London.

makeover
Change of image.

British Council
Independent body
responsible for
marketing British culture
throughout the world.

worse weather and arcane traditions. The country evokes images of companies hamstrung by strikes, products that are badly designed, royal palaces and a wonderful history. To many outsiders, Britain may be fun to visit – if you want to step into the 19th century.

But look around Britain as it really is. It has been reborn as a self-confident, outward-looking, multicultural island with a new government and a lot of hope. That's the reality the new government wants to project, that's what 'rebranding' is all about. Is it worth the trouble?

The answer is yes, on several counts. The old image is bad for business. Three out of four of the world's largest companies (Fortune 500 companies) say that national identity is one of the key factors that influence them when they buy goods and services. This is just common sense: most people are willing to pay a premium for products from certain countries – whether it is engineering from Germany or consumer electronics from Japan. But research shows that when people think of Britain, too many either think of shoddy goods or wildly extravagant ones – like a Rolls-Royce or a night at the **Savoy**. In fact, many British companies have found the British image so damaging that they have dropped the 'British' from their names. The largest British consumer-electronics retail chain, Dixons, even calls its own brand Matsui to make it sound Japanese.

The national **makeover** also matters because the British government already spends almost £1 billion a year on promoting an image of itself abroad, through embassies, the British Tourist Authority and the **British Council**. The government has a network of more than 200 offices around the world that regularly runs advertising campaigns and organized trade shows to sell Britain to the world. But too often these activities have simply reinforced the worst stereotypes about Britain.

This is all set to change ... [T]he government [has] launched Panel 2000, a group of luminaries from business, fashion, sports and the media. Its charge: revamp all the government's efforts to project itself to the world – expos, trade fairs, embassies, government buildings – to make them embody the new reality of a country that is self-confident, creative, tolerant, ethnically diverse and connected to the world. The British Council is starting to restructure itself to better deliver a picture of the new Britain. The new British Embassy building in Berlin is a bold and self-confident emblem of 'Cool Britannia'. A government task force has recommended redesigning airports and train stations to give visitors the best possible introduction to Britain. And the Foreign Office has appointed business and cultural ambassadors to key embassies to promote practical schemes on the ground.

The recent European and world summits hosted by Britain were brazen exercises in cultural diplomacy. When **Bill Clinton** and other world leaders turned up in Birmingham for the G-8 summit, the Beefeaters and brass bands were nowhere in sight. Instead, the leaders were serenaded by All Saints, a chart-topping British band. Commonwealth leaders were subjected to a 15-minute video on 'Britain, the Young Country' in Edinburgh, and Asian and European leaders were given a guided tour of the futuristic 'Powerhouse: UK', a huge exhibition of British talent set up behind Downing Street.

Some of the local reaction to rebranding has been harsh, with the British press regularly attacking the term 'Cool Britannia'. Critics see it as the guitar-strumming Tony Blair and his ministers trying too hard to sound hip. They claim this new found energy as merely ephemeral: every 30 years the Americans discover we are cool. But the fact is that Britain really has changed. And rebranding Britain is not about trying to be cool, but showing the world who we really are. The millennium marks the 200th anniversary of the Union Jack and the 150th anniversary of the Great Exhibition. It is fitting that Britain should abandon the doom and gloom and the psychology of decline of the postwar years and look to the future. What made Britain great in the Victorian era wasn't that we stood still, nostalgically harking back to a golden age. We were the pioneers and inventors that other nations looked at to see their own future. We can do the same again.

■ ■ ■

In the face of criticism from the media, politicians and popstars, the Prime Minister (Tony Blair) has also tried to define the nature of Labour government 'modernization' and his aims for a forward-looking Britain, which combines the best of the past and the present.

6 *'Britain is on a roll, whatever popstars say'*
Tony Blair
(Author copyright, 29 March 1998) abridged

It was the American *Newsweek* magazine that first[10] coined the phrase 'cool Britannia'. Journalists from all over the world copied it because of the enthusiasm of those who visit our theatres, watch British films, eat at our restaurants, admire our young artists, buy British clothes, read our novels, listen to our

Bill Clinton
President of the USA
1992–2000.

top bands and orchestras, benefit from our scientific breakthroughs, or commission our architects to design their new buildings.

Businesses and tourists alike look at Britain today and see a country embarking on an exciting journey, not slowly coming to the end of the road. We can start to believe in ourselves again. We have a unique advantage over so many other countries. The next century will be dominated by brain, not brawn. Creativity and knowledge will be the key tools. And Britain has always been a world leader in creativity and innovation.

We are forging a new patriotism focused on the potential we can fulfil in the future. For me, this is not about being 'cool' or keeping up with the current trends in pop music. It is about being modern and forward-thinking and believing in the future.

Part of that modernisation is about the identity of a country. It matters what a country looks like and feels like. It matters what we think of ourselves and how we project it.

So when I talk of a modern Britain, it is a patriotic vision of a model 21st-century nation. It is a vision that is based on our national characteristics. We are tolerant and open-minded: a multicultural society that works. We are innovative and pioneering, with more than 90 Nobel prize-winning scientists. We are compassionate and fair-minded, giving large amounts to charity.

Another characteristic seems to be cynicism – at least from some. I don't know why we have to be embarrassed about Britain's success. I'm not. I love it. So let me take on some of the criticism.

To start with the obvious: people are surprised that some musicians and artists don't support the government. It would be a surprise if all of them did. Rebellion is part of any youth culture. But I think they are wrong to criticise a New Deal programme giving many young people their first chance to get real jobs – after all, unemployment was the main complaint that many of them had against the Tories. But I am relaxed about criticism. The important point is not their politics, but the fact that they are part of a new and exciting cultural renaissance in this country.

Some critics say that you cannot 'rebrand' a country as you can a product. That is obviously true. Identity is complex and cannot be handed down by politicians. But countries do have an identity. Say 'France', and we all have an immediate impression. Say 'Germany' and we have a different one. When people visit this country they take away an impression. When businesses choose where to open a new plant, the perception of a country matters. That means we should show a face of Britain that is forward-looking.

Others fear that modernising Britain means abandoning the past. That's not what this is about. I have always believed that it is by building on our history that we can be most successful. A country's identity cannot be started from scratch. It is an accumulation of centuries of proud history. Why should the nation of Shakespeare, **Elgar, Constable** and some of the finest castles and cathedrals and palaces ever wish to betray the richness of that heritage? I certainly don't.

But I make no apologies for wanting Britain to be a nation characterised by merit, not privilege or stuffiness. Not all tradition should be retained for its own sake. In a modern democracy it is surely right to say that **hereditary peers** who owe their power to birth, not worth, should not be allowed to vote on laws that affect our everyday lives.

The most patronising criticism is that this is a metropolitan, trendy idea that excludes most people. Ambition is not a London-based phenomenon. It is certainly not the preserve of the young. The champions of modern Britain are to be found in every community in the country, trying to turn their ambitions into achievements.

Finally, there are those who say that this is all just a passing fashion with no real substance or depth to it. My view is that creativity will be the key to success in the 21st century. What we can do now is to put down the roots to boost creativity in this country. That is what we have done since May 1 [1997], in discussion with those from the creative industries . . .

There is an energy about Britain at the moment. I've never used the word 'cool' myself, but far from being embarrassed about it, I am proud the rest of the world is talking about us and wanting to know more about the modern Britain we have started to build.

■ ■ ■

Contrasting images

Modernization, the 'Cool Britannia' slogan and Labour government policies have received conflicting responses, from home and abroad, as the next three texts illustrate. One supports modernization, one is against and *Newsweek* magazine points to the continuing disparities in British society that modernizing forces have not remedied. Britain, in its view, is a country of contrasts; part decaying, part surviving and part booming.

Elgar
Sir Edward Elgar, English composer (1857–1934).

Constable
John Constable, English painter (1776–1837).

hereditary peers
In the House of Lords.

Birmingham
The second-largest city
in Britain, situated in
the English West
Midlands.

de rigueur
Necessary, essential.

pollsters
Public opinion poll
organizations.

7 'A tale of two nations'
Stryker McGuire and William Underhill
(*Newsweek*, 6 July 1998)

> Tony Blair has a vision of a vibrant country that challenges and
> rewards its citizens. Too bad lots of ordinary Britons don't live
> there yet.

When Tony Blair speaks of 'New Britain' as 'the model 21st-century nation,'
he doesn't, frankly, have **Birmingham** in mind. The rusty birthplace of the
Industrial Revolution is a lovely enough city in its way. It's got canals (ah,
like Venice, it wants you to think). It's got bars in big, beautiful spaces where
high-street banks used to be and restaurants that serve sophisticated Indian
food in high style. It's got the *de rigueur* brick-and-glass art gallery, Ikon,
where you can see Rachel Whiteread's dental-plaster cast of a hot-water bottle.
But most of Birmingham is a postindustrial sprawl struggling to get back on
its feet – a home to low wages, a motorway system that has brutalized much
of the city centre, and the grim housing projects of Ladywood.

So when the city hosted the G-8 summit in May, the prime minister brought
new Britain to Birmingham. He gave the summit itself the enforced informality
of a corporate retreat. He treated the world's press to a sleek, high-tech media
centre. He took his fellow heads of government and their wives to a glitzy
concert led by the pop group All Saints. If only for those few days, Blair swad-
dled a bastion of very old Britain in the shiny foil of 'Cool Britannia.'

For anybody who looked closely, Birmingham had an important story to tell
about Blair's Britain. For all his talk about new Britain, and for all the blather
from others about Cool Britannia, much of the country remains old and uncool.
Witness the economic stagnation in some of the old industrial cities, which bear
little resemblance to the economic Seattle that Blair would like Britain to
become. Witness, too, the outrageous and violent behaviour of the football
hooligans England has exported to France this summer; not the best adver-
tisement for Blair's stated vision of Britain as 'the best place to live, the best
place to bring up children, the best place to live a fulfilled life, the best place
to grow old.'

Many Britons don't yet feel like they live in new Britain. Especially outside of
London and other relatively prosperous enclaves, they are bogged down in
the kind of worries that afflict all economies in transition. Blair knows many
people feel this way: **pollsters** have repeatedly uncovered the bad news in the

focus groups that are quietly but constantly being conducted for his Labour party. A political strategist who has seen the results coined a phrase to describe the disaffected: 'the insecure majority.' It's a term that could come back to haunt Blair, however popular he remains more than a year after his election in May 1997.[11]

The tensions that exist in Britain, however subtle, may not say much about Blair's popularity, but they say a lot about the country. Labour's extended honeymoon can't disguise the fact that an old Britain and a new one exist side by side. Older industries are taking a pasting. Interest rates have risen six times since Labour took power 14 months ago, driving up the value of the pound and persuading foreign customers to look elsewhere for supplies. Unemployment is edging up for the first time in two years. Britain remains Europe's healthiest big economy, but its growth has begun to slow. And wage inflation has risen to 5.2 per cent, summoning up the 1970s demon of stag-flation, where a recession meets rapid price rises.[12] For good measure, a study published in May by McKinsey, the consulting firm, said that output per worker in Britain is 40 per cent lower than in America and 20 per cent lower than in Germany.

'The British economy is experiencing boom and bust at the same time,' says Conservative Party M.P. David Heathcoat-Amory. The new Britain is a place of high-tech industries, whopping bonuses in the financial sector, and peppy polenta-eaters alive to foreign influences and making plenty of money in imaginative new ways. All of that can be found in once unlikely places. A boom in high technology and in creative fields like advertising and design can be detected from Glasgow and Edinburgh to Manchester and Leeds and on to Bath and Bristol. Still, when Labour's theorists want to typify their new nation, there's no doubt what place comes to mind. 'The image they want to project is very, very London-based,' says Tony Travers, director of research for the Greater London Group at the London School of Economics. 'You can see why London matters so much to new Britain. London may be laid-back, dynamic, multicultural and liberal; the overwhelming majority of Britain isn't.'

Outside London, the long, and doubtless necessary, restructuring of the economy continues to hollow out old Britain. The number of hotel and catering employees (300,000) long ago overtook that of coal miners (13,000). In June, British Steel announced a 30 per cent plunge in profits and a 'radical manpower review'; according to analysts, that could mean the loss of a quarter of the 48,000 jobs that remain in an industry that employed 150,000 in 1980. But old Britain also includes the rural shires, which, like the manufacturing towns, can feel left behind by the talk of prosperity in Blair's speeches in spite of government retraining schemes. A perceived urban bent in the Blair government's policies has already created a rift between Blair and rural Britain.

fox-hunting
The Labour government intends to introduce legislation that will ban foxhunting by horse and hounds. Supporters of foxhunting argue that this will lead to rural unemployment and the destruction of a rural way of life.

dumb down
To reduce knowledge, the lowest common denominator, cultural degeneration.

The Countryside Alliance, rallying around such issues as **fox-hunting** and excessive home-building in rural and semi-rural areas, has managed to organize two impressive recent protest marches on London; the larger drew 250,000 people. Last year farm incomes in Britain plummeted by nearly 50 per cent, according to the National Farmers' Union. The strength of sterling has hurt agricultural exports and made imports look like bargains. Farmers are quick to blame Blair whenever a bit of rural Britannia bites the dust. That was what happened last month when the Banbury livestock market in Oxfordshire – once the country's largest – went out of business. The government could have saved the market if it had wanted to, says Clive Aslet, editor of *Country Life* magazine. It didn't. 'That sort of example makes people think that this government doesn't really care much what happens outside London,' he says.

In a way that is beginning to be dimly understood, 'London' is turning into a problem [compare with text 7 in Chapter 3]. As the country's political, financial and cultural capital, London is New York, Los Angeles, Chicago and Washington all rolled into one. It dominates Britain and yet is the least British place of all. Its economy, driven by the City, is at the heart of an international web. For many Britons, the capital is another country; they do things differently there. In London during the first three months of this year, the number of homes that sold for £2 million or more was three times greater than in the same period a year earlier. The price of the average London residence is now more than twice its equivalent in Liverpool or Newcastle. A ballooning service sector – especially in finance – guarantees that a white-collar worker in London will earn 25 per cent more than he would outside the capital. But it is London that has imprinted itself on the vision of new Britain embraced by Blair and the party he chooses to call (inevitably) 'New Labour'.

Which brings us to Cool Britannia. Somewhere on the road to modernization, Blair's 'new Britain' project got mixed up with what sounds like an overused ad campaign. Blair has himself never uttered the phrase, except to say he didn't coin it. He has publicly claimed on at least two occasions that *Newsweek* did. We didn't. We wrote a 1996 cover story on London, which described the capital as 'the coolest city on the planet.' We didn't extend the adjective to the whole nation, because we knew it would have been crazy to do so. In fact, 'Cool Britannia' turns out to be a dangerous phrase; it can be used to **dumb down** Blair's whole campaign to modernize the economy, deconstruct the welfare state, adopt constitutional reform and rebrand the nation with 'a clear identity and role for ourselves in the outside world.' But just as bands of English hooligans marauding through World Cup venues do not advance the cause of rebranding Britain, the lightweight 'Cool Britannia' does no service to serious reforms.

The biggest potential Cool Britannia albatross of them all sits along the Thames in Greenwich, in east London. With a price tag of between £750 million and £1 billion, the Millennium Dome will be not only the world's most expensive building but the perfect monument to Blair's success or failure in moulding old and new Britain into the model nation he likes to talk about. Now a giant structure shielding 20 acres of dirt from the rain, the space is meant to house an ambitious high-tech, multi-media exhibition. It will be a celebration of the old and the new, of 'our past achievements and confidence in the future,' as Blair said in a topping-off ceremony at the site last week. Blair promised that, when its times comes, the Dome will out-Disney Orlando and out-Eiffel Paris – and be 'the greatest day out on earth.'[13] Birmingham will be watching it: it lost out to London in the competition to become the home of the Dome.

■ ■ ■

The next text, from the mid-market right-of-centre *Daily Mail* paper, also criticizes the Labour government's modernization project. This is seen as engineered change for change's sake and is apparently unrepresentative or untypical of the evolutionary nature of British history. The text, as well as suggesting the creation of a new 'Establishment', questions the nature of change in Britain and people's response to it, while doubting the Conservative Party's ability to construct an alternative view.

8 'This insidious urge to reshape Britain'
Stephen Glover
(*Daily Mail*, 23 June 1998) abridged

[The] characteristic representative of the new [British] establishment . . . is based on money, business and popular culture . . .

. . . [Often this representative] . . . [b]esides being metropolitan and rich . . . is essentially non-ideological . . .

Throughout our history colourful men have battened on to the establishment of the day. What is different now is that Tony Blair, allegedly the most conservative of politicians, is in the throes of building his own new establishment . . . Mr Blair is deliberately altering the landscape of our society. A new élite is being created, quite different from the old.

Union
The union of the United
Kingdom (England,
Scotland, Wales and
Northern Ireland).

big dipper
Rollercoaster ride.

William Hague
Leader of the
Conservative Party.

If Mr Blair's creation of this new establishment were merely a little sideline, one might not complain too much. In fact it is part of a wholesale transformation of our society. Everything must be changed. In this Mr Blair is the faithful disciple of Margaret Thatcher who, untypically for a Conservative, saw politics as a never-ending long march, a permanent revolution. But whereas Thatcherism used economics as its engine of change, whose effects admittedly spread far throughout our institutions, New Labour plans to shake up the whole of our society from top to bottom.

On the surface it looks like business as usual. The economy is run on generally prudent lines. But the Blairites are addicted to the idea of change for change's sake. Their only ideology is change. They want to change our image and our view of our history. They want to change the nature of the **Union**, and in so doing risk that very Union itself, so that within a year of a referendum Scotland is almost visibly breaking away. They want to change our relationship with Europe, whatever they may say.

So far New Labour's project has found no disfavour with the British people in their present mood of stupefaction.[14] I doubt whether this will continue to be the case. I believe that Mr Blair's craving for ceaseless change will eventually contribute to his undoing. For more than any generation that has ever lived, we already inhabit a world of change. I don't just mean technological change – CDs, computers, the Internet and all the other wonders of modern life. I mean the cultural and social change of which these things are part. I mean our feeling that our world is being transformed before our eyes.

Most of us feel ambivalent about these changes. In our hearts we recognize that there is little we can do about them. We seize upon some innovations and reject others. But only those who naturally head towards the **big dipper** whenever they see a fun fair are likely to want their government to pile changes of its own upon those which are already happening. The rest of us yearn for some measure of stability. Far from providing a still centre in a turning world, Mr Blair is himself an agent of change, egged on by a media class for whom politics is a form of entertainment in which change is the ultimate thrill.

Is it too much to expect **William Hague** and modern Conservatives to turn this to their advantage? The old Tory Party – the party of Knights of the Shires and gentlemen with stiff collars – is dead and nothing is going to revive it. But that does not mean the Tories' natural scepticism about engineered change should be disowned. It is, after all, called the Conservative Party, and has been since 1830 . . .

. . . Yet I fear that Mr Hague, while perhaps a natural Conservative at heart . . . is surrounded by spin doctors and management consultants who are almost as addicted to change as Mr Blair . . .

We are not the first people to be bewildered by the disappearance of familiar landmarks. The Victorians were devastated by the pace of change. Towards the end of a life that had seen more change than most, **W.E. Gladstone** wrote: 'I am for old customs and traditions against needless change. I am for the individual as against the state. I am for the family and the stable family as against the state.' This from a man who began his political life as a High Tory and became a Liberal, and who himself presided over many upheavals.

... A country cannot be reshaped like a political party and relaunched like a detergent. We will eventually tire of Mr Blair's appetite for change and Mr Hague, if he has any sense at all, will be on hand to deliver us.

■ ■ ■

However, some defenders applaud the main planks of the Labour government's modernization project, indicating that tradition for its own sake is self-defeating. The following text argues that change is happening and must be embraced. But this does not involve totally destroying the traditions of the past.

9 *'The bit of politics that led Ben Elton astray'*
Melvyn Bragg
(Author copyright, 20 April 1998) abridged

Ben Elton has joined a growing line of notables from the arts world who are attacking a Government which they feel has already fallen too far below their expectations ... But the Government of Tony Blair ... [has] more of a case than [it is] given credit for ...

The Government is surely saying that there is a Britain which is not only beefeaters and country houses and **Black Rod** walking backwards and villages determined never to go forwards, but also a place where young people rave through Saturday night to the best dance music in the world; where inventions still tumble out (although too often they are pirated away from us); where computer penetration in schools gathers pace – where, above all, there is a growing number of younger people happy and easy in a post-imperial democracy. In short, the Government wants to emphasize newness and change. Not to fabricate it, because it is already here. Not to give it precedence, because this is a government sensible of tradition. But to give it a profile. To give it

W.E. Gladstone
Liberal politician and Prime Minister, 1809–98.

Ben Elton
Alternative comedian, media person and writer.

Black Rod
The royal official who summons the House of Commons to the House of Lords to attend the State Opening of Parliament by the Queen, usually every autumn.

Silicon Valley
The common name for the collection of computer industries in California, USA.

the oxygen of approval. To blow away the loving cobwebs. To show Britain itself that this is what is happening now.

There is no doubt of this Government's belief that the only rich future is one which embraces the new. That is also the philosophy from **Silicon Valley** to Sydney. The 21st century will surely see an explosion of change when the three great 20th-century revolutions – the quantum, the biomolecular and the computer – mesh together and transform work, wealth and play. We need to be at that party.

But in this country to wave a flag for the new is to wave a red flag . . . [A]n attempt to change the perception of our culture, which is what this Government is up to, needs to be appreciated as much as criticized.

The Prime Minister is sending out a new message and it is bound to be raw and stumble a little in its first steps. The problem, I think, is that as a country we have become rather proud of our resistance to the new. Most people who can afford a wider choice of housing do not build new places but look for old, the older the better. In a country stacked with strong traditional arts, the new has to bulldoze its way in.

Our past is very fine and very secure and we are proud of it and sometimes over-addicted to it. Blair is right: it is no good for the future if the image of Britain is irredeemably fustian . . . As the multiplicity of television channels grows, image will be a crucial part of any success.

It is far too easy to bypass Olde Britain with the excuse that it prefers to be a happy little village undisturbed by the heavy traffic of the future. Although that holds great truth for me and for others it will be of very little use for our children and their children. The relentless promotion of the greatness of the past could become like a burden of debt around their necks. 'Cool Britannia' has had a short shelf-life – so what . . .? The substance of this Government's attempt to realise change does not hang on the slender thread of that phrase . . .

■ ■ ■

The people's images

In the light of the divided opinions about modernization and change, public opinion polls on how the British actually see themselves and their country also produce conflicting results. These are often at variance with ideas promoted by the media and politicians. For a time, they were also tied to questions of whether the death of Diana, Princess of Wales in 1997 had had a significant impact upon British people and had produced permanent changes in British society.

10 'Going soft? Britain is still a nation of hard-headed people'

David Smith

(*The Sunday Times*, 19 April 1998) abridged

When he agreed to submit an eight-page chapter on 'Diana, queen of hearts', for a **Social Affairs Unit** book[15] on the sentimentalization of Britain, **Professor Anthony O'Hear** did not expect to get his 15 minutes of **Andy Warhol-style notoriety**.

But there he was, last Friday, caught like a rabbit in the headlights, insisting he had not meant to cause any offence with his comments that, on her death, 'feeling was elevated above reason, caring above principle, personal gratification above commitment and propriety'. Unworldly professors of philosophy from Bradford should not mess around with Diana's memory.

But was there a serious point to O'Hear's claim? Has Britain, as the Social Affairs Unit argues, become a fake society, riddled with sentiment, and was Diana's death a defining moment in its creation? Are we living in a country where politics is by gesture, not substance: 'done for show, to strike a pose, and not for the benefit of anyone'? Are people now so prey to **faddism** and self-indulgence in healthcare, education, religion, literature and even eating, that it is right to describe Britain as a fake society?

With the anniversary of Labour's election victory coming up, **Opinion Leader Research** (OLR) organized a series of focus groups in London, Birmingham and Edinburgh to test the national mood ... After a year of Tony Blair, and in this post-Diana age which, according to O'Hear had changed Britain into 'another country', had people become different, more sentimental, more touchy-feely?

'One of the things we had thought was that the British psyche had changed,' said Deborah Mattinson, director of OLR. 'This was absolutely rejected.'

'They felt that British people don't change, and certainly not in a short time. They are quite cool, quite reserved, quite conservative. The national character

Social Affairs Unit
A right-of-centre think tank that produces pamphlets on social, political and economic issues.

Professor Anthony O'Hear
Professor of Philosophy, Bradford University.

Andy Warhol-style notoriety
Andy Warhol, 1928–87, American artist, who argued that every individual deserved 15 minutes of fame.

faddism
Temporary fashions.

Opinion Leader Research
Public opinion poll organization.

soundbite
A short, inclusive quote
usually for the media.

does not alter. Regarding Diana, the chin might have wobbled a little, but the stiff upper lip was still very much there.'

Indeed, people resented the suggestion that, post-Diana, they were different. 'It brought the people together at the time but it's soon forgotten isn't it,' said one Birmingham man. 'It's not there anymore – people are still trying to pull on it and it doesn't exist.' A London woman agreed. September 1997 was, she said, 'a strange phenomenon which will never happen again'. Another woman thought the national outpouring of grief at Diana's death was 'very much encouraged and engineered by the media'.

Are there other manifestations of the 'nation of sentimentalists', prey to every passing trend, claimed by the Social Affairs Unit? Far from it. The OLR research reveals, instead, a nation peopled by the nostalgic yearning for the return of traditional values and not at all keen to turn Britain into a colder version of southern California.

People want fewer out-of-town supermarkets and more local shops. They are concerned about the number of women with children who are working, because of its impact on the family. And they would like more people to stay in their own home area, to rebuild the communities of the past . . .

The public mood is also determinedly unsentimental when it comes to education and parenting. They want both to reflect traditional values. 'If you look at some of the younger parents, they have no respect for their children,' said a London woman. 'The way they speak to their children, the way they treat their children. Those children aren't going to have any respect and they will grow up into the same sort of adults.' Another bemoaned the fact that 'teachers have got no authority as such'.

This government, like its predecessor, has moved firmly to restore traditional values in education. The Social Affairs Unit has yet to catch up: 'In schools, discipline and obedience have given way to false love and a general slackness.'

Even the Social Affairs Unit's easiest target, fake politicians, found surprisingly little resonance. 'You at least want a government that comes from the same planet as yourself,' said a London man, comparing the out-of-touch Tories with the Labour government. 'I get a good vibe about what Tony Blair and his government are doing,' said another. 'They're young, they're dynamic, there are women in the cabinet.' Blair may have become the master of the **soundbite** and the political gesture but, so far at least, he is getting away with it.

Even the apparent decline in the sexual morals of politicians receives little condemnation. 'They can go to bed with anyone they like as long as their politics are what I voted for,' said a Birmingham woman.

So who has got it right? The Social Affairs Unit, in truth, has managed some good publicity on the back of O'Hear's Diana observations, but its claims do not stand up to scrutiny . . .

The OLR's findings, on the other hand, leave you more than a little uneasy. If everyone is so hot on traditional values, how come society has changed, many would say for the worse? Do they yearn for local shops while happily taking their custom to out-of-town stores? Did they insist on high standards of education for their children?

Ordinary people are seen as having little influence on what goes on, but then neither are formerly powerful institutions such as the Church of England ('I don't think people have got time for the church now') or the royal family ('it's tourism that keeps royalty going').

There is, too, little sense of national pride. It has been said before, but if Blair wants to put the 'Great' back into Britain, he has to start on the people them-selves. 'We're not made to feel Britain is successful – they're telling others but not us,' said a Scottish man. 'Nobody feels proud to be British any more,' said a Birmingham woman.

Indeed, the overwhelming impression is of passivity. 'We don't have a say, we just get told,' said a Birmingham woman. Politicians and the media are seen to be stitching things up, 'in cahoots', said one participant, with voters barely getting a look in.

This is the couch potato society, unwilling to get involved apart from 'voting once every four years'. People want things to be better, but they don't plan to do much to bring it about. Passivity rules. When it comes to changing society, the British people aren't that sentimental. But they are probably more than a little lazy.

 # Exercises

Write short essays on the following topics

1   Do you have an image of Britain? What is it and why?

2   Discuss the nature of change in Britain.

3   Are 'images' and 'stereotypes' an adequate way of understanding Britain?

4   Do you consider that some of the images of Britain and the British in these texts are too harsh and unrepresentative? Or are they justified?

5   Comment on the contrasting views of Britain revealed by internal and external sources.

6   Critically examine Tony Blair's article (text 6).

Explain and examine the following terms

nostalgia	Special Air Squadron	pub culture
nationalism	muddling through	judiciary
underclass	conservatism	Maastricht
yobs	Dunkirk spirit	Britannia
fustian	'new Jerusalem'	rowing eight
soundbite	Countryside Alliance	fogey
stagflation	couch potato	civic culture
stoicism	Blimpishness	focus group

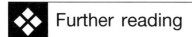 **Further reading**

British Social Attitudes, regular reports, Aldershot: Dartmouth Publishing Company.
Jacobs, Eric and Worcester, Robert (1990) *We British: Britain under the MORIscope*, London: Weidenfeld and Nicolson.
Marwick, Arthur (1991) *Culture in Britain since 1945*, Oxford: Basil Blackwell.
Storry, Mike and Childs, Peter (eds) (1997) *British Cultural Identities*, London: Routledge.

 **Notes**

1. Note that this quotation refers to England, not Britain.
2. Former London correspondent for *Il Giornale*, Milan.
3. Compare with text 4 in Chapter 8.
4. While this may be true on a comparative level, British politics in the 1990s suffered from sleaze and corruption allegations. External business and financial interests now have to be declared by politicians and are tightly controlled.
5. Scandals in the Conservative period (1990–97) were often concerned with money and financial sleaze.
6. See Chapter 3 for the difficulties of defining Britishness.
7. Reiner Gatermann (1999) 'Auf Wiedersehen, the England that failed', London: *The Sunday Times* 17 January.
8. See marginal note 'in France', p. 35.
9. *Newsweek* (1998) London: July 6, see text 5.

10. Opinions differ as to who coined the slogan 'Cool Britannia'. *Newsweek* denies it, see text 7.
11. The Labour government's initial popularity had been reduced by 2000 according to public opinion polls, which recorded some varying advances for the Conservatives.
12. Inflation and unemployment in 2000 continued to be relatively low.
13. The Dome has had technical and financial problems and has failed to attract large numbers of visitors since its opening to the public in January 2000. It exhibits have been described as tacky and its amenities as inadequate.
14. Public opinion polls in 2000 indicated that this situation was changing and there was a growing disillusionment with the Labour government's performance.
15. Digby Anderson and the Rev Peter Mullen (eds) (1998) *Faking It, the Sentimentalization of Society*, London: Social Affairs Unit.

devolution
Devolution is the
transfer of some
political power from
Westminster to a
Scottish Parliament and
a Welsh Assembly in
1999 and to a Northern
Irish Assembly and
Executive in 2000.

Chapter 3

National identities

This chapter expands upon the nature of image (how the British see themselves and are perceived by others) discussed in Chapter 2. It deals more specifically with the problematic question of national identity and the alleged tensions between the peoples of the United Kingdom (England, Scotland, Wales and Northern Ireland). Current debate in Britain in these areas mainly occurs at political, media and academic levels. But, following **devolution**, questions of identity are also obvious at a popular level in Scotand, Wales and Northern Ireland, and as a reaction increasingly so in England.

Is there a British nation, a British national identity or something called 'Britishness' and how long have these been in existence? Are there only mutually exclusive national identities in England, Scotland, Wales and Northern Ireland? Or are there dual nationalities, eg English and British or Welsh and British? Opposed theoretical models of what Britishness might mean continue to be developed.

National identity (of the individual nations or of Britain) is a multidimensional construction, formed by often competing forces. It derives from the events and accidents of history; the influence of central and local institutional structures; the existence of 'the Other' against which to measure oneself or one's country; ideals, folk memories and myths; alleged common ethnic origins; and a degree of invention and artificiality. Very often, it may be couched in terms of stereotypes and also be in conflict with more localized identities within nations.

The first text examines whether Britishness exists any longer, either in its arguable former state or in changed form. It emphasizes the tensions inherent in such a concept.

■ ■ ■

Britishness

1 'British unity in diversity'
Mary Ann Sieghart
(*The Times*, 22 April 1995)

What is Britishness? Is it more than the sum of its parts – or less? Many Scots and not a few Welsh believe that Britishness is no more than a disguised version of Englishness. Exploring the questions of national identity for the BBC,[1] I have just visited three towns with the same name – one each in Scotland, Wales and England – to try to discover whether there is an overarching sense of identity that it still makes sense to call British.

Nobody in Newport, Shropshire [England], had a problem with Britishness. In Newport, Gwent [Wales], some of the Welsh felt British, though others prefer to call themselves European. But it was in Newport-on-Tay, near Dundee [Scotland], that we found the greatest reluctance to sign up to a common identity of Britishness.

**long-standing
allegiance to region**
The notion of region or
local area within a
nation has been and is
an important primary
constituent of identity
for many people. This
may lead to tensions or
even conflicts between
region or local area and
nation.

Here is Billy Kay, a local writer: 'The British identity that I'm supposed to feel part of I see as being first of all an imperial identity through the Empire and then an identity which has been forced by the idea of people coming together to fight two world wars. I don't think that's a healthy identity to carry into the 21st century.'

This is a common complaint – that Britishness is something from the past that has little relevance today. When the Act of Union [uniting England, Wales and Scotland] was signed in 1707, people had to be persuaded to attach an extra loyalty to their **long-standing allegiance to region** or nation.

Protestantism
Arising from the
European Protestant
Reformation in the
sixteenth century.

Successive governments used the common religion of **Protestantism** as a propaganda weapon to encourage the English, Scottish and Welsh to unite around a common flag – and against Catholic enemies.

The Empire – which was always the British, not the English Empire – was also a unifying force. It drew heavily on the expertise of the Scots and Welsh as doctors, traders, explorers and administrators.

Battle of Britain
The air battle with the
German air force in
1940 during the
Second World War
1939–45.

Then there was the monarchy. Queen Victoria [1819–1901] perhaps perfected the art of being monarch to all of Britain and the Empire. Meanwhile, successive wars have brought Britons together in defence of the Empire and the Union. It was the **Battle of Britain,** not the Battle of England, that took place over the Channel and southern counties.

Scottish nationalists
The Scottish National
Party, which campaigns
as an ultimate aim for
complete national
independence for
Scotland.

But history is history; the Empire has gone, the Church no longer binds us, the Armed Forces are shrinking and the monarchy is troubled. Some people feel that the glue of nationhood has dried up. Alex Salmond, leader of the **Scottish nationalists**, no longer wants to be attached to what he sees as a Britain in decline. He looks to Europe as Scotland's new stage.

So do a surprising number in Newport, Gwent. Alan Richards, a sales director, has found that doing business with Europe has changed his outlook. 'I see our future very much as being linked to Europe as a whole; that includes England. I see England merely as part of Europe.'

But he is still unusual: probably a majority of the Welsh still think of themselves as British too. We are all capable of overlapping loyalties and identities – Britishness need not detract from Welshness. And as a nation we have a surprising amount in common. We are good at winning wars together. We are all good explorers, travellers, traders, philanthropists and inventors. We share a sense of fair play, and probity in public life. We respect the law.

These British values and ways of thinking that we all share have been some-what eclipsed by **Scottish and Welsh strivings for national identity**. So frustrated are they by English political domination that they have allowed themselves to forget how much the nations of Britain still have in common.

Some people see the devolution of power to Scotland and Wales as a threat to **the Union**. But it could be that, by venting their differences through poli-tics, the Scots and Welsh would feel more comfortable as part of the joint enterprise called Great Britain.[2]

■ ■ ■

The above text argues that there is still a Britain (or United Kingdom) with a distinctive British identity composed of common characteristics and values. But Britishness, and the difficulties of defining it, have to be seen within a historical context. Before 1707, the history of the geographical 'British' Isles is arguably not about Britishness or Britain. It is about Scotland, England, Wales and Ireland, which were different countries, often hostile to one another and, importantly, with substan-tial differences within their own borders. Britain (or Great Britain), as a political unit and arguably as a nation, is a relatively recent union of three older nations. Wales and England were formally joined in the 1530s. The Act of Union of these two countries with Scotland to create Great Britain came about in 1707, although there had been a Union of the English and Scottish Crowns since 1603. The later United Kingdom (to include Great Britain and Ireland) was formed only in 1801.

Historical developments, common institutional structures and alleged values have maintained this inherently unstable union. The growth of a British identity, for some historians such as Linda Colley,[3] began largely in the eighteenth century and was conditioned by Protestantism in England, Scotland and Wales, the expanding empire, military victories in Europe and a central monarchy. Others, however, argue that a collective sense of Britishness was already in existence before the eighteenth century, based on legal traditions, a belief in 'national' uniqueness, parliamentary government and a linguistic cultural history.[4]

One side of the debate maintains that Protestantism in England, Wales and Scotland promoted a sense of difference from the Catholicism of most of continental Europe (especially France). European military victories in the eighteenth and nineteenth centuries persuaded the British that they were morally and constitutionally superior to European states and helped to create a worldwide empire. The establishment of foreign markets expanded trade and job opportunities, promoted wealth and economic strength and increased a sense of national identity. The English, Scots, Welsh and (partly) the Irish all participated in and accepted the notion of a British empire.

Scottish and Welsh strivings for national identity
The movement towards devolved self-government for Scotland and Wales.

the Union
The union of England, Scotland, Wales and Northern Ireland to form the United Kingdom. Supporters of the Union are called Unionists, eg the Ulster Unionist Party in Northern Ireland.

But, for some historians such as Linda Colley, the ties of this common British identity have weakened. The empire has disappeared and Britain has experienced a reduced world role since 1945. Protestant belief and strength have decreased in modern Britain as secularism has grown and as the country has become more multicultural and multi-religious. A sense of British national confidence and cohesion has allegedly declined, to be replaced with confusion. Arguably, a reassessment of Britishness within Europe is required.

However, while some critics see Britishness as a flimsy and temporary construction based on historically created institutions, monarchy, the empire and Protestantism, others (such as politicians in the Conservative Party) see a more firmly based system of common values and shared history as constituting Britishness. National identity, in this view, is more durable and robust than some academic commentators allow.

Nevertheless, the next text suggests that the current movement is away from Britishness (which allegedly was a late flowering only from the nineteenth century) and towards a renewal of the identities of the four ancient nations within a European and global context. It points particularly to a potential reawakening of Englishness and its strengths, as well as indicating the difficulties in defining what is meant by a 'nation'. It also suggests nationalist reactions to a globalization of economies and culture and the easy assumption that global effects are inevitable and overpowering.

2 'Disunited we stand'
Brian Deer
(*The Sunday Times*, 5 February 1995) abridged

[There are] subtle differences of meaning between 'nation' and words such as 'people', 'society', 'culture', and even 'race' . . .

. . . a nation . . . has a defined space – an economic and social life that is rooted in rules and conventions, that endures in the face of the comings and goings of its various personnel. It has a common language and narrowly codified relationships that extend not only horizontally, but also from the captain down.

Even more crucially . . . nations are caught up in history and traditions, extending back to forebears whose examples are invoked today . . .

... **leviathans** ... slumber in national cultures. They symbolise something of the 'state', but more of 'tribes' and 'clans'; their lairs are in the eddies of the past and the currents of fable and myth. From time to time emerging in high art or heroic poetry, they are nevertheless often near the surface of what appears most everyday. Passed down more as collective sentiments than distinct entities, they live in the language, customs and creativity that ordinary people feel are theirs ...

... [But] there is not now, and never has been, a *British nation* at all.

... around the turn of the [nineteenth] century ... the notion of 'British' featured little in [society]. Not long before, **Benjamin Disraeli** ... was using ['English'] in his popular oratory [and omitting references to 'Great Britain' and 'British'] ...

But even as Disraeli's words were telegraphed to London, printed in newspapers and distributed by the new railway network across the United Kingdom, the ruling class knew that the moment had come to engineer a historic change. England was simply not big enough to satisfy new mass-production industries. Business needed a common market in which it could expand. The empire needed armies and administrators to sustain overseas profits. The government needed legitimising in bids to levy taxes. So the nation needed expansion – and the concept of 'being British' was born.

Élite political and military structures had long been in place, but otherwise 'Britain' in the 19th century was still the geographical feature it [had been earlier]. James I had declared himself king of Great Britain ... in 1603, and the two national parliaments had united in 1707, but the people were still of different cultures: they were English, Scottish or Welsh.

What Disraeli's people sought were new symbols to help with cultural colonisation. 'British Empire' was strong and 'British Army' powerful, but one was too abstract and the other too controversial to be the centre-piece of any initiative. What was wanted was something ... which would not only stir *Rule Britannia* emotions, but was world class and tangible enough to make the peoples feel as one ... So a 'British' brand celebrity was enlisted: Victoria, the miserable queen.

Although 'British' was cropping up more often as industrialisation gathered pace ... it was test-marketed in 1877 – but only in India ... 'British' was launched in Delhi at an elaborately planned 'Assemblage' ...

The cohesion that this provided was soon developed for Great Britain itself. A decade later, as the start of the wholesale manufacture of pageantry, Victoria

leviathans
Mythical and biblical sea- or river-monster, symbolizes something of great size and power.

Benjamin Disraeli
Conservative Prime Minister 1868 and 1874–80.

Rule Britannia
A patriotic song composed by Thomas Arne (1710–78) with music by James Thomson (1700–48). Sometimes sung as an unofficial British national anthem.

nationalised industries
Industries and services owned and controlled by the state.

eisteddfod
Annual gatherings in Wales that celebrate Welsh language and culture, allegedly dating back to the twelfth century.

personally moved centre-stage for her 'golden jubilee'. That day, June 21, 1887, was the symbolic fabrication of what, barely 100 years later, [is called] the 'British nation'. As Victoria made her way to Westminster, escorted by a bobbling phalanx of German princes, the capital was dragooned into a frenzy of the new patriotism.

Though it was still an age of minimal media, hardly anybody in the United Kingdom could avoid this event . . .

The cultural shift that this helped along cannot be overestimated, but complete English domination was still decades away. Although 830,000 people enlisted in Scotland and Wales to fight for the English ruling class in the first world war, it was not until the foundation of the British Broadcasting Company, in 1922, that London fully extended its grip across the United Kingdom. And not until the 1940s would another war and the new **nationalised industries** and health service cobble the island's peoples into a unitary block.

Yet one of the laws of nature and life is that all change contains within itself some element of contradiction . . . [T]he upheavals of industrialisation and empire not only brought the 'British' together, but also started a kind of back-wash, which would one day pull them apart. As the Scots and Welsh were roped more tightly by the English into the new British thing, they went looking, in compensation, for more potent symbols of themselves.

In this there also proved to be an aspect of invention. The Scottish short kilt, for instance, only appeared in the 1730s, and it is attributed to an Englishman, Thomas Rawlinson, who ran an iron forge – while the variegated clan tartans took off a century after that. Similarly, the 'traditional' Welsh women's national dress of tweed shawl and high hat was fashioned by one Augusta Waddington and some friends in the 1830s. Druidic Welsh **eisteddfod** rituals, assumed to date from the dawn of time, started in about 1790 on London's Primrose Hill.

But these were so keenly seized on that they must have been seen to symbolise something: they were not mere fashion statements. For Scotland, it was as if 'highland dress' was a form of defiance, mythically reaching back even to the glory of 1314, when their ancestors defeated England at the Battle of Bannockburn. For Wales, the new traditions echoed the fabulous days of Owain Glyn Dwr, who in 1400 also led his people against hated English rule. It was as if the rise of the 'British' thing also lifted 'Scottish' and 'Welsh'.

The feelings behind these symbols have continued to extend their power – and are at the heart of the problem with talk of the British 'nation' today . . .

. . . But, whatever the pretensions of politicians (and especially the vocal hard right) . . . [Britain must now speak] to European and global ideas.

Business naturally leads the European drift, just as it did with that to 'British' . . . For the movement of money, national boundaries no longer seem to count.

On the same giant stage is the ever more rapid globalisation of culture. Despite the hankering for lost British glory . . . it is America which, in communications, entertainment and even language, is spreading the veneer of Anglo-Americanism rapidly across the planet . . .

But though these changes seem overwhelming, the big yawn of familiarity that they produce conceals another trend. Since 1962, when Marshall McLuhan published his book *Gutenberg Galaxy*, people have talked in clichéd terms, about the rise of a 'global village'. Yet, despite the relevance of McLuhan's point, his catchy expression has spread an idea that, in a vital respect, is wrong.

What these words distract from is the lesson of the backwash that we should have learnt from the 19th century. People have a primary need to *belong*, to have sense of place, context and safety. And in the same way that the growth of empire and industry paradoxically raised interest in tartans and eisteddfods, so today we are seeing a similar contradiction in European and global expansion. Accompanying the rise of a world economy and culture, we are seeing a kind of collapsing going on, a pulling-in, a coming together.

. . . it is revealed once more (and most powerfully) in the mass emotion of nationalism. As people feel more than ever surrounded by expanding, uniform horizons of often cruel seas, they more keenly hunt out sheltered coves in which to feel secure . . . Everybody is looking for symbols on which they can get a hold.

Nothing reveals this better than Britain, which led the world into the industrial age and now faces something new. People from this island had the leading role in shaping America. The success of their language means that, around the world, 1.5 billion speak some English (including 60 per cent of scientists and 80 per cent of e-mail users). Yet, in 1993, parliament yielded to pressure for a law to promote the use of Welsh.

It is not to slight an ancient people to point out the irony. Since Wales was annexed in 1536 and its peasant population yoked into a proletariat in the 19th century, there has always been a Welsh resilience that English rulers could not crush . . .

ratings
The number of people
who actually watch
specific programmes.

The resurgence of Welsh in Wales is something that the champions of 'global village' ideas would have trouble explaining. Although the population is only 2.9 million and the number of native language speakers has halved in 60 years, the 1991 census shows that the underlying trend has reversed. During the previous two decades, the number of *young* speakers rose from 14 per cent to 25 per cent among 5- to 9-year-olds; and from 17 per cent to 27 per cent among those aged 10 to 14.

In the Scottish Highlands, Gaelic still dies, but the Scots have other symbols of themselves around which to mobilise. Whether it is the 'national drinks' (whisky [etc]), ... the images are of something distinctively alive.

A System 3 survey last year [1994] among the 5.1 million people in Scotland showed that when they are asked if they are 'British' or 'Scottish', three-quarters say the latter. In an ICM poll, 44 per cent said that they want their own parliament and 38 per cent full independence – both figures an increase on similar surveys the year before. If you go into Dillons or Waterstone's book-stores in Glasgow you will see Scottish literature proliferating ...

But the Welsh and the Scots are a minority of Britons – they must be seen against their neighbours. Despite the energy behind their identities, they are also forged negatively: out of being not English. People may not wage wars ... but in the search for belonging in the different countries of Britain there is often evident a sense of difference, of distrust or even disdain. In these low-key oppositions, the construction claimed to be the 'British nation' starts to come apart at the seams ...

But the speed of change is breath-taking, and as usual is led by profit. Not only is business becoming European and global, but it is also getting nation-alistic in the Welsh and Scottish sense. A survey carried out for the Leith Agency, an advertising firm, for instance, found that an amazing 40 per cent of Scots say they 'always prefer to buy Scottish products', while another 40 per cent would buy them 'if everything else were equal'. Commercial television has found that by boosting stations' Scottish identity, they can edge their **ratings** up.

These drives to cash in on the need to belong are now combining with globali-sation to break the remnants of 'British nation' ideas. Westminster politicians will deny this phenomenon – as will 'national' newspapers, which prefer the economies of a standardised pan-Britain market. But 'British' is effectively finished already because it does not make any money ...

... the United Kingdom has always been England with ... appendages ...
[T]he Scottish and Welsh are [now] seizing their chance to have somewhere
to belong.

With the fall of the sign saying 'British', moreover, an older one saying
'English' is revealed, legible and intact. Here is a true nation, which has less
imperial rust on it than at first sight you might suppose. And as the 48.5m
people living in England will discover as they watch their smaller neighbours,
there may be plenty to be gained by asserting identity as a distinct European
element.

They might also discover that England, not Britain, has things of value to
show the world. Since the Romans defeated some two dozen resident tribes,
the people who are now the English have been bastardised by conquest, incur-
sion and immigration. Perhaps more than anybody they have blazed a trail
for diversity and multi-culturalism – and although they have often been
suppressed by British notions of superiority, there is a strong undercurrent of
pragmatism and ethnic tolerance ...

■ ■ ■

Tensions

There have always been historical tensions between England on the one hand and
Scotland, Wales and Ireland on the other. Variations of these are visible in contemporary Britain, although they can be exaggerated and may exist merely as
stereotypes. While they reflect the argument that Britishness is fragmenting, they
do not alter the fact that there is still a political union called the United Kingdom,
nor that different identities and conflicts are also apparent *within* the four countries
themselves. These latter can stem from regionalism, language diferences, local
customs, religious emphases and competing histories.

The next text looks at the contemporary relationship between the English and the
Scots. Scotland was initially joined to England through a dynastic alliance based on
a common monarchy in 1603. In theory, and although conflicts and skirmishes continued between the two countries, the Scots were therefore equal partners with the
English and maintained their own legal system and many of their institutional structures. This situation allowed them to maintain a strong sense of Scottishness and
a distinctiveness from the English.

Braveheart
Film loosely based on William Wallace (c. 1274–1305), Scottish knight and champion of the independence of Scotland.

Rob Roy
Film based on Robert MacGregor (1671–1734), Scottish outlaw and the object of many legends.

The Bruce
Film based on Robert Bruce (1274–1329), hero of the Scottish War of Independence.

Bannockburn
The Scottish king Robert the Bruce defeated the army of the English king Edward II in 1314, allowing Scotland to remain an independent country.

Trainspotting
Scottish-based film, 1996.

3 'Hooked on hatred of the English'

Fergus Kelly
(*The Sunday Times*, 3 March 1996) abridged

It is said that Scottish fans always support two teams: Scotland and whoever is playing England. The rivalry dates back centuries.

However, the antipathy, if not outright hostility, now evident towards all things English has not been so prevalent since more than 1,000 weak and starving Highlanders were slaughtered by the English Redcoats[5] – far superior in number and weaponry – on a remote tract of moorland near Inverness called Culloden [1746]. Next month marks the 250th anniversary of Britain's last big land battle.

This weekend, meanwhile, sees the premiere of yet another film glorifying a Scottish national hero, at the same time as vilifying its southern neighbours. While produced on a much smaller budget than the Hollywood epics **Braveheart** and **Rob Roy**, the British-made **The Bruce**, about the Scottish king Robert ... [the Bruce] who famously smashed the English at **Bannockburn**, is expected to play to packed houses north of the border.

The film includes a reworked version – which has just gone on sale – of *Flower of Scotland*, the 1960s folk song that commemorates the same victory over the Auld Enemy. It has become the country's unofficial national anthem [with its concluding words] 'We can still rise now and be the nation again'.

Earlier this week, Jim Telfer, Scotland's rugby coach, declared in forthright terms his dislike of certain English traits. 'They still see themselves as superior, condescending and arrogant, but that's not just to us; it is to the whole world. They tend to think that they are the masters of everything, whether it be soccer, cricket, rugby, economics or politics. They tend to think they are the ruling class. I feel other countries resent that.'

Even in the ultra-trendy new film **Trainspotting**, the main character breaks off from its defining mordant humour and drug excess to launch into an anti-English diatribe.

The roots of this animosity stretch back at least 700 years and the recent rash of celluloid Scottish legends has served merely to reactivate ancient grievances. Not that the Scots need much excuse. After their rugby team's last win over

England in 1990, one Scottish newspaper ran the headline 'Bannockburn 1314, **Murrayfield** 13–7'.

Both these celebrated fields of battle, however, represent rare successes in what is otherwise a history of reverses at the hands of the Scots' most traditional adversaries. Certainly Scotland's other great patriot, Sir William Wallace, as memorably portrayed on screen by Mel Gibson, slew the English Sheriff of Lanark for the murder of his sweetheart, and then, though vastly outnumbered, massacred enemy forces as they crossed a bridge at Stirling in 1297.

The next year, however, he was decisively beaten by Edward I at Falkirk, leaving his military reputation in tatters, and was eventually betrayed by one of his own countrymen into the hands of the English. After refusing to pay homage to Edward at his trial in the Great Hall of Westminster in 1305, Wallace was hung, drawn and quartered.

Known as 'Longshanks', because of his lofty appearance, and, more pertinently to those above **Hadrian's Wall**, as 'the Hammer of the Scots', Edward is said to have called his son to his deathbed in 1307 and made him swear that, after his demise, his bones would be preserved and carried into battle in front of his armies until the Scots were vanquished.

Fortunately for the Scots, Edward's son, Edward II, was an ineffectual and limp-wristed successor, whose weakness contributed as much as the **exemplary spider** to Robert the Bruce's spectacular rout of an English army three times as large as his own.

They then enjoyed three centuries of freedom, until the two crowns were united in the person of James VI of Scotland (James I) in 1603.

However, it is the memory of Culloden that haunts the Scottish imagination. In the space of 40 brutal minutes, the English under William Augustus, Duke of Cumberland, destroyed Bonnie Prince Charlie's forces and put the Young Pretender to flight – for the loss of only 50 men. It is a sign of Culloden's lasting legacy that the flower named 'Sweet William' in honour of Cumberland's military exploits is still referred to as the 'Stinking Willie' or 'Sour Billy' in Scotland.

If the English sometimes feel the Scots remain obsessed with the nature of their relationship, some 250 years after it last caused them to take up arms against one another, Alex Salmond, leader of the Scottish National party [SNP], says they should not be so surprised.

'Any country that has a larger, more powerful neighbour is going to have that attitude to some extent. The second point is that Scotland has a very unusual

Murrayfield
Rugby Union stadium, Edinburgh, headquarters of Scottish rugby.

Hadrian's Wall
Wall built in 122 AD across northern England on the orders of the Roman emperor Hadrian. Its purpose was to prevent tribes from the north invading the Roman province of Britain.

exemplary spider
The legend that Bruce, hiding in a cave, was strengthened in his resolve to struggle against the English by watching a spider continually trying to complete its web after frequent failures.

Adam Smith
Adam Smith, Scottish philosopher and economist, 1723–90.

and unhealthy relationship with that neighbour because of the subservience of the Scottish political system to the Westminster one.'[6]

Salmond suggests that the fervour specially reserved for sporting clashes between the two countries might also diminish if the Scots won independence. 'It's because national sentiment doesn't find expression elsewhere,' he says.

Modern historians, such as Linda Colley, in her book *Britons: Forging the Nation*, however, have observed the rise of anti-English sentiment in parallel with the decline of the British empire. The extraordinary contribution by Scots to the conquest, settlement and administration brought lucrative gains to the old country. Once Britain's status declined in the world, the links to Westminster began to loosen.

Similarly, antipathy towards the English helps unite a country that is itself divided between highlander and lowlander, Catholic and Protestant, east and west.

Among the more surprising adherents of Scottish independence, perhaps, is Alan Clark. The maverick former [Conservative] trade minister, all of whose male forebears since 1725 were born in Scotland, says: 'I think there are perfectly respectable historical antecedents for the Scots to believe that the English have conned them.' Clark, whose son (described as 'card-carrying SNP') lives in Scotland, says he finds little evidence that the Scots actively dislike the English. 'You have to make allowances for the proximity, and also for the fact that ritual enemies have an important place in the folk history of peoples.'

He adds, however: 'You cannot really take Scottish independence seriously until they take it seriously themselves.' He claims that by talking about 'Scotland in Europe', the nationalists funk the issue.

While independence might not still command majority support, the case for greater self-government gains even greater backing . . .

As a straw poll on the streets of Glasgow last week showed, it is the perceived condescension and arrogance of the English that so infuriates their neighbours.

'They are ludicrously dismissive of Scotland,' said Robert McInnes, an electrician. 'We gave the world the telephone, the television and **Adam Smith**. They gave us a nation of slums and took our oil in return.'

Shirley Girdwood, an artist, cited another much repeated source of irritation. 'If a Scottish athlete loses, it's a defeat for Scotland; if he wins, it's a victory for Britain. I find the English very sly. They don't have the courage of their convictions like we do. They stand back and watch and, if things go right, jump in and say it was their idea all along.'

According to Margaret Watson, a cleaner, it was not always thus. 'There was a time when I thought this was all one country. We would sing the national anthem at the cinema. We respected the royal family. That's all gone now. Thatcher ripped this country in half. It was obvious she thought the Scots were just savages. Now I'd rather sing *Flower of Scotland* at **the pictures**.'

She is not alone. Since it was written in 1966 by the late Roy Williamson, of folk band the Corries, the tune has usurped *Scotland the Brave* as the national song. The latest to adopt it is the Scottish Football Association, and its strains will be heard before Scotland take on England in the European Championships at Wembley on June 15 . . .

■ ■ ■

The relationship between the English and the Welsh has also historically been problematic and hostile. The contemporary tensions contribute a further dimension to the difficulty of defining Britishness, although Wales itself is divided linguistically, politically and geographically. Many Welsh people (such as Jan Morris[7]) feel that the English do not understand or take them seriously, do not appreciate their culture and history and, in their ignorance of Wales, treat the Welsh as a source of mockery.

Historically, the Welsh were a conquered and subject people, enemies of the English crown and treated by the English authorities as untrustworthy. This resulted in an often bitter antipathy towards the English. However, although some Welsh people share a mixed English–Welsh descent, many have retained their own linguistic and cultural distinctiveness. Commentators, like Jan Morris, feel that the antagonism between the two peoples today is unfortunate, and is based partly on misunderstanding and partly on imbalance.

Morris argues that a numerical imbalance between the English and the Welsh (population of 2.9m) has historically contributed to a Welsh lack of confidence and a sense of inferiority. Devolution for Wales in 1999 (an elected assembly) after eight hundred years of English rule was not as generous as that in Scotland. But this limited measure of self-government is helping to promote a sense of Welshness. According to Morris, a minority of Welsh people might want a Welsh republic. But most would probably accept a bilingual, self-governing nation within a federal United Kingdom.

The English treatment of Ireland and Irish responses (in Northern Ireland and the Irish Republic) to England are open to conflicting interpretations and arguments.

the pictures
The cinema. The national anthem (or song) used to be played at the end of an evening's film entertainment.

Green
Irish national colour.

Paddy
A common name
(sometimes regarded as
derogatory) for an Irish
person.

shamrock
The national emblem of
Ireland: a clover-like
plant with three leaves
on each stem.

Saint Patrick's Day
17 March: the patron
saint of Ireland.

red
Colour of English
military uniforms: also
blood.

caubeen
An Irish hat.

**country that lies
beyond the sea**
USA: the main target
for Irish emigration in
the nineteenth century.

Erin
Poetic name for Ireland.

History, myth and political ideology have fuelled opinions, hatreds and tensions on both sides. They contribute to the difficulties of assessing whether a sense of Britishness can meaningfully include Northern Ireland (see text 8). English behaviour to the Irish over the centuries, and the Irish perceptions of it, are captured in the following song.

4 *The Wearing of the Green*
Dion Boucicault (c. 1820–90)

Oh, **Paddy** dear, and did you hear the news that's going round?
The **shamrock** is forbid by law to grow on Irish ground;
Saint Patrick's Day no more we'll keep, his colours can't be seen,
For there's a cruel law against the wearing of the green.
I met with Napper Tandy, and he took me by the hand,
And he said, 'How's poor old Ireland, and how does she stand?'
She's the most distressful country that ever yet was seen;
They're hanging men and women there for wearing of the green.

Then since the colour we must wear is England's cruel **red**,
Sure Ireland's sons will ne'er forget the blood that they have shed;
You may take the shamrock from your hat, and cast it on the sod,
But 'twill take root and flourish there, tho' underfoot 'tis trod.
When law can stop the blades of grass from growing as they grow,
And when the leaves in summer-time their verdure dare not show,
Then I will change the colour that I wear in my **caubeen**;
But till that day, please God, I'll stick to wearing of the green.

But if at last our colour should be torn from Ireland's heart,
Her sons, with shame and sorrow, from the dear old isle will part;
I've heard whisper of a **country that lies beyond the sea**,
Where rich and poor stand equal in the light of freedom's day.
Oh, **Erin**! must we leave you, driven by a tyrant's hand?
Must we ask a mother's blessing from a strange and distant land?
Where the cruel cross of England shall never more be seen,
And where, please God, we'll live and die still wearing of the green.

■ ■ ■

Change and reaction

The sentiments and stereotypes in the above texts and commentary contribute to the difficulties inherent in coming to terms with Britishness and even the viability of the term. But some perspectives are now arguably changing. For example, there has recently been some revisionist writing (or re-evaluation) in Northern Ireland, the Irish Republic and England that attempts to strike a balance in the perceptions of the connection between England and Ireland and that also re-examines Northern Irish identities.

Life in Northern Ireland is diverse and complicated by the relationship between Catholics and Protestants and by these groups to the British state. Both communities (Catholic and Protestant) have experienced violence and upheavals, especially since 1968–69. The people are influenced by their ancient conditioning but also by the contemporary biases through which their histories are remembered and passed on to succeeding generations.

Commentators, such as Colm Toibin and Fionnuala O Connor,[8] argue that this selectivity has played an essential part in creating a sense of victimhood for Northern Irish Catholics. Their community has above-average rates of unemployment and deprivation while the Republic of Ireland is allegedly indifferent to their condition. But the Catholic middle class has now increased in numbers, wealth and influence so that, while a class-division is starting to develop between affluent and deprived groups, some Catholics feel that they can play a part in the future of the country.

O Connor points to the complexity of Catholicism, nationalism and republicanism in Northern Ireland and suggests that these have changed in the last 25 years. Arguably, such elements of identity are being redefined as modern, intelligent and reasonable. This re-evaluation influences changing attitudes towards the feasibility (or otherwise) of a united Ireland and the existence of Northern Ireland as a separate, viable country in which Catholics have a role. O Connor feels that this suggests, at least, a sense of possibility for Northern Irish Catholics, although its precise nature and direction remains unclear.

Such positive and cooperative re-evaluations do not seem to be affecting the Protestant/Unionist side to the same degree, nor its problematic identity–relationship with Britain. But there are indications of a more sympathetic or revisionist treatment of the Protestant arguments by some commentators. The next text, while not denying that deep-seated animosities still continue, examines the Protestant Orange Order and tries to place it within the context of Northern Ireland. Although influential, however, the Order is not representative of all Protestant/Unionist thinking there.

5 'Unpeeling the Orange'
Peter Taylor
(The Daily Mail, 2 July 1999)

With energy and patience exhausted by this week's epic **negotiations in Belfast**, Tony Blair now faces a potentially calamitous weekend. **Portadown**'s Orangemen are determined to march home down the nationalist **Garvaghy Road** after their church service at Drumcree – although the parade has been banned.

After such a dramatic week, emotions are running at fever pitch. Once again, Orangemen will be depicted as bone-headed bigots in bowler hats prepared to take their beloved Ulster to the brink of civil war. But Ruth Dudley Edwards does not see it like that.

To her, the 'Faithful Tribe'[9] has been grossly misrepresented and her history of the Orange Order is designed to set the record straight.

The author is an unlikely guide – a Roman Catholic Dubliner from the nationalist 'tribe' with a doctorate in Irish history.

From the outset, she makes no secret where her sympathies lie. 'I have never known a community as misrepresented and traduced,' she writes. 'The members of an organization mainly composed of decent, Christian, law-abiding people have been represented throughout the globe as violent bigots.'

She accepts that the perception is partially due to the Order's traditional inability to make its case to the world outside, in particular to its fellow citizens in the rest of the United Kingdom.

At last in Ruth Dudley Edwards, Orangemen have found a powerful voice to champion their cause. In the process, she makes no apology for going native.

What Dr Edwards writes about the nature of Orangemen when in the company of their own brethren is undoubtedly true. Most are not the monsters of popular myth.

I remember queueing for tea in Drumcree church hall during the 1996 stand-off, bewildered at the contrast between the ugliness of the growing confrontation outside and the atmosphere inside the hall. Matronly ladies in neat pinafores dispensed tea, sandwiches and cakes as if they were serving at the **WI** or village fete.

---

negotiations in Belfast
The attempt to establish a devolved power-sharing Assembly and Executive in Northern Ireland, following the Peace Agreement in 1998 was resurrected in 2000.

Portadown
A small town in Northern Ireland and focal point (Drumcree church) for conflict in recent years.

Garvaghy Road
A street bordered by Catholic areas.

WI
Women's Institute, an English organization of women.

But Drumcree was no picnic. Suddenly, the mood changed as the notorious loyalist paramilitary leader Billy Wright ('King Rat') entered the hall. (Wright was later shot dead by republicans inside the Maze prison.)

With neatly pressed denims, gleaming white T-shirt and single gold earring, Wright, flanked by large minders, epitomized the darker forces the Orangemen's protest has unleashed. The tea queues fell silent and the crowd parted as Wright made his way to an upstairs room for a private meeting.

Shortly afterwards, David Trimble – Orangeman, local MP and recently elected leader of the Ulster Unionist Party, thanks to his controversially high-profile support of his brethren at Drumcree the previous year – followed Wright up the stairs to try to avert certain bloodshed. I have no doubt that the vast majority of those inside and outside the church hall wanted Trimble to succeed. And he did – at least as far as paramilitary provocation at the protest itself was concerned.

Shortly afterwards, however, Wright is thought to have ordered the sectarian killing of a Catholic taxi driver. Orangemen were horrified, appalled to think blood should be shed in their name.

To the bewilderment of most outsiders, Orangemen are driven to act as they do, in particular at Drumcree, because they see their heritage, culture and ultimately their country, Ulster, being crushed by the nationalist and republican tide that they believe successive British governments have made precious little effort to stop.

Drumcree has become symbolic, the line in the sand. If they lose the right to walk down Garvaghy Road – the route, according to Dr Edwards's research, they have followed since the first recorded march in 1827 – they and Ulster are finished. That is why emotions run so high.

The other side – the **residents' group** led by the Order's bogey man, Breandan Mac Cionnaith – is equally determined that the marchers shall not pass for equally symbolic reasons, on the grounds that the days of Orange triumphalism are over. That's why Drumcree has become High Noon, with neither side prepared to back down.

The most revealing chapters in a very readable book are those in which Dr Edwards not only chronicles the four successive crises over Drumcree (1995–98) but perceptively analyses how and why the confrontations have been manipulated by the Republican Movement – the IRA and Sinn Fein.

Its purposes, she writes, is to use residents' organizations, orchestrated by its supporters, to make **loyalist** parades 'the focus for republican discontent which,

residents' group
Mainly Catholic.

loyalist
Protestant; supporters
of the Union.

with careful management and clever propaganda, could be made to spread to the wider nationalist community'.

This is precisely what has happened and why, with both sides equally entrenched and fired up after such a momentous week, confrontation seems inevitable this Sunday at Drumcree. Dr Edwards has ensured that even if readers don't agree with the Orangemen's stand, at least they may better understand it.

■   ■   ■

Although there was no disturbance in 1999, there were serious outbreaks of violence at Drumcree, Portadown and throughout Northern Ireland in June–July 2000. The leadership of the Orange Order appeared to have become more hard-line and paramilitaries were becoming influential in the Protestant cause. For many Protestants, the marches celebrate what they feel is their British identity. Any attack upon that identity results in greater efforts to assert it.[10] But some Northern Ireland people, raised in the Protestant faith, are ashamed of their tradition and what they see as its paranoia, bigotry, intransigence, myth-making and explicit sectarianism.[11] Opinion polls suggest that mainland Britons are increasingly disaffected with Northern Ireland and successive British governments have been disenchanted with Protestant leaders. Such developments have obvious implications for any discussion of Britishness and the identities of the two traditions.

The increased feelings of national identity aroused in Scotland and Wales by devolution have resulted in a continuing reassessment of Englishness and the future position of England, whether within the United Kingdom or as a separate country. This debate has been carried out mainly at the political and academic levels, but there are signs of a growing popular and media response. The following text assesses the possibilities of what has been described as an 'English backlash', as well as commenting on Scottishness.

6 'Scotland rouses the beast of English nationalism'
Andrew Neil
(*The Sunday Times*, 28 April 1996) abridged

English nationalism has started to stir. It is unorganised, unfocused, uncertain of its purpose, unsure of its future. It is not quite yet an 'idea whose time has come', nor does it deserve to be dignified by the term 'movement'. Rather it is an awakening after decades, perhaps centuries, of quiescence. It was a backlash waiting to happen; now it is under way. The Scots have only themselves to blame.

When I went to school and university in Scotland in the 1950s and 1960s there was no conflict in being Scottish and British. We were taught to be proud of being both. Being Scottish was something special; but we were not encouraged to think ill of the English. We revelled in victories over them at **Hampden Park** and Murrayfield (though they were rarer than we cared to admit) and we did not take kindly to being patronised by posh English folk. But we had no reason to hate the English, who seemed on the whole well-disposed to Scots.

We were confident in our roots. We could reel off a long list of Scottish inventors, explorers, entrepreneurs, engineers, doctors and philosophers – the names by which a small, barren cold country on the periphery of Europe made such a hugely disproportionate contribution to the success of the United Kingdom and the British Empire. They were proof we were better educated, more meritocratic, harder working than the class-obsessed English.

But we relished being part of the UK: being British gave us a far larger playing field on which to exercise our skills and made us part of a great endeavour with global achievements, in which we took as much pride as the English. They were not our enemies; the English were our allies, our fellow citizens in the great British nation; and together with the Welsh and Northern Irish we were part of a whole which was greater than the sum of its parts.

That has all changed. Since the early 1970s a new Scottish nationalism has taken root which goes far beyond the ranks of the Scottish National Party. It emphasises being Scottish and downgrades being British. Despite Scotland being more prosperous than ever – Aberdeen is one of the richest cities in the world, Edinburgh one of Europe's most beautiful capitals and Glasgow has gone from slum to city of culture – it thinks Scotland is hard done by.

The end of empire and the relative decline of Britain in the post-war world has made many Scots question the Union. The feeling has been exacerbated by a parting of the ways in political traditions. In 1955 more than 50 per cent of Scots voted Tory and the two-party system in Scotland was as alive and well as it was in middle England. No longer: as England became more Tory, Scotland remained wedded to a dull municipal socialism. Since 1979 socialist Scotland has increasingly bridled at being ruled from Tory England. A clear majority of Scots want independence or home rule.

Hampden Park
National football stadium, Glasgow.

St George's Day
The English national
day, with Saint George
as the national patron
saint.

London has continued to pick up the tab for Scotland's addiction to collectivism but that has not stopped Scots from blaming London for whatever ails them, even when the problems are self-inflicted, or from thinking that maybe the Union is holding Scotland back – that there is indeed a conflict between being Scottish and British. At its worst this has manifested itself in unpleasant anti-English sentiments which have infected even the Scottish middle class . . .

This is the nasty underside to Scottish nationalism, fuelled by a media which panders to all manner of Scottish prejudice about England. Until recently the English have remained remarkably immune to this festering hatred among a section of the Scottish population, particularly the young. However, even the slow-to-anger English were bound to react: historians may one day mark the start of the English nationalist backlash as **St George's Day**, April 23, 1996.

Last Tuesday those two quintessential voices of middle England – the *Daily Mail* and the *Daily Express* – carried leader-page articles urging the English to take greater pride in their national heritage. 'The English must be more English,' wrote Derrick Hill in the *Express*. Richard Littlejohn, in the *Mail*, urged the English to stop being 'a race in denial'. Their English populism had already been given academic credence by David Starkey in last Saturday's *Times*, who bemoaned the 'disintegration of [English] national feeling'.

These English calls to arms were not explicitly anti-Scottish. But Scotland is bound to be caught up in the backlash: 'The Scots demand their own assembly,' wrote Mr Littlejohn. 'Let them have it – but also let us tell them they can pay their own way.' We face a lot more of this talk before the decade is out.

. . . a [future] Labour government will face a Tory opposition ready to wrap itself in the flag of English nationalism. It will be strongly Eurosceptical and relish the chance to defend English interests against both Brussels and Edinburgh. Whereas the Tories in power have demurred, for the sake of the Union, from asking the tough questions about Scottish devolution, they will feel under no such restraint in opposition.[12]

They will want to know, if Scotland is to have a large measure of home rule, why Scottish MPs will still be allowed to vote on English domestic matters in Westminster (the famous 'West Lothian' question, to which Labour has no answer). They will ask why a devolved Scotland needs to remain so grossly over-represented in the House of Commons when it will be running its domestic affairs from Edinburgh . . . There are also bound to be harsh questions about why public spending per capita in Scotland is 24 per cent more than in England, even though Scottish unemployment is lower. If Scotland wants to be the last socialist country in Europe, the Tories will say, it can pay for it.

The Scots will bridle at such sentiments. But Scottish nationalism was never going to be a one-way street.

The English were bound to be roused. A strident Scottish nationalism now risks colliding with a newly assertive English nationalism and Britain looks like being the main casualty. We are entering dark days for the Union.

■ ■ ■

The next text, as with many other recent books on the subject,[13] tries to assess what is distinctive about Englishness. It suggests that Englishness differs from the other national identities and should be encouraged. It also argues that there is a con-siderable inventiveness and artificiality involved in the creation of national identities.

7 'Mongrels not Angles'
Matthew Parris
(Author copyright, 21 November 1998) abridged

Who are we, in England? Are we a people at all, a collective 'us'? Without Scotland and Wales and the umbrella of Britishness and empire, is there anything south of Hadrian's Wall that could call itself a nation now, or could one day call itself a nation, or should?

This is the last of three essays written during the autumn. In the first I suggested that the Union as we used to know it was coming to an end, and that competing nationhoods were taking over in Scotland and perhaps Wales. It is too late to draw back from this. In the second I argued that national iden-tity, like ivy, is a fast-growing plant which generates an often fanciful aura of antiquity. Myth, convenience and political usefulness are core-ingredients in the making of nationhood. Scotland has faked it magnificently and what she has faked is now real and strong.

Responding to this deconstruction of *Braveheart* Scotland, some readers have supposed my intention was to disparage. Not so. I admire – respect – the way a tartan mantle of nationhood has been spun into being by **Sir Walter Scott**, a kilt-maker, a shared resentment of **Sassenachs**, two generations of canny populist politicians and one big-screen movie. The enterprise is well on its way to creating a world-class nation.

Sir Walter Scott
Scottish novelist and historian 1771–1832.

Sassenachs
Scottish name for the English.

The Scots are being rebranded faster than they know. But the brand has limitations; it pinches – and we should acknowledge as much when we consider how an English nationhood might be forged. I want an Englishness that does not pinch. I want an Englishness freed from the grip of blood and soil. In some measure I want a nationalism freed from the grip of history . . .

England is one of the most open places in the world, and always has been. After the Celtic, Anglo-Saxon and Norman mix (a collision not just of tribes but of languages) came Flemish Huguenots and a steady drip-feed of Protestant refugees from the Continent, and, later, Jewish immigrants. The Irish, Scots and Welsh are in England in numbers so huge and so intermingled that it hardly makes sense to refer to them as distinct. The Second World War brought smaller but significant arrivals from Poland and Italy; the Cold War brought a steady trickle of brave people from behind the Iron Curtain. Readers who recall how it used to be impossible to get takeaway food except in the larger English cities will remember the arrival, from the Sixties onwards, of the Chinese. Many of these groups have shaped our culture out of all proportion to their number.

But far greater numbers of West Indians, Indians, Bengalis, Greeks and Turkish Cypriots have come too. Nigerians and Albanians are here in larger numbers than we officially know. This is no place for a disquisition on the racial tolerance of England – big problems remain – but I challenge anyone to name a European nation that has absorbed, with less difficulty, anything like these numbers of people of wholly different culture or colour [See text 4 in Chapter 8]. About 20 per cent of the population of London, and nearly 15 per cent of the West Midlands, are from what are loosely called the ethnic minorities.

London is critical to all this, and, I contend, critical to our modern sense of what we in England are [compare with text 7 in Chapter 2]. London is a world in itself, and part of England's soul. No longer larger, wealthier, or the centre of more power than any European rival, London remains in a league of its own: incomparably 'bigger'. Bigger as an idea, bigger as a sensation, wider as an experience than Frankfurt, Munich, Berlin, Rome, Turin, Madrid or Paris. Like New York, London is a world city. Though the empire has gone, our capital remains an imperial capital. The word 'cosmopolitan' has been flogged to death in its description. Paris remains quaintly – charmingly – French. London defies categorization.

For all that many in England do not live in London, I believe that the idea of our capital is important to the way we see ourselves in England. Manchester, Liverpool, Leeds . . . all have attracted to themselves something of that same impression of openness and mixture, of modernity, experiment, initiative and cheek. A staggering 90 per cent of the English live in urban areas . . .

Scotland, too, is an overwhelmingly urban nation, and enormously diverse in race, origin, religion and culture. But she has saddled herself with a nation-hood ineradically stained by blood and soil. Most nationhoods are.

England can embrace something better. We can embrace concrete and steel. We can find a picture of ourselves in which the truth – that we are mostly city-dwelling mongrels not rural pure-breds – is not an embarrassment. Alone on these islands, we can choose a nationhood that is not rooted in romantic mis-conceptions. We can go with the grain of what we are. It is empire that has given us that chance. As I argued in the first of these essays, the English have unwit-tingly conflated England with Britain. We find little difficulty in feeling British, even if the Scots or the Irish don't want to [contrast with text 8].

That luxury is not available to our Celtic neighbours. They associate Britain with outside domination. As they draw back from the Union, they cannot take with them much that the idea stood for. We can. An open, world-wide iden-tity is with us already, ready for the wearing. England can wear it. And we can wear it lightly. There is a great deal to Britishness, to the heritage of empire, that is positive; but there was an unpleasant side. But Empire also burdened our spirit. You cannot wear the ownership of two-fifths of the Earth's surface lightly; you cannot bully, subjugate, defend and govern lightly. Self-righteous arrogance creeps in. With empire went ugly attitudes, ludicrous uniforms and silly walks – things which people as English as **D.H. Lawrence**, **George Orwell**, **E.M. Forster** or **Monty Python** could detest without ceasing to be English. We can drop the aggression, lay aside the plumes and brocade, and lower the rifle.

But we can keep the cultural inclusiveness. We are used to ownership of a language that others share. We are used to seeing accessibility as strength. We are used to a trading culture that not only accepts but depends upon a reaching out from our borders. All this we can keep.

We can keep the idea of a people rooted in something other than shared blood, shared soil – or even shared history. My England, my Englishness, includes the millions of Scottish, Irish and Welsh people for whom this is their England too. We are well on our way already to this. But my England will be a place where it becomes as natural to talk about being black English as it has become to call yourself black British. No blood, no race, no soil should dye our banner.

So where does this leave St George, warm beer and old maids cycling to church? We should not jettison the past . . . The strands of Englishness **Jeremy Paxman** identifies – marmalade and **Marmite**, tweed and church bells – matter too. 'Heritage' means a lot to many. But it is part of the picture, not the whole; not even the half of it. Jamaican heritage, though the thread starts in

D.H. Lawrence
English novelist and poet 1885–1930.

George Orwell
English novelist, essayist and journalist 1903–50.

E.M. Forster
English novelist 1879–1970.

Monty Python
1969–74, a television series noted for its surreal humour. The group later made several films.

Jeremy Paxman
British broadcaster and writer.

Marmite
Sticky brown mixture of yeast and vegetable extracts used by the English as a sandwich spread.

lift
Create, invent.

Dick Whittington
Sir Richard Whittington returned to London when on the point of leaving and eventually became Lord Mayor (died 1423).

Dickens
Charles Dickens, English novelist 1812–70.

Dixon of Dock Green
Popular BBC television series of the 1960s dealing with a traditional policeman.

Eastenders
Contemporary BBC television soap opera dealing with East End (London) characters.

Coronation Street
Long-running commercial ITV television series dealing with north-west English working-class characters.

Brookside
Contemporary commercial Channel 4 television series.

Emmerdale
Contemporary commercial ITV television series dealing with rural and farming characters.

Only Fools and Horses
Popular BBC comedy series dealing with East End (London) characters.

Jamaica, is now woven into the cloth of England. Anyone British can see that, see what England might come to represent.

So how do we do it? Probably not with Downing Street steering groups or Tory or Labour think-tanks. Unselfconscious mythmaking and storytelling are integral to the generation of nationhood. Our modern English narrators are television producers, print journalists. We have the talent to entertain, even to mesmerize. Now we should learn how to **lift**. Robin Hood did. **Dick Whittington** did. Tales of piracy, adventure and exploration did. Tales of kindness and mercy did: **Dickens** could. So did *Dixon of Dock Green*. So, sometimes, can *Eastenders* and *Coronation Street*, *Brookside* and *Emmerdale* – *Only Fools and Horses*, even.

So spare me too much St George; spare me an English *Braveheart*; give me *Eastenders*, tolerance, self-deprecation, humour, darts, rude newspapers, sentimentality, individualism and cheek for my England. We can build it if we want; the bricks and foundations are already there.

■ ■ ■

Public opinion

Public opinion polls, while sometimes producing contradictory findings, are frequently taken of the population's attitude to national identity, as in the following text. This suggests that the very notion of Britishness is changing and developing positive connotations, shorn of the allegedly negative characteristics of its earlier form. It is apparently being embraced by the Scots, the Welsh and the Northern Irish as an umbrella identity, with which their individual national identities can coexist. But the English, at least in this poll, appear to be confused about who or what they are.

8 'Confident Celts put England in shade: Welsh and Scots find new pride as English face identity crisis'
Mark Henderson
(*The Times*, 1 February 1999)

The English are a dull, petty and insecure people who are increasingly reviled by their proud Celtic neighbours, according to a survey into national identity published today.

While **devolved** Scotland, Wales and Northern Ireland are emerging as confident nations with a strong sense of local identity, Englishness is in crisis, the report by the brand consultants Springpoint says.

The [English] national character is seen at best as quaint and boring and at worst vulgar, materialistic and loutish. It is summed up by football hooligans, staid City gents and 'people just talking about nothingness', and is disdained by the rest of the United Kingdom.

The English find none of the inspiration that Scots, Welsh and Irish derive from their nationhood and are often 'dumped with all the least desirable traits and characteristics of Britishness, including the less attractive colonial ones'. Positive aspects of Englishness – tolerance, the Royal Family and fine public services such as the health service – are now seen as part of a new British identity that embraces Scots, Welsh and Irish as well.

The report, *I? UK – Voices of Our Times*,[14] finds an affinity for a wide range of national symbols, such as fish and chips, Wimbledon and Big Ben, but these 'do not add up to a national identity that connects with people, feeds and inspires them and makes them feel proud'.

Instead, there is widespread insecurity and self-consciousness. The English see themselves as 'people just talking about nothingness' in **Laura Ashley** sitting rooms, who are 'petty, envious, obsessed with money, small-minded, divided'. They feel that 'Englishness is increasingly irrelevant as a notion, and something from which they distance themselves'.

The traits are most marked in the South East, which attracts opprobrium both from the Celtic fringe and the North [of England]. Those from the North of England have a strong regional identity, which they often place ahead of an Englishness they can find alien and embarrassing. Many feel closer to the other nations than the English of the South.

The report concluded: 'Combine the energetic defiance and criticism of the English and England from newly confident Scottish and Welsh; some English people's own insecurity and defensiveness about their own identity; the possible fragmentation of the United Kingdom through devolution; and hints of a more positive, emerging identity for Britain which co-opts some of the positive values of England – and you have a recipe for a "crisis of Englishness."'

The research involved in-depth interviews with a socially representative range of adults in regional centres across the United Kingdom. Fiona Gilmore, managing director of Springpoint, said the 'crisis of Englishness' was a thread that ran through the 77-page report.

devolved
The creation of self-governing assemblies in 1999 and 2000.

Laura Ashley
A company producing mainly chintzy fabrics.

good crack
Talk, gossip and
entertainment.

leprechauns
In Irish folklore, a fairy in
the shape of a little old
man.

'I was amazed at its strength,' she said. 'The English are seen – and see themselves – as insular, restrained, pompous and obsessed with money. Their positive qualities are shared by Scots, Welsh and Northern Irish, but these nations have lots of particular qualities as well.'

Scots felt by far the strongest separate national allegiance. They have a clear idea of who they are – 'tough and hardy, outdoor, friendly, warm'. They are enthusiastic about their history and traditions, and their identity is well-understood and respected outside Scotland.

The success of the film *Braveheart* and impending devolution have helped to fuel a burgeoning sense of nationhood that 'can provide an emotional uplift, an inspiration, even spiritual feelings'.

Wales is less aggressive in its national feeling, and its people are more vague about how they identify it. Even so, there is a strong underlying sense of common identity. The Welsh emphasize the strength of communities, a friendly, welcoming character and a sense of social responsibility. 'In some ways this can be difficult to pin down, but it seems to be about genuineness and integrity, a real sense of caring,' the report found.

Many Welsh felt their country was re-emerging after years in England's shadow, as the language revives and devolution and economic regeneration progress. 'We're rediscovering ourselves through the language and culture, the beauty of the country,' one Cardiff respondent said.

Northern Irish identity was also distinct, both from Irishness and the rest of the United Kingdom, though the bulk of the research focused only on Ulster Protestants. They had an easy-going and down-to-earth character, a hard-working streak and a love for '**good crack**'. Others said they identified neither with the 'shamrocks and **leprechauns**' of the Republic nor 'Brits' from the mainland.

Britishness was picked out as an increasingly powerful concept that encompassed opportunity, respect, tolerance and supportiveness, as well as some sense of national decline. The notion of being British has become acceptable to Celts and ethnic minorities as well as the English – indeed such groups get intensely annoyed by the continuing English tendency to try to appropriate its qualities for themselves.

Britain is seen to have 'nicer connotations' than England: it has shed its imperialist image and is seen as a force for progress and decency, in contrast to the insularity and conservatism of England. It 'adds up to an inclusive identity', the report found.

Europe, however, scarcely gets a look-in. British people of all backgrounds have little *communitaire* spirit, and most saw it as 'distant and not part of their everyday lives'.

■ ■ ■

The findings on England in the above poll arguably reflect a confusing moment of transition in which Englishness is having to be reinvented along the lines described in text 7.

England is now occupied by many Celtic groups and its cities and towns are composed of very varied multicultural, multilingual and cosmopolitan communities. Commentators maintain that the traditional English stereotypes or a simplistic notion of English national identity no longer satisfy in the light of these relatively new, multi-layered features. They argue that the alleged crisis of Englishness marks, in fact, the beginnings of a new society that is complex, cosmopolitan, sophisticated and diverse and that is in the process of developing a new identity.

Despite the apparent emergence of a new 'Britishness', as reflected in the above poll, it would seem that the national identities in the various countries are still dominant. A *Sunday Times* poll[15] in 2000, for example, suggested that schoolchildren clearly see and define themselves as English, Scottish or Welsh rather than British or European. The figures were 79 per cent for Wales, 82 per cent for Scotland and 66 per cent for England. Some 84 per cent of English schoolchildren regarded England as their home (rather than Britain) and 75 per cent felt that their nationality was important to them. But there was little interest in the creation of regional English assemblies (which might promote regional identities rather than Englishness) and little desire, significantly, for a break-up of the United Kingdom.

Commentators felt that these findings indicated that the English are increasingly concerned to define their Englishness (whatever that may be) as a reaction to manifestations of Scottishness and Welshness. This situation could result in growing tensions between the countries of the devolved United Kingdom. It was pointed out that the poll findings coincided with an internal cabinet report from the Performance and Innovation Unit, which argued that a majority of Britons believed that the British identity is breaking up.

■ ■ ■

Exercises

Write short essays on the following topics

1. What is meant by the concepts of 'nation' and 'national identity'? Could these be validly applied to Britain?

2. Attempt to define 'Britishness'.

3. How would you characterize the relationships between the English and the Scots, Welsh and Northern Irish?

4. Examine some of the contradictions exposed in the texts dealing with 'Tensions'.

5. Place text 8 within the context of the other texts in this chapter.

Explain and examine the following terms

myths	'the Other'	Victoria
eisteddfod	Culloden	*Rule Britannia*
stereotypes	the Union	Great Britain
clan tartans	shamrock	Murrayfield
Drumcree	'global village'	sassenachs
Anglophobia	Orange Order	St George's Day
SNP	Sinn Fein	Englishness

Further reading

Bardon, Jonathan (1992) *A History of Ulster*, Belfast: The Blackstaff Press.

Black, Jeremy (2000) *Modern British History since 1900*, chapters 12 and 15, London: Macmillan.

Boyce, D. George (1995) *Nationalism in Ireland*, London: Routledge.

Clark, J.C.D. (2000) 'Protestantism, Nationalism and National Identity, 1660–1832', *The Historical Journal* 43, 1 March, pp. 249–276, Cambridge: Cambridge University Press.

Colley, Linda (1996) *Britons: Forging the Nation 1707–1837*, London: Vintage.

Davies, John (1993) *A History of Wales*, London: Penguin Books.

Giles, Judy and Middleton, Tim (eds) (1995) *Writing Englishness 1900–1950*, London: Routledge.

Grant, Alexander and Stringer, Keith J. (eds) (1995) *Uniting the Kingdom? – The Making of British History*, London: Routledge.

Harvie, Christopher (1998) *Scotland and Nationalism: Scottish Society and Politics 1707 to the Present*, London: Routledge.

Robbins, Keith (1998) *Great Britain: Identities, Institutions and the Idea of Britishness*, London: Longman.

Notes

1. *The Big Picture: The Break-Up of Britain?* (1995) BBC2, 23 April.
2. This is one of the arguments for devolution; the granting of greater powers of self-government to Wales, Scotland and Northern Ireland will preserve the United Kingdom. The term 'Great Britain' strictly means England, Scotland and Wales.
3. Linda Colley (1994) 'Britain 1994: a country in search of itself?' London: *The Times* 31 January. See also Linda Colley (2000) 'Britishness in the 21st Century' http://www.number-10.gov.uk/default.asp?PageId=1190, 30 March.
4. Leader (2000) 'The Strip of History' London: *The Times* 17 June.
5. Historical research argues that the English army was in fact largely composed of Lowland Scots.
6. This situation was improved with the granting of devolution to Scotland in 1999.
7. Jan Morris (1995) 'Why do we love the Scots but laugh at the Welsh?' London: *The Sunday Times* 10 December.
8. Colm Toibin (1994) 'Keeping the faith', London: *The Sunday Times*, 9 January. Fionnuala O'Connor (1993) *In search of a State: Catholics in Northern Ireland*, Belfast: Blackstaff Press.
9. Ruth Dudley Edwards (1999) *The Faithful Tribe*, London: HarperCollins.
10. Michael Gove (2000) 'Orange Order has lost its way over march for British identity' London: *The Times* 8 July.
11. Susan McKay (2000) 'This paranoid and unloveable people' London: *The Sunday Times* 6 July. See also Susan McKay (2000) *Northern Protestants: An Unsettled People*, Belfast: Blackstaff Press.
12. This has happened as the Conservative Party under its leader William Hague is addressing the consequences of devolution and the question of Englishness.
13. See Jeremy Paxman (2000) *The English: A Portrait of a People*, London: Penguin Books.
14. *I? UK – Voices of Our Times* (1999) London: Springpoint.
15. Jack Grimston (2000) 'Young Britons lose sense of nation' London: *The Sunday Times* 19 March.

Chapter 4

Political ideologies

This chapter is concerned with contemporary political developments in Britain. It illustrates, in particular, changes in political ideology, new directions in policy and the attempted creation of 'modern' images by the main political parties (Labour, the Liberal Democrats and the Conservatives). These are the national parties that fight in most parts of Britain for seats in the Westminster Parliament. They also participate in local elections, European Parliament elections and elections to the Scottish Parliament and the Welsh Assembly. Parties such as Plaid Cymru (the Welsh National Party), the Scottish National Party and the Northern Irish political parties campaign in their own territories, although they do have seats in the House of Commons.

The traditional ranking placed the Conservatives roughly on the right of the political spectrum, the Labour Party on the left and the Liberal Democrats in the centre.
Each tried to develop distinctive political programmes. But ideology and political
opportunism are often inter-connected, with the latter appearing to be the dominant factor in Britain today.

Following the modernization of the Labour Party and its supposed distancing from
what is called Old Labour social democracy, the Labour government (despite
alleged current tensions with Old Labour activists and grassroots members in the
party) has arguably moved to the right (or at least the centre). But the Prime Minister
(Tony Blair) is impatient with the old parameters of left and right (see text 7 in
Chapter 8) and is attempting to chart a 'third way' in British politics. Opinions differ
on what this means and also on whether the Labour government has a distinctive
ideology beyond pragmatic managerialism. Opinion polls in 2000 indicated
increasing dissatisfaction by Britons with the Labour government and some of its
programmes.

The Conservative party under its leader William Hague and following its crushing
defeat in 1997 is attempting to generate new policy directions and a new image
in order to appeal to the electorate. Without clear programmes, which distinguish
it from Labour and other political parties, it will have difficulty in returning to political power. Nevertheless, during 2000, the party has been developing agendas on
crime, law and order, asylum seekers, pensions, taxation, Europe, education and
public spending, which, while they have been criticized for their alleged oppor-
tunistic populism, are proving attractive to voters. The Conservatives are trying to
capitalize on Labour's reduced support and have closed the gap between Labour
and themselves in public opinion polls. But such improvement is not decisive and
they face an uphill struggle prior to a possible general election in 2001.

The Liberal Democrats have traditionally seen themselves as a left-of-centre party.
They have recently cooperated with the Labour government on certain issues such
as reform of the electoral system and the constitution, although this cooperation
has caused tensions within the party. But the Liberal Democrats are also trying to
present a set of policies under their new (1999) leader Charles Kennedy, which are
different to those of the Labour and Conservative parties.

Nevertheless, Tony Blair is keen to cement a progressive centre-left movement that
would heal the historic split between the old Liberals and the Labour party in the
early twentieth century. The possibility of coalition or minority government after
the next election is being actively discussed in the media, particularly if the Labour
government does not win an overall majority of seats in the House of Commons,
resulting in a hung Parliament. On the basis of (and projecting) current public
opinion polls, it is conceivable that Labour could lose a significant number of seats;
the Conservatives could gain some, but fail to obtain a decisive amount; while the

Old Labour
Used here to indicate what is regarded as the former doctrinaire, ideological and socialist-based Labour Party.

Liberal Democrats may improve their share of the seats and hold the balance of power.

All the political parties are therefore positioning themselves for electoral advantage and the ears of the voters by attempting to develop attractive programmes prior to the next general election. But it might be queried whether the traditional ideological distinctions between the three parties are any longer strongly in evidence.

■ ■ ■

The Labour Party

The first text critically examines the political policies of the Labour government, one year after its overwhelming success in the 1997 general election. It identifies the Labour Party's movement away from Old Labour and suggests that it has in practice embraced and built on many Conservative ideological positions.

1 'The strangest Tory ever sold'
(*The Economist*, 2 May 1998) abridged

On the evidence of its first year, Britain's new Labour government may yet make the country safe for Thatcherism

When Tony Blair's remodelled Labour Party came to power a year ago, we gave it a less than rousing welcome. Despite the revolution Mr Blair had wrought within the party, despite his remorseless efforts to assure traditional Conservative voters that **Old Labour** was dead, two risks seemed to remain. One was that New Labour in office would nonetheless slide back into bad Old Labour ways. The other was that Mr Blair's efforts to define a distinctive non-Conservative vision of Britain's future would collapse into muddle. We doubted that both risks could be avoided, but if they were, we argued, a good outcome might be possible.

This good outcome was not that Mr Blair would guide Britain to his distinctive non-Conservative future: in our view the vaunted 'third way',[1] which is neither left, right nor in between, but something on a higher and altogether different plane, is so much waffle. The optimistic case was rather that he would succeed in reconciling Britain to the Thatcher revolution – consolidating it, perhaps even extending it, in ways that post-Thatcher Tories could not contemplate.

One year on, we aren't so worried. Labour has had a busy time. It has recast monetary policy, granting the **Bank of England operational independence** as almost its first act; it has implemented a **'New Deal' for the unemployed**; it is promoting reform in education; it has revived the search for peace in Northern Ireland; and more. Then come the big things that Labour has not done, such as raising income taxes,[2] increasing public spending,[3] empowering the unions . . . and so on. There is plenty to criticize, much may yet go wrong, and plainly one year is far too short a time to come to any firm conclusion – but judged by his record so far Mr Blair is proving a pretty good Tory after all.

Something borrowed, something blue

This assessment of New Labour in power is hardly novel. It commands wide support among ordinary Britons, whatever their political preferences; and this, by the way, is precisely what accounts for the new government's popularity. Last year the British electorate wanted a change of faces and a change of style, a sense of energy and purpose, something fresh and new – but no essential change in political direction. Mr Blair promised them exactly this, and so far he has kept his word. But here's an odd thing. This simple judgement is almost universally regarded as merely simple-minded by political commentators and other sophisticated types. In their view, the idea that New Labour in power is just Tory government by other means is, as one leading thinker put it recently, 'hopelessly wide of the mark'. This is a puzzle.

One answer is simply that Britain's leading thinkers never much liked Margaret Thatcher – they couldn't forgive her for being lower middle class. Tony Blair, on the other hand, is of their tribe, very upper middle, a true man of the People. To leading thinkers, therefore, the two are chalk and cheese – but clever unsnobbish reasons (the third way and all) must be found to legitimize the prejudice. Also, a related point, leading thinkers tend to judge politicians by the complicated things they say rather than the more straightforward things they do. Margaret Thatcher was harsh, confrontational and divisive (she was a true revolutionary, so she needed to be). Except when he is speaking to his party, Tony Blair is smooth, consensus-seeking and **'inclusive'** (he is a consolidator, except when he is speaking to his party, so he needs to be).

Apart from this, the two are proving quite alike. If it seems otherwise, it is partly beccause the fog of social-justice third-way communitarian post-modern post-neoclassical rhetoric laid down by New Labour is so amazingly dense – thick enough to keep the experts blundering around for years.

Bank of England operational independence
The Bank of England can now itself set interest rates in an attempt to control inflation and the national economy.

New Deal for the unemployed
The unemployed are offered education, training and work opportunities in order to get them off unemployment and into jobs.

inclusive
The attempt to include all sections of British society in the new Labour 'project' or the 'big tent', excluding no section of society.

Heathite

Ted Heath,
Conservative Prime
Minister 1970–74.

Nigel Lawson

Former Conservative
Chancellor of the
Exchequer or Finance
Minister.

David Blunkett

Labour Secretary of
State for Education and
Employment.

**Framework
Document**

Drawn up by the British
Prime Minister John
Major and the Irish
Prime Minister John
Bruton as part of
advancing the Northern
Ireland Peace Process.
It emphasized the
establishment of all-
party negotiations and
the decommissioning of
terrorist weapons.

Devolution

Transfer of some
political power from
Westminster to a
parliament in Scotland
and assemblies in
Wales and Northern
Ireland.

centralize

Political power
centralized in
Westminster and
Whitehall, London.

New Labour is not Thatcherism unadulterated, of course. In some ways it is an older, softer style of conservatism, with **Heathite** one-nation highlights. Mr Blair will not press on, as Margaret Thatcher might have, to roll the state back further – more's the pity. The fact remains that Tony Blair has spent his first year as a Tory prime minister. This applies almost as much to what the government has done as to what it has not done. Independence for the Bank of England? **Nigel Lawson** campaigned for it as chancellor. The 'New Deal'? It extends Tory initiatives, but overturns no basic thinking. Reform in education? **David Blunkett** is telling teachers things that Tory ministers would have loved to, but didn't dare. Northern Ireland? Mr Blair's bold leadership played a crucial part, but the ground was laid by Tories and the agreement reached drew heavily on the **Framework Document** designed in 1995. Did somebody say Europe? Labour is as confused as the Tories.

The only big exception is constitutional reform. Here, Mr Blair is radically anti-Tory, perhaps more so than he intends. **Devolution** is meant to bind the United Kingdom together; it seems as likely, for good or ill, to break it up. Be that as it may, if Labour's constitutional plans formed a coherent part of a broader political strategy, then talk of a third way – not Tory, not Labour but something quite new – might start to mean something. As yet the plans not only fail to form part of that bigger whole, they are incoherent in themselves. Does Mr Blair want to **centralize** power or disperse it? He is a centralizer by instinct and a disperser by (current) intellectual conviction. He is trying to have it both ways, and it won't work.

It is true, in sum, that the differences between New Labour and watered-down Thatcherism are far more of style than of substance. But to say this is not to criticize the government. Look, in politics, presentation really matters. Tiresome as the third-way nonsense is to curmudgeons such as *The Economist*, its success as a marketing device is not in doubt. Voters are happy, leading thinkers are happy, everyone except the bewildered souls who believed in Old Labour is happy.

Thatcherism's main defect was that it was badly sold. Britain needed it, and knew it needed it, but never much liked it. Britain likes New Labour, and so far there is little not to like.

■ ■ ■

In 2000 the large lead in public support for Labour over the Conservatives had narrowed (but not decisively) by varying amounts in public opinion polls. The Labour government was having difficulties in presenting a positive picture of its policies to an increasingly sceptical electorate. Support was being replaced by disillusionment and many of the respondents indicated in polls that they were unhappy with the Labour government's performance and style. According to some critics,[4] it had since 1997 been genuinely radical in reforming the constitution but less radical in attacking the actual structural weaknesses of public services such as health and education. It has instead pursued cautious, pragmatic policies based on increased public spending and indirect taxation, together with an alleged growth in central control.

The Labour government's 'third way', which still appears to be the foundation of its political policies, has also been treated critically, although it has been followed with positive interest in Europe and the USA. Attempts have been made, as in the next text, to evaluate what the third way actually means in terms of political philosophy and practice and whether it amounts to a new distinct ideology.

2 'Ideology: beyond left and right'
(*The Economist*, 2 May 1998)

> As part of our researches into Tony Blair's 'third way', we sent
> somebody to attend a seminar of New Labour intellectuals. Here
> is the memo he circulated on his return.

You will recall from your schooldays **Aristophanes**' play 'The Poet and the Women'. The hero, disguised in **drag**, gatecrashes an all-female festival, only to be exposed and ridiculed when the suspicious women strip him of his clothes. I felt a similar discomfort after being identified at the **Demos** seminar as a one-time employee of the last Conservative government.

The purpose of the seminar was not revealed until we arrived. The government had decided that the third way was important, we were told, but ministers didn't know what it meant. So they were keen to encourage seminars like this one to help them find out.

Anthony Giddens, director of the London School of Economics [LSE], was the main speaker. He said that the third way was an attempt to go beyond (not, he stressed, between) the neo-liberalism of the old right and the social democracy of the old left. He suggested seven different dimensions along which this could be tested.

Aristophanes
Greek comic dramatist
c.410–350 BC.

drag
Men dressed as
women.

Demos
Left-of-centre think
tank.

subsidiarity
A term, often used in connection with the European Union, to signify that if something can be done adequately at a lower level, then it should be done there and not at a higher level of bureaucracy. The essence of local democracy.

democratic deficit
The argument that if political power is too centralized at a higher level then it loses democratic legitimacy and there is a deficit at the grassroots level.

multiple sovereignty
The traditional notion of a state having absolute power or sovereignty over its own affairs has developed into ideas of shared or pooled sovereignty.

redistribution
The movement of money (usually from the richest) to the poorest in society, often by means of taxation.

Beveridge
William Beveridge produced a report in 1942 that became the blueprint for the Welfare State in Britain.

five negative giants
Ignorance, want, squalor, idleness and disease.

1) Politics: The old left and right were based on class. But class was no longer a driving force in politics.[5] So the third way had to be based on new coalitions, which could not easily be categorised as either right or left.

2) State and government: The old left sought to maximise the role of the state, the old right to minimise it. The third way should seek instead to restructure government, at all levels. It should promote **subsidiarity** and address the '**democratic deficit**'. Measures included constitutional reform, greater transparency, and more local democracy.

3) Civil society: The old left was suspicious of civil society, as it reduced the role of the state; the old right thought civil society would only flourish if the state got off its back. The third way values civil society, but sees the state as having a valid role in promoting it.

4) The nation: The old left distrusted the idea of the nation; the old right equated nationalism with jingoism. The third way endorses a 'cosmopolitan nation', which recognizes that nations are still important, but also appreciates the complexity of the modern nation and the distinction between the nation and the state, embracing 'fuzzy nationalism' and '**multiple sovereignty**'.

5) The economy: The old left supported a mixed economy to humanise capitalism; the old right exalted the market. The third way favours a 'new mixed economy', where the emphasis is not on ownership but on competition and regulation.

6) The welfare state: The old left welcomed the welfare state as the main vehicle of **redistribution**; the old right demonised it. The third way aims to reform the welfare state into the 'social investment state', which shifts the emphasis away from spending money on benefits and towards 'investment in human capital'. Whereas **Beveridge** envisaged the welfare state as an attack on **five negative giants**, the social investment state should have positive aims such as the reduction of environmental toxicity.

7) The global order: The old left had no global theory, simply a proletarian internationalism; the old right's approach to international relations was based on the need to fight wars: the third way recognises that we no longer live in a bi-polar world and realises that states no longer face enemies, only dangers.

After this presentation, the chairman kicked off a discussion by asking whether future politics was more likely to be based on ideology or pragmatism.

A lively debate followed. Participants confidently employed terms like 'a learning society', 'knowledge-based politics', 'communitarianism' and so forth, to murmurs of approval. I found it hard to work out whether they were addressing the original question, ignoring it, or, like me, had simply failed to understand it. The wisest course, I thought, would be to keep a low profile. But my plans were thwarted by the chairman, who identified me as an employee of the last government, and asked my opinion. Caught on the hop, I rashly asked whether there was a danger that the government's third way could end up like the Conservatives' 'back to basics': a slogan not defined by its inventors and interpreted unhelpfully by everyone else. They seemed disappointed and the discussion moved on.

Some participants did seem to share my difficulty in progressing beyond left and right. One thought that the government's record so far could be summed up as 'indicate left, turn right'. Another responded that, on the contrary, it was the other way around. Somebody asked why the government should bother with promoting the third way in the first place, as it were. After all, if the opinion polls were so favourable without a coherent ideology, why bother to develop one?

Asked to sum up, Professor Giddens said – and I have this almost verbatim – that the seminar showed there was a new cultural sensibility emerging, based on the collapse of neo-liberalism and post-modernism, and the start of global cosmopolitanism. The chairman, not to be outdone, concluded that we had ended the era of endings and begun the era of beginnings.

■ ■ ■

Some commentators argue, as in the next text, that there is nothing new about the 'third way' in terms of the Labour Party's history and that Labour would benefit by jettisoning it. The text also criticizes the use of the term 'Old Labour' and suggests that the Labour Party has always been characterized by adaptability and different schools of political thought.

3 'Third Way, Old Hat'
Ross McKibbin
(London Review of Books, Volume 20, Number 17, 3 September 1998) abridged

[T]he increasingly desperate attempts by the Government's leading members, particularly the Prime Minister himself, to discover a Third Way, represent an important moment in the history of New Labour. The hunt for the Third Way, which has been going on more or less since Blair announced the birth of New Labour, is in many respects paradoxical. It is not obvious why a government which prides itself on its pragmatism and freedom from ideological baggage should spend so much of its time trying to acquire a new ideological encumbrance. Furthermore, the Government is at the moment under no electoral pressure: on the contrary, its lead in the opinion polls remains formidable – without precedent in our modern history. The Prime Minister continues to be enormously popular. In these circumstances, it seems surprising that he should wish to tamper with a winning formula . . .

What is most curious about the search for the Third Way and the debate about the policies which are supposed to constitute it is how unhistorical they are. Few of the participants seem to have much sense of the history either of the Labour Party or of the country it now governs. The rhetoric of the Third Way is, in fact, very misleading in its assumptions. It seems to suggest that the Third Way is a *via media* between two polar opposites – an uninhibited free market at one pole and 'socialism' at the other – and that these opposites themselves are complete entities which occupy all the space at each pole. But this has never been the case, at one pole or the other. In Britain there have this century been few defenders of the uninhibited free market as a basis of society and there has certainly been no such thing as 'Old Labour', if by that we mean a political party whose ideology was set in stone and therefore unquestionable. The history of the Labour Party has been one of almost constant ideological and political adaptation. In this sense there are many 'Old Labours' . . . We should, therefore, at least in part, see New Labour – both as practice, what it does in government, and as ideology, what it says it stands for – as one strand in the Labour Party's traditions . . .

The Labour Party only stands to gain if the quest for the third way is abandoned, and there are three reasons why it should be. The first is that there is no such thing as one Old Labour to which New Labour can be opposed. There are, rather, a number of Old Labours, of which New Labour is one, and these various forms of social democracy have always been in competition. New Labour has a long history and its various bits and pieces are very familar to the historian. The director of the LSE, Anthony Giddens, is quoted as saying that the 'ideas of old-style social democracy' no longer work. But which old-style social democracy is he talking about, and which ideas? Some ideas clearly no longer work: but others do – as has always been the case in the history of social democracy. Furthermore, historical competition has had an outcome: the policies which are thought to be unique to New Labour are those which in the history of the Labour Party have been the ones most prone to fail.

The second reason is that the quest has been very disorientating, particularly to those whose roots within the Labour Movement are deep enough for them to feel that its policies should be grounded in an organized body of principles. It would have been much better had the Labour leadership stuck to the

Kinnock–Smith Party – if the Party wants a Third Way that is it. The most successful policies of the Government – devolution, for example – were those it inherited from Smith and which it carried forward, not always enthusiastically . . .

The third reason is that a Third Way, as an organized body of principles, is really not possible. No political theorist, however distinguished, can act as though the country has no history, as though we can simply start afresh. The fact that we have a history and that Old Labour is so deeply a part of it is largely why the quest has been so fruitless. Everything we know of popular opinion in Britain suggests that most people still hold to the two basic propositions of Old Labour: that society should be based on some notion of fairness but that the rich and the powerful can only be made to acknowledge this by political action. The British hold to these propositions rather loosely – more loosely than in many other democracies – but they do hold to them . . . If, however, the Third Way has any distinguishing characteristic it is the premise that everyone can agree on everything. Unfortunately for its proponents that premise flies in the face of both social and political reality . . . New Labour has a past and members of the Government cannot escape it. And they will be much happier if they do not try.

■ ■ ■

The Labour government has attempted to explain 'the Third Way', if only in economic terms and within the context of European and international cooperation. Its elements include lower rates of income tax, strict controls on public spending, flexible labour markets and more freedom (deregulation) for business. But these are also Conservative Party goals.

Some commentators see such policies as pragmatic and ask whether British politics has lost its ideological thrust and become merely a managerial concern. They argue that the Labour government seems to believe that government is about management, not ideology or great issues of principle, is apparently happy to govern without old-style ideology and is concerned with what works on a commonsense level.[6]

■ ■ ■

The Conservative Party

The Labour party had modernized and won convincingly in the 1997 general election. The Conservative Party, on the other hand, has tried to recover after its defeat.

Kinnock–Smith
Previous leaders of the Labour Party.

sleaze
Scandals associated with financial and sexual irregularities.

red
Traditional Labour Party colour.

blue
Traditional Conservative Party colour.

It is generally accepted by most British commentators that it lost because of tax rises, 18 years of rule, **sleaze**, divisions over Europe, the perception that it was tired and the emergence of a 'new' Labour Party. Opinions differ on how successful the Conservatives have been in re-evaluating their policies and in becoming more attractive to the electorate. The weakness of the Conservatives leaves a gap in the traditional picture of British two-party politics in which they and Labour have fought each other for parliamentary power on the basis of different political programmes and ideologies.

The Conservatives are trying to establish policies that will distinguish them from Labour and the Liberal Democrats. Critics argue that the party must move away from automatic opposition to everything that Labour proposes; emphasize that it has in fact learnt something of value from its defeat; demonstrate its willingness to change; and formulate new and fresh policies. In this view, it also needs to understand the different political and more pluralistic social conditions that have developed in Britain in recent years, to which it will have to adapt in order to achieve government office. Conservative policies must radically and realistically address tax and spending, the welfare state, personal lifestyles, constitutional reform, the EU common currency (euro) and Europe in general. The next text addresses these matters and the splits within the Conservative Party.

4 'Mods and Rockers: the real division in the Tory party: and the right course'
(*The Times*, leader, 6 July 1998) abridged

The wise politician knows that fortune's wheel always turns: but the truly gifted knows that patience is not enough, that positioning is all. When governments decay, as they inevitably do, there is nothing inevitable about who the beneficiary will be. Already once this century the principal party of Opposition has found itself out of joint with the times and then locked out of office for generations. Accumulating constitutional change, which may blur the hard certainties of alternating **red** and **blue** into a new mosaic, makes the future all the harder to discern.

Tony Blair's Government has formidable reforming energy but its defects are becoming apparent. A taste for meretricious novelty, an itch to intervene, a populism tinged with cynicism and a capacity for feuding all stain the fringes of this administration. The crusading edge to its policies has also been corroded by suggestions of sleaze . . .

But the Conservatives will not be able adequately to exploit those weaknesses until they first tackle their own. A start has been made. But there is still a great deal to do. The most important of the tasks facing **William Hague** on his return to Westminster today is the stripping away of the comfortable myths to which too many Tories still cling, and which, far from providing protection, only hold them back.

The Tory party which Mr Hague must change is a party split in twain. The most important division, however, is not between Left and Right, **Europhile** and **Eurosceptic**. The real division is between liberals and reactionaries, modernisers and traditionalists, those armed primarily with principle and those whose first instinct is to take shelter in institutions. If the Tories are to win office, then liberals must first win the battle of ideas within their party . . .

It may seem odd to assert that Europe is no longer a cause of fundamental division within Toryism. **ERM** and **BSE** were engraved on the heart of **John Major's administration**. But the real arguments were buried alongside that unhappy Government. Europe, in particular a deep but pragmatic scepticism on **EMU**, is now a cause which unites the overwhelming majority of the Tory party. The party's leader articulates an opposition to further integration which is fluent, internationalist, rooted in economics and anchored in democracy. A small number of hoary-locked veterans may object but they are a dwindling band, all too conscious of their fading powers.

Sensing the new mood, the party's wiser MPs have hurried to endorse their leader's position rather than making a virtue of their distance from him. Quarrels do not fade just because arguments have been won. There will still be rumblings over Europe. But they come from exhausted volcanoes.

The more important argument the Conservative Party still needs to have is between those sensitive to changing times and those inclined to nostalgia. It is a battle, we believe, between Tory **Mods and Rockers**. In the Sixties the former were those comfortable with change, the latter those who followed old fads. It is the difference between those with a gaze fixed on new horizons and those either blinkered or still dreaming.

There are a number of issues on which this new division asserts itself, but one of the most telling, for it hangs on how the party adjusts to the modern world, was the vote on the age of homosexual consent [1998]. William Hague has always been a supporter of **equality** and was one of a small group of ministers who voted for it in 1994. Although illness kept him away from the division lobby two weeks ago, those Tories who voted for equality included young left-wingers with a pro-European tinge . . . and flintily sceptical right-wingers

William Hague
Leader of the
Conservative Party.

Europhile
Supporters of closer
British identification with
the EU.

Eurosceptic
Opponents of closer
British integration with
the EU.

ERM
Exchange Rate
Mechanism of the EU,
from which Britain was
forced to withdraw in
1992.

BSE
So-called mad cow
disease, which led to
the banning of the sale
of British beef.

**John Major's
administration**
1990–97.

EMU
European Monetary
Union.

Mods and Rockers
Opposed members of
youth cultures in the
1960s.

equality
16 as the age of sexual
consent for both
homosexuals and
heterosexuals.

Unionist
Preserving the UK: the United Kingdom of Great Britain and Northern Ireland.

Good Friday Agreement
Easter 1998: the basis for a power-sharing Assembly and Executive (between Catholics and Protestants) in Northern Ireland.

Heath
Conservative Prime Minister 1970–74.

Edmund Burke
British statesman and philosopher, 1729–97.

... Those opposed to any change included older men of the Right ... and also moderate men of the Tory Left ...

In attitudes to Ulster, a keystone issue of Conservatism, another dichotomy exists. The party is, and should remain, **Unionist**. But in their responses to the **Good Friday Agreement**, two Tory sensibilities conflicted. Many of those who were inclined to oppose the Agreement ... had honest objections. But their distaste for the devils in the detail blinded them to the prospect of peace. Other Tories preferred to swallow their doubts and wish the Agreement well. In so doing they aligned themselves with the deeper yearnings of the majority of citizens across the United Kingdom. Principled efforts to develop the deal in the right direction are squarely in the Tory tradition. But too strong an attachment to a traditional expression of the Union can weaken the cause of Unionism in the eyes of potential supporters.

There is another matter, of great constitutional significance, which forces Conservatives to examine whether inherited positions or durable principles matter more. Although reform of the House of Lords [see Chapter 5] should be a trial for the Government rather than a headache for the Opposition, the Tories have given themselves a migraine over the matter. All can agree that it is wrong of the Government to remove hereditary peers without also making other changes to the chamber: but after that confusion reigns.

Some Tories want to die in the same ditch still stained with their ancestors' blood. Others wish to emphasise the distrust Labour has of proper parliamentary scrutiny by proposing reforms more than Mr Blair has, in an effort to strengthen the second chamber. In this issue, as in others, the simple filter of Left and Right is inadequate. Leftish figures ... and men of the Right ... are wary of changes while enthusiasts for reform include sons of Thatcher ... and **Heath**'s heirs in the current Tory Reform Group.

A reactionary stance on the Lords has an appeal for anyone with the disposition towards conservatism ... But true Tories know that institutions sometimes become inadequate vessels for the principles and virtues which they cherish.

... the current presence of hereditary peers in the Lords weakens the capacity of the second chamber to hold the executive to account and unbalances the constitution.

A stronger revising and checking chamber would embody better the principles of wisdom, caution and limited government which are the true mark of the Tory. **Edmund Burke**, no friend of change, sympathised with the American

Revolution, because a decayed form of government no longer guaranteed that conservative virtues would flourish in a New World. It is one old insight of lasting power.

The Tory leader knows his principles are popular in a way that his party and some of its old causes are not. There will be a temptation for Mr Hague to march to an antique drum because it is banged with such vigour elsewhere in **Fleet Street**. Those parts of the Tory press which have stayed loyal to the party, right or wrong, speak for a constituency which no Conservative should neglect. Reaction has a claim on any Tory heart. But middle England no longer defers to **ermine** or pulls on its boots to the sound of the hunting-horn.

Any political party which is to have a hope of recovering must reach out to voters who live in a world of accumulating choice, increasing diversity, diminishing deference and deeper-than-ever scepticism towards extravagant claims. Wise Conservatives deal with the world as it is, not as it should be or once was. They respect the changing landscape and are sensitive to its contours. Having spent the Eighties telling other British institutions that they must adapt to compete the Tories must now make the same transition.

The Tories can do that by showing a liberal face to the electorate and extending an emancipating hand to all voters. Labour is, still, a party which trusts to government first. That government may be modernised, taskforced and target-led but it is still a leviathan which squeezes out choice. The Tories should oppose the reach of government and champion the role of people. They should not argue for 'the People' as an abstract licence for a swollen state, but real people liberated by greater ownership of their own lives and institutions.

The Conservatives should take government out of the boardroom and the bedroom, with a bonfire of businesss and social regulations as well as a plan to slim government itself. The Tory party could liberate business from a new tangle of red tape and individuals from restrictions on what and when they can consume. Parliament should be saved from an over-population crisis with a **cull** on the number of MPs and ministries. A party that was pledged to cut the number of jobs for its boys would establish a clear ethical advantage.

The party should find new ways of encouraging a human capitalism that creates incentives for saving and extend independence. They must develop a more sophisticated family policy which supports marriage but acknowledges the diversity of human love. The Tories should resist the reach of the State into family life, recognising ... that the family is a wisely subversive institution

Fleet Street
The former centre of the British newspaper industry in central London.

ermine
The material out of which peers' robes are made.

cull
Reduction in numbers.

which flourishes best when interfered with least. Tangible support in the tax-ation system but a proper horror of intrusive social policy is the wisest course.

The family is the safest shelter for future generations but those generations should grow up with a widening vista of opportunities. To that end, the Tories should seek to celebrate the achievement of British women, promote them in their party and consider how their lives can be made fuller.

The arguments are primed. The troops, arranged around new groups and new publications within the party, are ready to be led. The structures are re-organised; now is the time to listen honestly to the new Britain. It is up to Mr Hague to show that his understanding of what modern conservatism means extends beyond the tentative steps his party has so far taken.

■ ■ ■

Commentators argue that the Conservatives should listen, and pay more atten-tion, to the developing views of the British people and rethink their policies in a changing, more fragmented world.[7] According to this argument, many who voted for the Labour Party in 1997 disliked what the Conservative Party had become, but approved of its fundamental principles. The Conservatives, under their leader William Hague, seem to have taken some heed of such views and engaged in consultation exercises throughout the country from 1998. The next text reflects their progress.

5 'Hague pledges to remake Tories'
Philip Webster
(*The Times*, 20 January 1999)

William Hague promised last night to remould the Conservatives as a modern forward-looking alternative to new Labour that would avoid harking back to past glories and embrace the country as it is today and will be in the future.

In the most comprehensive statement he has given of his political philosophy, Mr Hague accepted that the Tories would have to take on and beat Labour on some of its most favoured territory if he was to achieve another 'great Conservative revival'.

The party faced a huge cultural change. 'We must never be a nostalgia party. We must do more than grudgingly accept Britain here and now: we must celebrate it.'

Outlining for the first time the key policy areas that will be reviewed over the coming months as he attempts to present a new agenda for Britain, Mr Hague acknowledged that winning battles over efficiency and the economy would no longer be enough.

Instead the Conservatives would have to win battles over generosity, charity, compassion, tolerance, fairness, social institutions and the community, all areas that Tony Blair has claimed.

Mr Hague used his speech to the right-wing Centre for Policy Studies to flesh out his credo of the British Way, which he claimed was threatened by Mr Blair's Third Way philosophy. 'The Prime Minister is in effect holding a dagger at the heart of what it is to be British,' he said. 'If he is left to carry on unchecked he will drive it right through that heart.'

The task of the Tories was to offer the British people an alternative – 'a British way for the 21st century that is founded on the experiences of the British people, a British way that builds on what is strong about Britain rather than trying to rebrand us or turn us into something else'.

But to succeed the Tories had to embrace the Britain of the future. 'Not just the sleepy villages, polite manners, friendly vicars and novels of **Scott** and Jane Austen that have always been Britain.' They had to embrace the Britain of 'big industrial cities and housing estates, the Britain proud of its world-class designers and good restaurants, the Britain where hundreds of thousands go to the **Notting Hill carnival** and the **Eisteddfod**, the Britain which watches MTV and *Changing Rooms*, and which is fascinated by **Ricky and Bianca**'s ups and downs, the Britain which turns to the sports pages before the political news, where more people go on holiday to Florida than **Butlins**, the Britain in other words that has always been Britain too – urban, ambitious, sporty, fashion-conscious, multiethnic, brassy, self-confident and international'.

He raised the fear that under Mr Blair people would wake up and 'find themselves living in what feels to be a different country'.

'People did not elect a Labour Government because they wanted to make Britain into a foreign country. But the impact of the Blair agenda will make people strangers in their own land – with an **alien voting system** and Parliament and an overmighty state.'

Scott
Sir Walter Scott, Scottish novelist and poet, 1771–1832.

Notting Hill carnival
Originally a West Indian, now multicultural, festival of music and dance, held each August in Notting Hill, west London.

Eisteddfod
Welsh festival of song, dance and poetry.

Changing Rooms
Popular television programme about interior decorating.

Ricky and Bianca
Characters in television soap opera *Eastenders*.

Butlins
Traditional English holiday camps on the coasts.

alien voting system
Proportional representation. This particular reform of election procedure has not been accepted by the Labour government. Instead, it seems to prefer the Alernative Vote (AV) system. See note 9 in Chapter 5.

The Tories are preparing a preliminary new policy programme, *Agenda for Britain*, for later this year. Mr Hague made plain that it would cover areas such as the constitution, including proposals to reduce the powers of Scottish MPs at Westminster after devolution; Europe, where it would come out against any further transfers of power and sovereignty from Britain to outdated European institutions; and a fundamental review of the welfare state favouring families and reducing dependency on it. There would also be new policies on education to give choice to schools and parents and 'get central government off the back of teachers', on health where the aim would be to get more doctors and nurses into a modern health service, and the next stage of the 'enterprise revolution' in which the Tories would again try to free business from over-regulation from Europe and the state.

Attacking Mr Blair's plans, Mr Hague said British identity could not be treated like 'some passing fad that can be repackaged, rebranded or simply consigned to the dustbin. It is my profoundest belief that if the Conservative Party is not in touch with the identity and values of the British people then it cannot be authentically Conservative. The British people came to think that the Conservatives had lost touch with them. They felt that in important areas of our national life we had become detached from the British Way.'

He asserted that Labour was reversing the Tory enterprise revolution and heralding the return of the big state as an enemy of Britain's enterprise spirit.

■ ■ ■

Some commentators, such as the political analyst Peter Riddell,[8] argue that William Hague has begun to counter what might be called 'Blairism'. But his alternative of the 'British Way' (see above text) is undefined, unclarified and unsatisfactorily elusive. It does not answer the hard questions and choices about the future of Britain, such as its relations with Europe, the changing nature of the constitution and the structure of the public sector.

Riddell maintains that the Conservatives have to win battles of principle as well as pragmatism if they hope to achieve governmental power. He argues that while the party stresses Britishness, it appears to be more concerned with English interests. It recognizes the importance of constitutional questions, but does not seem to appreciate the reality of devolutionary changes or Scottish, Welsh and Northern Irish hopes within the Union. The Conservatives may clearly oppose membership of the EU single currency. But their claim to be in Europe, while not being run by Europe, conflicts with those EU countries that seek further political and economic integration. It is argued that the Conservative position on Europe could result in the country's isolation, possible renegotiation of the terms of British EU member-ship, or ultimate withdrawal.

The Conservatives have begun to develop new policies in areas such as educa-tion, crime and the NHS. But it is felt that they still lack consistent policies over a wide agenda and indulge in negative reactions to isolated issues rather than positive politics. They give the impression of uncoordination, incoherence and uncertainty, with no overall vision. However, public opinion polls in 2000 showed that the Conservative rhetoric and perceived attempts at populist policies have persuaded the electorate as to their virtues in some, but not all, areas of policy.

■ ■ ■

The Liberal Democrats

It has long been argued that the Liberal Democrats suffer from an identity crisis because they have no realistic hope of achieving majority political power. They were once able to take advantage of their centrist position between Labour and the Conservatives to attract voters. But they have been squeezed by the Labour Party's alleged move to the right or centre ground, although they have benefited electorally by the weakness of the Conservatives, particularly at by-elections. The Liberal Democrats consequently face the task of creating an image and policies that could attract significant support from voters and lead to shared power.[9]

The Liberal Democrats have traditionally stressed constitutional reform (especially **PR**), local government, civil liberties, citizen participation in politics and society, higher taxes for public services, internationalism, the environment, federalism and a pro-Europe stance involving a more integrated European Union. Commentators maintain that the Liberal Democrats must either remain true to their traditional prin-ciples on the centre-left of the political spectrum or develop even more distinctive radical policies. The present leader (Charles Kennedy, 1999) is concerned to chart new courses for the party (see text 8).

The Liberal Democrats in recent years have been pursuing a policy of '**construc-tive opposition**' to the Labour government. This partial cooperation with Labour is arguably part of Tony Blair's ambition to forge a grand alliance of the progres-sive centre-left, that could potentially eliminate the Conservatives from future power. But, tactically, commentators feel that the Liberal Democrats have been unable to balance this cooperation on constitutional reform with opposition or criticism on issues such as health, schools, public spending and the environment. Ideologically, the policy of cooperation has generated Liberal Democrat condemnation from anti-Labour factions at local constituency and national parliamentary levels. Furthermore,

PR
Proportional
representation.

**constructive
opposition**
Opposition in specific
policy areas to the
Labour government
while cooperating in
others.

Mr Ashdown
Former leader of the
Liberal Democrats.

many Labour Party groups in Parliament and the constituencies also dislike the cooperation between the two parties. There is a resulting tension between Labour and the Liberal Democrats.

There is also a debate about the ideological position of the Liberal Democrats in the political spectrum. The left of the party often gives the impression that public sector problems can be solved merely by spending more on them and raising taxes to pay for the cost. But increased taxation is opposed by Labour and most of the electorate. The right or centre of the party argues that central government needs to be a monitor of better public services. These would then be delivered by providers rather than central government. But this entails huge structural reorganization.

Commentators maintain that the unconvincing nature of some Liberal Democrat arguments detracts from their innovative policies in other areas (which are often stolen by the other parties) and condemns the party to a permanent and minority third place in British politics.[10] The Liberal Democrats have not developed the kind of full policy agenda that could appeal to a broadly based electorate and allow them to gain more political power. Yet the party seems, if some present (2000) projections hold, to be capable of capturing House of Commons seats from both the Labour and the Conservative parties at the next general election. This might result in it holding the balance of power in a new parliament.

The next text argues that the Liberal Democrats should develop a principled or possibly left-of-centre position in British politics if they are to survive as a viable party (even though they may continue to play a minority role). This could be achieved by appealing to specific constituencies in the population, which are not being served by Labour or the Conservatives.

6 'Turn left for No. 10. The Liberal Democrats' best hope lies in outflanking the new Blatcherism'

Simon Jenkins

(*The Times*, 27 January 1999) abridged

For a decade **Mr Ashdown** has struggled to keep alive the fiction that there was room in British politics for a party that was both 'Centre Left' and to the right of Labour. He defied the common sense of history. He defied the

Kinnock-Smith-Blair invention of new Labour and the signing by Tony Blair of the Thatcherite covenant. He never came within a mile of power. Yet last year [1997] he could rejoice when the electorate showed a fine sense of humour and gave him 26 more MPs for fewer actual votes than in 1992.

Since then Mr Ashdown has been in a turmoil of indecision. Should he be nice to Mr Blair, perhaps get a Cabinet post, perhaps form a coalition if one is on offer? Or should he oppose, as his voters presumably intended him to do? Such Liberal floundering was meant as the outcome of Mr Blair's project. Never again should Labour be outflanked 'from the Centre' and never again thought spendthrift or fiscally punitive. Never should the party be thought soft on defence or foreign affairs. Efficiency and value-for-money should mark any Labour administration. The strategy has proved sound. William Hague's Tories are having enough trouble criticising it from the Right. For Liberal Democrats to criticise it from the Centre Left is impossible.

Slowly but surely Mr Blair is fashioning '**Blatcherism**' as Britain's national ideology. Butskellism, the welfare state Toryism of the **Rab Butler–Hugh Gaitskell** era of the 1950s and 1960s, has been reborn as the privatise-or-centralise authoritarianism that Mr Blair inherited on taking office. It is marinaded in clichés about One Nation, Third Way, social inclusion and aspirational society. But its appeal is as clear as a focus group memo, to offer a rigidly controlled state sector to the tax-conscious floating voters of Middle England.

On January 14 Mr Blair gave his celebrated eulogy of Labour's political target: 'a new, larger, more meritocratic middle class . . . millions of people who traditionally see themselves as working class but whose ambitions are now far broader'. The plea is to stakeholders who already have something at stake and something to hold, to voters who drive their **Mondeos** from out-of-town estates to hypermarket malls. After the Labour Party came the New Labour Party. Perhaps Labour will soon vanish altogether. The New Party has a politically appealing ring – and nobody reads history.

The political gap is obvious. Two weeks ago Mr Ashdown appeared to spot it. He made a bizarre intervention during Prime Minister's Questions, passionately attacking the Government for failures in education and health. 'The truth is,' he cried, 'that the Government are travelling in the wrong direction', away from a commitment to public services. I wondered if Mr Ashdown had suddenly found the plot. Somewhere in the fog of his mind he had sensed a mission for his party after all. Here he was on his feet, attacking a Labour Government from the Left, offering a choice not an echo. He was championing the outcasts, those excluded from Mr Blair's aspiring middle class. But the moment passed. Mr Ashdown sat down and shut up.

Blatcherism
A combination of Blair and Thatcher.

Rab Butler
Conservative politician, 1902–82.

Hugh Gaitskell
Former leader of the Labour Party, 1906–63.

Mondeos
Middle-of-the-range Ford motor car.

Lloyd George
British Liberal politician
and Prime Minister,
(1863–1945).

London mayoralty
Elections for the newly
created post of Mayor
of London.

Ken Livingstone
Left-wing Labour MP
who was elected as an
Independent as the first
Mayor of London in
May 2000.

workfare
A Labour programme
to get people off
welfare benefits and
into work.

The greatest threat for a political movement comes when it is in the ascendant. Labour should remember the strange death of Liberal England. It saw the mighty [Liberal] party of Gladstone and Asquith soar and then crash under the leadership of **Lloyd George,** who propelled his party from glittering success on the momentum of his image to a bickering rump of Westminster caucases . . . Lloyd George neglected his popular base and left the way open for Labour. Dazzled by his own light, he could not see the darkness until it overwhelmed him.

Mr Blair runs the same risk. He believes he has the poor in his pocket and that they are anyway no longer a political force. He need only remain 'open to the Right' to hold on to power. He is all red roses to Mr Ashdown. He invites him to meetings and listens to his views on Bosnia and electoral reform: politics has no nobler sacrifice. Meanwhile, he treats the Left with contempt. His national executive slaps down any dissent or requests for more open policy debates. He feels some strange urge to rig the shortlists for the **London mayoralty** and the Welsh assembly. He is terrified of **Ken Livingstone** and paranoid about the press.

These are small clouds on the horizon. But recession has yet to bite. The electorate has not experienced the full force of **workfare** and slashed social benefits, nor of cash-limited public-sector payrolls, nor of declining public transport . . .

There is still a huge section of the British population to whom the term 'middle class' does not remotely apply. They inhabit the vast housing estates and decayed industrial villages of the North and West. Their regions have lost economic viability. They are a geographical underclass, dependent either on welfare or on a surrogate welfare that is state employment. They are the reason why Britain is still not a rich European nation. Their income seems bound to decline as the welfare state comes under ever more stringent control. Mr Blair cannot be their friend and that of the aspirant middle class. There is not enough money to go round.

These groups are a political rebellion waiting to happen. The word betrayal is on their lips. They have never voted Tory. But their support cannot be taken for granted. Their attitude to Labour is likely to be the same as that of 'loyal' Tory voters in 1997. They are ready to break ranks if pushed too hard.

They are surely Liberalism's recruiting ground. If I were Liberal leader I would simply rerun history with the names changed. Like Labour at the turn of the century, the Liberal Democrats are far stronger in the cities than in Parliament. They are a plausible alternative to the local (Labour) mafia. The party has laid the ground for a leftward swing, having campaigned for higher taxes for better public services. It could demand local discretion to raise rates dedicated to schools, hospitals and public transport. Mr Ashdown was never a localist in this sense, any more than he was a 'liberal' on crime or drugs. His successor need feel no such compunction.

Liberalism should surely treat Blatcherism as an unequivocal enemy. It should gamble on Mr Blair doing a Lloyd George, sinking into Westminster cronyism, losing votes to the Tories on the Right and to a renascent, populist Liberalism on the Left. This Liberalism would champion the disadvantaged, those who want more from government, not less, those for whom higher taxes are no threat and public services a salvation. It should offer a home to public sector trade unionism, as the party of local autonomy and local expenditure. Ever since Lloyd George, Liberalism has been squeezed between Left and Right. Why not put new Labour in the same squeeze? . . .

■ ■ ■

In 1999, the Liberal Democrats elected a new leader, Charles Kennedy. Commentators[11] then argued, in a similar manner to the last text, that he should take the party in a principled direction in order to broaden British politics and to achieve a distinctive message. Meanwhile, and in this view, the party and its leader have to choose between closer links with Labour, outright opposition to this 'project' or demand better terms from Labour for their cooperation. Critics feel that attempting merely to balance between scepticism and acceptance in this relationship limits the Liberal Democrats' appeal and influence.

The current public opinion polls, which in varying degrees indicate a disillusionment and dissatisfaction with both the Labour government and the Conservatives, suggest that the Liberal Democrats could benefit from a different approach and thereby attract more support. But this would have to be based on a distinctive political programme.

In such a view, the party should stress to a much greater extent, civil liberties, the environment and internationalism; propose greater spending on public services such as education and health; stand for intellectual and political nonconformism; embrace controversial issues that the main parties will not consider; and emphasize the moral dimension in politics. It is argued that Britain needs such a principled party to carry on important public debates.

Commentators, as in the next text, have tried to itemize the options for the Liberal Democrats in British political life, including the principled and left positions.

Kenneth Clarke
Conservative pro-
European MP.

Michael Heseltine
Conservative pro-
European MP.

7 'Kennedy's dilemma. The Liberal Democrats' new leader cannot face all ways'
(*The Times*, leader, 10 August 1999)

The Liberal Democrat leadership campaign ended yesterday, as it had begun, polite to a fault. Although Charles Kennedy had to fight for his party's crown, his victory had never been seriously questioned. Mr Kennedy's progress will still have been closely watched in Downing Street and Conservative head-quarters. For the new Liberal Democrat leader, anxious to lead 'a serious party of government', has yet to show his hand on the central question, which the contest failed to resolve: should the Liberal Democrats co-operate more with Labour, or chart a new, distinctive course of their own.

The result showed that Liberal Democrat activists are far from united on how far to help Tony Blair to 'modernise' Britain. Only when the votes had been counted four times, to take account of voters' second preferences, did Mr Kennedy win the required majority over his main rival, Simon Hughes. Mr Hughes's strong showing was partly thanks to his doubts about cuddling up to Labour, a position that grates with Mr Kennedy's more friendly approach.

As the new leader picks over the embers, he faces four possible courses. First, he may choose to reaffirm his party's fundamental tenets – safeguarding civil liberties, support for higher taxes and a radical agenda on the environment. Yet this is unlikely to win the Liberal Democrats more votes in Conservative-held marginal constituencies where they are needed most. Nor is it likely to provide new grounds of genuine agreement with Mr Blair.

The second option is for Mr Kennedy to shift his party to the left in an attempt to woo disaffected Labour voters. This may indeed succeed in winning some new votes, and would please Liberal Democrats who want to end their party's love affair with Labour. But, again, there are pitfalls. These votes are most likely to be found in Labour heartlands where the Liberal Democrats' chances of victory are slim to non-existent. And breaking up with new Labour might appal Liberal Democrats who believe that their participation in a Cabinet committee has paid dividends.

Mr Kennedy could therefore be tempted to take his party to the soft right, accentuating a pro-European liberalism of the kind that **Kenneth Clarke** or **Michael Heseltine** espouse. Appealing to disaffected Conservatives would be shrewd electoral strategy, yet convincing his party activists of its merits would test Mr Kennedy's leadership skills to the full.

Finally, Mr Kennedy might decide to turn co-operation with the Government into a more committed alliance. The temptations of ministerial office and the prize of proportional representation – if he believes he can count on the latter – would however be bought at a high price: that of the transformation of the Liberal Democrats from an independent organization into an appendage of the Labour Party.

Mr Kennedy has given many clues to the future; the trouble is that they cancel each other out. At yesterday's enthronement he declared that Liberal Democrats must distinguish themselves from Labour. 'That difference is needed now more than ever,' he said. Yet within minutes he was talking about areas on which he might co-operate with the Government. He cannot expect the electorate, or his own party faithful, to be anything other than confused.

■ ■ ■

Charles Kennedy's policy statements on becoming leader of the Liberal Democrats do not appear to solve these problems of ideological and pragmatic direction, as the next text illustrates. They also indicate the continuation of a balancing act between Labour and the Liberal Democrats (constructive opposition), based on the achievement of PR for Westminster and other elections.

But the Labour government in July 2000 rejected PR and holds out only the possibility of changing to an Alternative Vote (AV) system.[12] The AV procedure falls short of the pure PR that the Liberal Democrats have been fighting for and arguably is only a small refinement on the 'first-past-the-post' simple majority electoral system that is currently in operation. The Liberal Democrats might, however, see AV as the possible first step on the road towards PR.

Nevertheless, Tony Blair appears keen on the possibility of a progressive centre in British politics, which would banish the traditional right and left from the political scene (see text 7 in Chapter 8). This could involve an alliance between Labour and the Liberal Democrats and might lead to potentially endless coalition government in the event of no overall majorities. Such a situation could happen even under the present system and would not need new electoral procedures. The Liberal Democrats might achieve shared power, but this could be at the expense of their identity and influence.

dump PR

In July 2000 the Labour government in effect ruled out proportional representation (PR) for parliamentary elections. It seemed, however, that it might be discussing the possibilities of the Alternative Vote (AV) system with the Liberal Democrats. See note 9 in Chapter 5.

8 'A sickness at the heart of our nation'
Charles Kennedy
(*The Times*, 11 August 1999) abridged

In the era of the catch-all Third Way, so beloved of the Prime Minister and the No 10 policy unit, there is a greater need than ever for the Liberal Democrats to provide a distinctive and principled voice. The Third Way's mix-and-match politics makes gestures to both the Left and the Right, and it is easy to be seduced by this approach.

But the Third Way leaves a vacuum in politics, for its shifting sands threaten to engulf those who pass its way. And shifting sands cannot offer a solid basis for the new constitutional structure that we need to build in Britain.

Faced with this, we Liberal Democrats must get our strategy right. While wary of being swamped, we should take advantage of the Government's willingness to listen to ideas from a range of sources. On key constitutional issues, the game is there to be played and won. No 10's public assurances yesterday chime with my own view that the Prime Minister is not preparing to **dump PR**. I believe his mind is open and he is willing to be persuaded. So we must engage constructively with Labour on the constitutional agenda, showing that we are businesslike – and are ourselves ready to listen to others, just as we have been listening to each other over the course of a unifying leadership election.

Make no mistake, there is a sizeable agenda for co-operation with the Government on the constitution. In addition to fair votes for Westminster, the country needs PR for local government in England and Wales.

There is much work to be done on British entry to the euro, democratizing the House of Lords, and meaningful freedom of information legislation. This is an agenda for constructive and adult dialogue right up to the next election and beyond.

In winning the PR case, I will have several weapons in my armoury. The first of these is that fair votes have delivered constructive and co-operative politics in Scotland, where Liberal Democrats and Labour govern together.[13] We have seen that in both Scotland and Wales PR has resulted in fair representation for the views of all. Politics is better for it, and people actually seem rather to like that.

The second will be the hard electoral truth that to enact a long-term programme of modernization there must be an electoral system that truly represents the views of the people. We must not forget that Margaret Thatcher was elected on 42–43 per cent of the votes[14] and tore civic Britain apart.

That could happen again. Without fair votes, a similarly damaging Conservative administration may be a possibility. Without fair votes, there will be little support for greater partnership with Labour among Liberal Democrats.

Under my leadership, the Liberal Democrats will reconnect with Britain as a strong and independent party, opposing Labour where it fails to deliver. I will be taking my colleagues in the parliamentary team beyond Westminster. I want us to be seen – visible, active and in touch – in every corner of Britain.

In particular, I will be highlighting the deep social divisions between rich and poor in Britain. These are worsened by inadequate health and education services in many of our poorest areas, which deny many the life chances that the better-off enjoy.

Some have said that this means a return to tax-and-spend social policies which will place us to the left of the other parties. Nonsense. All parties agree that we need to tax to pay for the activities that we as a nation decide are right and necessary, and that the better off should pay more.

The clear difference between the Liberal Democrats and the others is about being straight with the British people. We are prepared to face up to the choices involved when it comes to paying for the decent services which people expect in health and education. That means being honest, ensuring that people understand that higher taxes are sometimes necessary if schools are to have books, and hospitals are to have beds.

But tax revenue is not the only solution to social divisions in Britain. Far from it. Last month, I outlined in *The Times* my idea of a social justice audit, which would change the nature of our political discourse, placing concerns about poverty [see texts 2 and 3 in Chapter 7] at the heart of political debate.

I also want to debate how to provide decent public services, going well beyond discussing levels of expenditure. We need to think seriously about whether monolithic state provision is the answer to all our problems. Mutual societies may offer the way forward ... where mutually-owned companies provide services on the basis of contributions made by members.

Beveridge
Author of the Beveridge Report (1942), which helped to create the British welfare state.

These kinds of organizations have deep Liberal roots back into the last century, and the contributory principles which underpin them have much in common with **Beveridge**'s original vision of the welfare state. They could enhance consumer choice and bring public service provision into the 21st century.

This engagement with the voters will help us to strengthen the party, increase membership, and put in place a strong, national campaigning force. It will also demonstrate to one and all that we are a serious force to be reckoned with.

We should be ready to work with the Government where it is willing to deliver a modernized constitution and fair votes. But we will widen and deepen our criticism where they fail to tackle the inequalities that still divide Britain. Not only is this approach philosophically the right one for our party, it also makes strategic sense. In my view, it is the best way to obtain fair votes for Westminster.

■ ■ ■

In the light of the above texts and although public opinion polls fluctuate considerably in the run-up to a general election, a MORI poll in May 2000 indicated that the Conservatives were gaining on Labour in terms of respondents' voting intentions and support.[15] Labour obtained 48 per cent of the poll (its lowest level for six years); the Conservatives received 32 per cent (their highest level since 1996); and the Liberal Democrats remained stable on 15 per cent.

However, the poll also showed that three-quarters of the respondents did not consider that William Hague was ready to become Prime Minister. Some two-thirds did not think that the Conservatives were ready to form the government at the next general election.

■ ■ ■

 Exercises

Write short essays on the following topics

1   What is meant by ideology?

2   What, if anything, distinguishes the three main political parties in Britain in terms of ideology and policies?

3   Is the Conservative Party in terminal decline? If so, why?

4   Does New Labour have an ideology? What is the Third Way?

5   Is there any room for the Liberal Democrats in the British party-political arena?

6   Critically examine Charles Kennedy's article (text 8).

7   The term 'centralization' appears in many texts in this book. What does it mean?

Explain and examine the following terms

left-of-centre	workfare/New Deal	consensus
'inclusive'	Bank of England	coalition
social democracy	subsidiarity	jingoism
sovereignty	welfare state	pragmatism
free market	Old Labour	deregulation
sleaze	pluralism	executive
public sector	Opposition	Unionism

 Further reading

Dunleavy, Patrick *et al.* (ed.) (2000) *Developments in British Politics 6*, London: Macmillan.
Jones, Bill *et al.* (2000) *Politics UK*, London: Prentice Hall.
Kingdom, John (1999) *Government and Politics in Britain: An Introduction*, Cambridge/Oxford: Polity Press/Blackwell.
Ludlam, Steve and Smith, Martin J. (eds) (2000) *New Labour in Government*, London: Macmillan.
Marr, Andrew (1995) *Ruling Britannia: The Failure and Future of British Democracy*, London: Michael Joseph.
Pilkington, Colin (1998) *Issues in British Politics*, London: Macmillan.

 Notes

1. See next text.
2. But it has substantially raised indirect taxes (stealth taxes) on items such as pensions and insurance and abolished marriage allowance and mortgage relief, all of which affect its middle-class supporters.
3. The Labour government has been forced to increase public service spending on education and the National Health Service after widespread concern about their inadequacies.

4. Leader (2000) 'Intimations of mortality' London: *The Economist* 17 June.
5. A MORI public opinion poll, (2000) London: *The Times* 27 June, indicated that a majority of respondents felt that class was still very much a reality in Britain, despite the Labour government's attempts to promote a 'One Nation' philosophy.
6. Peter Riddell (1999) 'Managing without the vision thing. Tony Blair is happy to govern unencumbered by ideology', London: *The Times* 3 August.
7. Leader (1998) 'All Ears. The Tories should listen to Britain, but be true to their beliefs', London: *The Times* 13 July.
8. Peter Riddell (1999) 'but begs the big questions' London: *The Times* 20 January.
9. Peter Riddell (1998) 'Ashdown's task is to create new Liberalism' London: *The Times* 26 June.
10. Leader (1998) 'Fated to be third. Decent Lib Dem ideas ripe for snatching by Labour' London: *The Times* 4 September.
11. Tim Hames (1999) 'Making a pitbull out of a poodle' London: *The Times* 8 August.
12. See note 9 in Chapter 5.
13. In fact, this is an uneasy alliance, with conflicts between the two parties, as there are at local levels throughout Britain.
14. The Labour Government in 1997 was also elected on a minority of the votes (44.4 per cent of the popular vote).
15. MORI (2000) London: *The Times* 25 May.

Constitutional reform

Public opinion polls suggest that constitutional reform in Britain does not rank high on the list of most people's personal concerns about the country. But, nevertheless, constitutional issues continue to play a significant part in British life and could increasingly and directly affect greater numbers of citizens. This chapter is concerned with recent significant reform processes initiated by the Labour government. It focuses on devolution (a degree of self-government for Scotland, Wales and Northern Ireland); the reform of the House of Lords; the creation of a Human Rights Act and progress towards a Freedom of Information Act.

Most countries have a written document (a constitution) that sets out the powers and duties of government institutions, and the relationship between them. Britain has no written constitution contained in any one document. Rather, it has a collection of written and unwritten constitutional sources that have evolved over the centuries. They are supposed to provide a balance between government institutions and to act as restraints upon the holders of power.

The sources of the British constitution today consist of 1) the common law (judge-made law); 2) laws (or statutes) passed earlier by the monarch and now by Parliament (the House of Commons, the House of Lords and formally the monarch); 3) conventions (informal agreements); and 4) European Union law.

The original powers of the monarch were gradually reduced over the centuries. The House of Commons became the dominant force in the parliamentary structure and the legislative powers of the House of Lords were curtailed by the Parliament Act, 1911, leaving it with authority only to amend and delay legislation. The Act was intended to be the prelude to a complete reform of the House of Lords.

Parliament historically has been accorded an absolute power ('sovereignty') that is not constrained by any other body. This means that a government (executive) with a workable majority in the House of Commons is normally able to pass its policies through Parliament without any opposition.

The main exception to the so-called 'sovereignty of Parliament' is European Union law. As a result of membership of the EU in 1973, European law in some areas, and where there is conflict between it and British domestic law, takes precedence over British law.

Historically, there was also a gradual union between the four nations of the British Isles. Wales was united with England in 1536–42, Scotland was also joined to England/Wales by the Act of Union, 1707 and a common Parliament was established for the three nations. A further Act was passed in 1801 to unite Great Britain and Ireland to form the United Kingdom of Great Britain and Ireland (UK). The current process of devolution gives increased self-government (but not independence) to Wales (1999), Scotland (1999) and Northern Ireland (2000) within the existing structure of the UK.

■ ■ ■

The British Constitution

There has been a continuous debate on possible reform of the British constitutional system for many years, especially by the campaign group Charter 88. The Conservative Party generally wants to preserve the existing arrangements, while the Labour Party and the Liberal Democrats press for radical change. The next text sets the general scene for reform and comments upon the nature of the British constitution.

1 'Reclaiming Britain's constitution: Power in Britain is far too concentrated. This must change'

(*The Economist*, 14 October 1995) abridged

What a peculiar thing is the British constitution. Its defenders regard it not so much with approval as with reverence. Its critics see not a structure in need of repair here and there, but a rotting monstrosity requiring outright demolition. The constitution's most distinctive characteristic – the fact that no one ever bothered to write it down, so no one is sure what it says – again divides the camps. Traditionalists marvel at this ineffable quality: Britain's constitution is, literally, too wonderful for words. Modernisers find that infuriating. How British can you get? Mystical mumbo-jumbo . . . blind deference to outmoded institutions . . . blithering complacency.

If there is to be an intelligent debate about reforming the British constitution, it will be necessary to break out of these modes of thought. The traditionalists need to realise that the rules by which Britain is governed are a legitimate object of scrutiny and revision. Without reform, the constitution will not remain a thing of unchanging beauty. It will be revised by stealth, as it has been already, and in ways that serve the government of the day rather than the wider interest of good government. Modernisers, on the other hand, need to understand that it is neither feasible nor desirable to adopt the root-and-branch reform of a written constitution and all that goes with it. Without a crisis of improbable proportions, or the widespread conviction that Britain's system of government is a much greater failure than its democratic counterparts abroad, change must be both cautious and incremental.

separation of powers
Between executive,
legislature and judiciary.

cabinet
A small body of senior
ministers within the
government who are
supposed to collectively
discuss and initiate
government policy. This
model is no longer
entirely true of the way
in which programmes
are developed.

Bagehot
Walter Bagehot, British
economist and
journalist, author of *The
English Constitution*,
1826–77.

It's broke, so fix it

... Our goal is not to write a blueprint. That would be to side with angry uncompromisers bearing final solutions. It is, rather, to show that Britain's constitution does need repairing, and to offer some ideas for putting it right. Up to a point, we will argue, it is possible to regard these proposals as a menu of choices, to say yes to some and no to others – though we regard each reform as desirable in its own right.

This newspaper has already argued the case for abolishing the monarchy. We view that change in the same light – as one of several possible reforms, desirable on its merits, feasible (by and large) with or without the rest ... With or without the monarchy, Britain must reclaim its constitution.

Why 'reclaim'? Because ... the greatest virtues of the British constitution have been the very ones which time and successive governments have diminished. Traditionalists are fond of saying that the British constitution has been the country's most successful export: how can principles that have been so widely imitated require revision? Unfortunately, the ideas that Britain pioneered and others adopted – the **separation of powers**, the notion that basic liberties must be sheltered from the power of the state – are precisely those which the British constitution, as it evolved, failed to embody. Other systems copied the best things in the British tradition; Britain let them wither.

This happened in the name of an idea lauded as the cornerstone of Britain's system: the sovereignty of Parliament. At first sight, it seems an impeccably democratic concept. The House of Commons is accountable to the people; what could be more democratic than to concentrate formal political power there? But the sovereignty of Parliament means that whatever the House of Commons says (by simple majority) goes. Never mind whether it is revising traffic regulations or denying blue-eyed citizens the vote. Britain's constitution makes no distinction between the two, and grants virtually no say in the matter to anybody else.

True in theory, you might say. In practice, parliamentary scrutiny offers the best testing-ground for government proposals, the best restraint against abuse, the best source of popular legitimacy and, above all, a system that can adapt flexibly to changing times. If only that were so. In practice, parliamentary sovereignty has served these goals badly. By degrees, the idea has become a mere disguise for the sovereignty of **cabinet** – a profoundly undemocratic concept. The House of Commons is, to use **Bagehot**'s words, ever more 'dignified' (jarring though the term will seem to any modern observer of its proceedings) and ever less 'efficient'. Thanks to party discipline, its debates are a sad charade, and its committees are largely ineffective.

The government, established on the basis of a minority of [the popular] votes, has huge executive powers, yet faces very few formal constraints. Its powers are not untrammelled: elections, the press, **judicial review** and the **European courts** all act upon it. But these checking forces work slowly, weakly and unreliably. Britain's constitutional defences against an overmighty state are far too flimsy. They need strengthening.[1]

That view is gaining ground. The Labour Party has committed itself to an ambitious programme. It promises a bill of rights (initially by incorporating the European Convention on Human Rights into British law), regional assemblies, a referendum on proportional representation [PR],[2] and reform of the House of Lords. We shall examine such ideas in detail over the coming weeks; in principle, we favour them, because they disperse political power. The Liberal Democrats also seek reform. But the Conservative Party flatly opposes it – which is odd, in a way. Limiting the role of the state is a cause you might expect to arouse the sympathy of the right and the suspicion of the left. Political leaders seem to love the constitution when in power and loathe it otherwise. This is one reason to take Labour's promises with a pinch of salt.

Look around the democratic world and you see a great variety of constitutional arrangements and a uniform disenchantment with politics. This cautions against expecting too much of constitutional reform. And it is true that the best guarantor of freedom is a political culture that demands it. Without that, constitutional reform serves little purpose. With it, as in Britain, it seems less urgent – but, if undertaken, might be all the more effective. The case for change in Britain is strong. The constitution is broken, and needs fixing.

■ ■ ■

judicial review
The power of the senior courts and judiciary to examine government actions to see whether they accord with Acts of Parliament.

European courts
Eg the European Court of Human Rights and the (EU) European Court.

Constitutional reform is often advanced by opposition politicians. Governments, however, have little incentive to restrain their own powers by such changes. Advocates press for reforms that have the effect of promoting checks and balances against the government of the day. However, the Labour Party in opposition was committed to constitutional reform and has implemented some of its policies since 1997. The next text represents the party's views on constitutional issues.

canard
Something false, or a hoax.

chattering classes
Derogatory expression referring to people (often mainly middle class metropolitan professionals) who wish to promote widespread changes in British society.

2 *'Democracy's second age'*
Tony Blair
(*The Economist*, 14 September 1996) abridged

We are now in the Second Age of democracy. It is time to give it a second wind. After a long battle, the First Age established universal suffrage, in 1928, when the vote was extended to all adult women.

Nearly 70 years later, however, Britain has changed radically. The attempt to change prevailing social and economic conditions (and the need to fight two world wars) hugely extended the scope of central government. In 1900, central government spending as a share of GDP amounted to 9.7 per cent; in 1930 it was 13 per cent. Today, it is over 42 per cent – steady at that level since 1979.

In mid-century the majority of the country was self-consciously working class, and paid less than 10 per cent of their income in tax. Today, the largest grouping is the middle class; the groups classified as 'ABC1' by pollsters make up 52 per cent of the electorate, and pay over 35 per cent of their incomes in taxes . . . So government now spends more public money and the majority of the population fund the expenditure.

These changes raise serious questions for democracy. Is it still supportable that the power to decide how these vast resources are spent should reside exclusively with a highly centralized national government? And do the more educated and wealthier citizens of today, albeit all of them with the vote, really have power over the system?

To make matters worse, some British institutions have not yet caught up even to 1928 . . . Think of the way Parliament works, sometimes seeming more private club than modern democratic forum; or the composition of the House of Lords; or constitutional conventions established in the 18th and 19th centuries.

The consequence of ignoring these questions is that politics becomes less respected, less accountable, more remote from people's lives. That is bad for Britain and bad for democracy.

Contrary to the Tory *canard*, constitutional reform is not an issue for the '**chattering classes**', irrelevant to most people. Properly done, it will go to the heart of public concerns. It is important not only for its own sake, but because it makes possible the attainment of other vital goals: a stronger economy, better transport, good schools and crime prevention.

Walter Bagehot, the great Victorian editor of *The Economist*, declared at the outset of his classic text *The English Constitution*: 'Every constitution must first gain authority, and then use authority'. It must, he went on, 'first win the confidence and loyalty of mankind, and then employ that homage in the work of government.' These are wise words, and they summarize very well my approach to constitutional reform (or democratic renewal, as I prefer to call it).

Changing the way we govern, and not just changing the government, is no longer an optional extra for Britain. So low is popular esteem for politicians and the system we operate that there is now little authority for us to use unless and until we first succeed in regaining it.

For three decades the standing of Britain's constitution has been declining. Barely a third of the people now declare themselves satisfied with their system of government. Parliament's very *raison d'être* is to express and redress popular grievances. When it has itself become the focus of those grievances, it is obliged to act.

We do not need to exaggerate to make the case. Britain is not recovering from war-time defeat or social collapse, nor is it tainted by totalitarianism. We are not faced with the necessity of building a new constitution from scratch, as for example was post-war Germany.

Britain is, however, struggling to find its way after the collapse of the grand 20th century ideologies of left and right. These too often placed ends above means, grand projects of social or economic reconstruction above the democratic requirement for consent, self-government and respect for rights. The result has been 80 years since the first world war of a steady accretion of power to ministers.

New Labour's aim is a partnership between people and politicians based on trust, honesty and a realistic assessment on both sides as to what government can deliver.

The Economist
British political and economic weekly magazine.

The challenge facing us is that which confronted the Victorian reformers in the last century who, almost uniquely, gave Britain democracy without revolution. It is to take a working constitution, respect its strengths, and adapt it to modern demands for clean and effective government while at the same time providing a greater democratic role for the people at large.

raison d'être
Reason for being, or existence.

due process
Openness and the
correct procedures of
law which are to be
followed in any given
case.

Bourbons
A French royal house or
dynasty associated with
absolutist political
traditions.

de facto
In practice or reality

referendums
Giving the electorate a
direct vote on a
particular issue.
Referendums have
been seen as reducing
the sovereignty of
Parliament, but are
increasingly used in
Britain (eg on
devolution proposals).

Labour's programme for democratic renewal is threefold: to strengthen the rights and obligations of citizens; to take decision-making closer to the people; and to improve the democratic credentials of Westminster.

Democracy can flourish only as part of a rich culture of rights respected and duties performed. Most of the rights and duties relate to community life beyond the sway of the politician or the ordinary scope of the courts. But the duty of the state's constitution to safeguard freedoms, and encourage the performance of duties, remains profound.

The British state presently does too little on these counts. Basic rights, to information, legal equality, **due process** and security of property, are too often flouted. And little attempt is made to encourage people to take more than a cursory part in their own governance. The idea that the people at large might play a greater political role is instinctively alarming to many in the élite for its implication of greater 'direct democracy'. It ought, instead, to be seen as critical to developing a richer notion of democratic citizenship.

Tory Bourbons

The case for a freedom of information act and the incorporation of the European Convention on Human Rights into British law is now generally agreed outside the Conservative Party and even by some within it. The onus must always be on public authorities to explain why citizens should not have access to information and not vice versa. Britain already has a *de facto* bill of rights through its ratification of the European Convention underpinned by a court in Strasbourg which delivers more hostile judgements against Britain than any other state. Only the strange mentality of the modern Tory Bourbons could think it satisfactory to force British citizens to go to France to enforce their rights because their own courts are incapable of doing so.

More information and guaranteed rights are only two means of achieving far broader democratic objectives. Greater use of **referendums** is another, to give citizens a veto over proposals to change their system of government, and to give legitimacy to the changes to which they do agree ... Informed public participation is the key, complementing not replacing established decision-making by elected representatives.

Most political decisions of concern to citizens affect their immediate locality. The revival of local government must be the prime means for achieving the second objective of taking government closer to the people. Local government's democratic voice needs strengthening, by establishing a closer engagement between local authorities and their electors. This is why I am so strongly attached to the principle of elected mayors for London[3] and our leading cities[4] – generating local chief executives with a direct mandate, able to mobilize their communities behind urban renewal as mayors across Europe and the United States do.

Strengthening the intermediate tier between London and the localities is also necessary. Here again our agenda is one of sensible, incremental change to meet modern democratic demands.

The Scottish Office was established as long ago as 1885 to provide a Scottish dimension to administration north of the border. But it is Westminster-controlled and Westminster-oriented. The Scottish people rightly insist on something more democratic, in the form of a Scottish parliament with **legislative powers**.

The Tories claim that this would threaten the unity of the United Kingdom, yet they rightly consider their proposals for **devolved government in Northern Ireland** as perfectly compatible with the union. Their opposition to our decentralization plans ignores the wisdom of the ages, as well as concrete experience in other countries. As **William Gladstone**, the Victorian prime minister, said: 'The concession of local self-government is not the way to sap or impair, but the way to strengthen and consolidate unity.'

Precisely this rationale has led every other large European democracy, including France and Spain with centralizing traditions as strong as Britain's, to create a regional tier between central government and local authorities [devolution] . . .

We are proposing a similarly refined approach for the United Kingdom. Scotland with its distinct national, legal and cultural institutions is manifestly in a class of its own . . . once a Scottish parliament is established, it will be here to stay. In their own separate ways, Wales and London also have powerful claims to – and their people want – their own authorities.

Across the rest of England, popular enthusiasm for a regional political voice varies greatly. Our policy reflects this, allowing greater regional government as people demand it. In the north-east and north-west demand for greater powers is strong. In other places, there is less demand. So be it.

Shaking up Westminster

Westminster has for too long insulated itself from change while imposing it on everyone else. Here again, Labour must settle some important unfinished business from a century ago, starting with the House of Lords. It delights and astonishes me that we are about to fight an election [May 1997] in which the

legislative powers
Devolved self-government in many policy and legislative areas.

devolved government in Northern Ireland
The creation of a power-sharing Assembly and Executive in Northern Ireland and the end of direct rule from Westminster. This process, after initial problems, was completed in May 2000.

William Gladstone
British Liberal politician and prime Minister, 1809–98.

minority votes
The Labour government
itself was successful in
the 1997 general
election on a minority
(44.4 per cent) of the
popular vote.

**proportional
representation**
MPs elected to the
House of Commons
and elsewhere on the
proportional distribution
of the popular votes
cast by electors.

inter alia
Among other things.

Tories will be defending the right of ancestral dukes, marquesses, earls and barons to make the law in a modern democracy. And this in a society which John Major claims he wants to make 'classless'!

Labour will remove the right of hereditary peers to sit and vote in the Lords[5] and introduce a more open system for nominating life peers. We will consult widely about an appropriate second-stage reform,[6] but we should be clear that removing the absurdity of the hereditary element will be a huge step forward in itself.

Effective democracy depends, above all, on the quality of the House of Commons. Electoral reform for the Commons has a totemic status among some of Britain's constitutional reformers. I appreciate the reasons for this, not least 17 years of 'elective dictatorship' by Tory governments returned on **minority votes**, pushing through divisive and destructive policies such as the poll tax and rail privatization, which is why I have confirmed John Smith's pledge to hold a referendum on the issue.[7]

However, I personally remain unpersuaded that **proportional representation [PR]** would be beneficial for the Commons.[8] It is not, as some claim, a simple question of moving from an 'unfair' to a 'fair' voting system. An electoral system must meet two democratic tests: it needs to reflect opinion, but it must also aggregate opinion without giving disproportionate influence to splinter groups. Aggregation is particularly important for a parliament whose job is to create and sustain a single, mainstream government.[9]

Whatever the electoral system may be, something has to be done about the House of Commons itself, which, to more and more voters, seems arcane and ineffective, or worse. We need to improve the way we scrutinize and debate legislation, how MPs hold the executive to account, how we organize the legislative programme and how we deal with European legislation . . .

We shall fight the [1997] general election *inter alia* on democratic renewal. More important still, with the support of the people we shall deliver what we promise on democratic renewal as an essential element in our project: the modernization of Britain.

■ ■ ■

Devolution

The Labour government has legislated, following referendums of the populations, for an elected Assembly in Wales and an elected Parliament in Scotland (1999).

Following a referendum in Northern Ireland a power-sharing Assembly was formed in 1998 and an Executive in 1999. Although the Northern Ireland arrangements collapsed due to difficulties over the decommissioning of IRA weapons, they were restored in May 2000. May 2000 also saw the first directly elected Mayor of London and the establishment of a Greater London Assembly to run the capital. The next two texts contain some of the early arguments for and against devolution, which are still part of the ongoing debate as tensions emerge in the new arrangements. The Conservatives support the Union of the UK and tend to be sceptical of devolution, while the Labour Party and the Liberal Democrats support devolved government.

3 'A house devolved against itself'

Lord Mackay of Clashfern (Lord Chancellor in former Conservative government)

(Author copyright, 7 February 1996) abridged

There is no shortage of people proposing what they believe to be perfectly-formed means for constitutional change. But those would-be reformers wrongly assume that our present arrangements are inadequate. To lose sight of the strength and ends of our constitution could lead to lasting harm.

Of course, there is no human institution which could not be made better. But it is false logic to argue that any change must therefore be an improvement. First, it is necessary to see the value of what we have. Central to what we have is the Union [United Kingdom of Great Britain and Northern Ireland], developed over a long and important period of our history.

For me, as a Scot, the value of our union is beyond price. It is the means through which all the citizens of the United Kingdom can live together in unity and diversity. Our diversity is not in doubt. The Union consists of nations of very different sizes. It accommodates two distinct systems of law, three of education, two established churches, different languages, and many distinctive traditions. Its unity is our strength. Under the Union we have built common institutions which reconcile order with liberty under the law, national differences and common citizenship. I feel no less a Scot for having the privilege of being Lord Chancellor of Great Britain.

To 'sleepwalk into separatism' would diminish us all – not only the Scots. I look at proposals on devolution and ask four questions: What are the

The Opposition
The Labour Party at the time.

constitutional ends that should be served? What would devolution offer me, as a Scot? What would be its practical consequences? And is there a better way?

First, the end must be to ensure that power is exercised as close as possible to the people. Civil society works when it has institutions with which people have a historic affinity, which are close to them and through which they know they can exercise power: a vigorous society in which citizens do more than pay their taxes and then abdicate. Despite all the criticism, I believe the House of Commons serves our people well, and that we should cherish the direct relationship between constituents and their MPs.

Devolution would interpose a new layer of politicians between the people of Scotland and their MPs at Westminster. Yet Parliament would continue to have responsibility for what is vital for the United Kingdom – its economic position, its foreign affairs and defence. It would also retain responsibility for the distribution of the proceeds of the Union Exchequer between the parts of Britain. In short, Westminster would remain the centre of power. The proposed parliament in Edinburgh would be just a sop . . .[10]

Would devolution increase my sense of being a Scot? No. Would it change Scotland's distinctive legal or educational system for the better? No.

What then of the practical consequences of devolution? What the Scottish convention proposes is a separate, single-chamber parliament with tax-raising powers, able to legislate on virtually everything except what is really important for the United Kingdom. This raises three huge practical issues.

First, the West Lothian question – so-called because it was first asked by Tam Dalyell, the West Lothian MP – about the role of Scottish members at Westminster if there were a separate Scottish parliament. If English and Welsh MPs had no say in exclusively Scottish matters, why should Scottish MPs be allowed to vote on English or Welsh matters?

Some constitutional radicals pretend to solve the West Lothian question simply by ignoring it. **The Opposition**, with greater intellectual honesty, recognizes that the question exists and seeks to answer it by proposing English regional assemblies. This only equates Scotland with an English region. But in any event, the proposal for regional assemblies is a plant without roots. Are the Union and its institutions to be sacrificed for an unconsidered, unwanted patchwork of federalism? [see text 7] So the West Lothian question remains unanswered.

What of a Scottish parliament's tax-raising powers? Some argue that these need not be exercised. Then why propose them? To increase taxes uniquely in Scotland would, I believe, be profoundly bad for Scotland. But in the unlikely event of the powers being used to lower taxes, constitutional as well as economic issues would arise. Government expenditure in Scotland is nearly one-third higher *per capita* than that of England. How long would English MPs continue to vote more money to Scotland than to their own constituents, only to see it used to fund tax cuts north of the border?

A tax-raising Scottish parliament would soon be in permanent confrontation with Westminster. Break-up of the United Kingdom would then be but a step away. The devolutionists suggest that disputes would be resolved by judicial or appellate committees [of the House of Lords]. Better, surely, to avoid creating the disputes in the first place. From my position in the judiciary, I doubt whether this would bring government closer to the people, or make it more responsive. A field day for the lawyers would be a bad day for representative democracy.

Our living constitution may look untidy, but like the Wynds [narrow streets or alleys] in the old parts of Scotland's towns it is homely, it is ours, and it has grown through our history. It may need some repair and renovation, but how much finer and closer to us it is than the soulless constitutional tower blocks with which the radical reformers would replace it.

4 'Devolution is not a revolution'

Lord Irvine of Lairg (Lord Chancellor in the present Labour Government)
(Author copyright, 0 February 1996) abridged

My opponent on the Woolsack, the Lord Chancellor, has made a rare intervention . . . in the party political debate, with his attempt to take Labour to task over its proposals for constitutional change in general and devolution to Scotland in particular. But his attack is riddled with contradictions.

Lord Mackay of Clashfern rightly extols the virtues of the Union. As a Scot who practises law in England, I too value the bonds of friendship, common history and common interest which keep our two countries together. But Lord Mackay conflates the desire for reform of the Union and renewal of the friendship between Scotland and England through devolution with the breaking of the Union.

per capita
Per head of population; the number of people in a country.

Ted Heath
Conservative Prime
Minister, 1970–74.

poll tax
An unpopular property
tax based on the
number of people over
18 in a household,
replaced by the present
council tax.

quangos
Quasi-autonomous
non-government
organizations in public
life appointed by
government but
consisting of non-
elected members.

Devolution will establish a Scottish parliament firmly *within* the Union. It has, at one time or another, been supported by all the main political parties, including the Conservatives. In the Declaration of Perth in 1968, **Ted Heath** said: 'This then is our desire: to keep the United Kingdom united, but at the same time to see power more widely diffused within the framework of a united country . . .'

The Union is a partnership of the nations which would be strengthened if Westminster decides to respond to a deep sense of grievance in Scotland. The danger to the Union is to refuse to listen to the people, or to say, as the Conservatives do, 'you may vote for separation if you wish, but it is not legitimate to vote for a reformed Union'.

Lord Mackay is confident that a Scottish parliament could not improve policy in such areas as the Scottish educational or legal systems. How can this assertion be justified when the whole point of devolution is to bring decision-making closer to the people and to pursue policies which command popular support? It is precisely the feeling that central government ignores Scottish opinion that has given rise to the strong support for devolution.

Lord Mackay should remember how Scotland's sense of grievance was fanned to an unprecedented level of bitterness when his government used Scotland as a laboratory for the **poll tax** a year before England and against the wishes of practically every Scot. And does he for a moment believe that a Scottish parliament would have taken Scotland's water services out of local control and placed them in the hands of unelected **quangos**?

The great flaw in Lord Mackay's argument is his inconsistency in saying both that the Edinburgh parliament would be a sop and that 'break-up of the United Kingdom would then be but a step away'. The Tories cannot make up their minds whether or not devolution is a meaningless or a substantial reform, and in their confusion are left arguing that meaningful change is impossible. If Lord Mackay believes devolution is a sop, then why would it undermine the Union?

The truth is that Conservative rhetoric on this matter has lost touch with the reality. Devolution is a sensible, practical policy for the decentralization of government within the United Kingdom. This is acknowledged by the [Conservative] Government in its plans for a legislative assembly for Northern Ireland as part of a package designed to keep that part of the United Kingdom in the Union. It simply will not wash to advocate such policies but at the same time to argue that devolution proposed for anywhere else would be a constitutional catastrophe.

Scotland already enjoys a substantial degree of administrative devolution. The problem is that there is no direct accountability to the Scottish people. Labour proposes to make this extensive administrative devolution, and distinct law-making, properly accountable to the people while preserving the immense value of the Union.

Lord Mackay raises the so-called West Lothian question, which in truth is not a *question*, but a *consequence* of preserving the Union. The British constitution grows pragmatically, not by abstract theory. What Labour proposes is a constitutional settlement which will strengthen the Union, not imperil it.

A clear distribution of functions between a Scottish parliament and the United Kingdom Parliament should prevent disputes arising but if, over time, any should arise they would be dealt with either by the Appellate Committee of the House of Lords or the Judicial Committee of the Privy Council, which amounts to much the same thing.

On taxation, there is no constitutional reason why a law-making body should not have some room for flexibility over its budget. After all, this is a power which is granted to every local authority in the land ... Nobody in Scotland should pay a penny more or less in tax unless parties have placed such a plan before the electors. And ... we have no plans to raise taxes.

To try to polarize the debate between the unhappy status quo or separatism is absurd, as is the charge that devolution and separatism are blood relations. Many countries have devolved power successfully, and have unleashed the talents and diversity of the nations within them. In Britain there is great potential in following a similar path.

The Union has served us well, and it must be preserved for the future. Conservatives do it no service by arguing that reform is impossible in the face of the clamour for change from Scotland. Reform is both possible and desirable, and will be carried through by Labour. And when it happens, Lord Mackay and I, as Scots who spend our working lives in England, can be sure that we will have a Union better equipped to face the challenges of the future.

■ ■ ■

Devolution has attracted much criticism from those critics who argue that the constitutional reforms have been inadequately thought through, leaving loose ends and problems. The implications of devolution, such as alleged movements towards full independence (separatism) for the individual nations, the break-up of the Union and difficulties with the actual workings of devolution, are addressed in the next two texts.

new Scottish
parliament
The Scottish Parliament
was opened on 1 July
1999.

5 'Weakening the ties of a United Kingdom'
(Daily Mail, comment, 2 July 1999)

Behind the cheers and fanfares for the **new Scottish parliament**, a worm of
discord is beginning to stir.

Little by little, the Union is weakening. A new poll reveals that most English
people don't want Scottish MPs to vote at Westminster on matters affecting
only England. That is but one small sign of the resentment likely to grow as
the Scots, Welsh and Northern Irish go their own way.

Why, after all, should these countries receive more subsidies than the rest of
Britain? Why does London still have an expensive Scottish Office and Welsh
Office? Why should English taxpayers stump up on behalf of those who some-
times seem positively antipathetic to the idea of Britishness?

The tragedy is that such questions will grow more insistent in the years ahead.
Pressure is already mounting for an English parliament, even though it would
mean yet another layer of politicians and bureaucrats.

The Balkanisation of Britain would benefit nobody but the federalists of the
EU, yet that may be where our country is heading. It is increasingly possible
to imagine waking one day to find that the United Kingdom in its present
form no longer exists. If that tragic day ever dawns, New Labour will have
much to answer for.

6 'Blair's brave new Britain is a catastrophe'
David Davis (Conservative chairman of the House of Commons Public
Accounts Committee)
(Author copyright, 5 August 1999) abridged

Once it proudly stood as 'The Mother of all Parliaments', now the Palace of
Westminster sits at the centre of constitutional chaos – a fractured monument
to two years of Tony Blair's new Labour project. The opening of the Scottish
Parliament and Welsh Assembly marked the end of a truly United Kingdom

Parliament. In its place, we are now embarked on a massive constitutional gamble that could create mutual antagonism and destroy the United Kingdom as a single country.

William Hague [Conservative] is the first party leader to recognize that there is a real and deep-seated problem. The unfair treatment of England under our new dispensation requires new thinking. His call for English laws to be decided by English votes in the Commons was welcome and timely.

In contrast, Tony Blair . . . regards our constitution as merely a management problem. Blair still tries to pretend that devolution has little consequence for Westminster.

The [Labour] Government has buried its head in the political sand about what the transfer of so many powers to another **sovereign parliament** really means. It ignores the huge implications of one simple fact – that a large group of MPs, the Scottish, Northern Irish and Welsh, can now vote on English issues, while English MPs have no say in those same issues in Scotland, and to a lesser extent, Ulster and Wales. The Government has created a deliberately unfair system in which only the English will not be able to decide their own laws.

William Hague's response is a preference for a measured, careful, intermediate solution – the concept of English-only voting on English business. The problem with this intermediate solution of English-only voting is that it could, under some circumstances, lead to a constitutional crisis.

Imagine for a moment that we had such a procedure in place. What would happen when the Government elected to the UK Parliament has a majority in the UK, but not in England? Labour might conceivably form a Government which depended on Scottish and Welsh votes for its majority in Westminster.

Such a government would have been elected on a nominally UK **manifesto**. But the elements of its manifesto that applied to law and order, health, education and transport would be policies which could apply only to England (and to some extent Wales). These are the most important policies to the electorate – the ones that influence their vote.

A government with only a minority of the English Members of the UK Parliament would face an extraordinarily difficult situation. Under Hague's proposal, the Secretary of State for Health might bring his main Bills to the House of Commons – and be defeated by the Opposition's English majority. So might the Education Secretary, Home Secretary and Transport Ministers. The Government would face defeat after defeat on the main planks of its electoral platform.

sovereign parliament
The Westminster Parliament still has overall sovereignty.

manifesto
The programme of policies that a political party presents to the electorate before an election.

Euro election (1999)
On a very low turnout
of voters, the
Conservatives
increased their seats in
the European
Parliament while Labour
performed badly.

Imagine a Labour Government in that position. It would face a choice of two disastrous options. Either it contemplates the complete collapse of its main policies and almost inevitable subsequent election defeat, or the Labour Prime Minister could use his overall majority in the UK Parliament to change the rules and override the English. There could be few more potent scenarios for English nationalism than one where England's own interests were so explicitly subordinated.

The electoral system would only occasionally return a Government with a UK mandate but a minority of English MPs. But such a result has occurred in the past, could happen again, and would be disastrous when it did.

Hague has rightly identified that the current arrangements are unfair and unstable and the Government also knows that there is a problem. That is why it proposes to fracture England into artificial regions (although it is rumoured that Blair may be cooling on his commitment).[11] Hague has rightly swept aside these bogus and bureaucratic regional government solutions.

We now have to ensure that our solution is fair and stable – not a halfway house or a compromise that will not stand the test of time. And Conservatives should not be afraid that Tony Blair will paint them as English nationalists ... Blair tried to misrepresent us as extremists in the **Euro election (1999)**, and the British people saw through that. The same would happen on the question of an English Parliament.

It is possible that the Hague scheme can be modified to avoid the potential crisis I have outlined – but I find it hard to see how. Unless we resolve this problem, the best option remains an English Parliament – that would be fair, and avoid crises.

What is more, it will be more resilient than what we have now, and, because it is transparently fair, will reduce (rather than increase) the risk of break-up of the UK. From it will flow dynamic changes that will be beneficial to the Union – for example, more transparent taxation and funding arrangements.

Labour's ill thought-out reforms have posed a danger to the UK, and have posed deep problems to those who would preserve the United Kingdom. There is much debating yet to do – and the Conservative Party is the only major party willing to take that debate on. It will be the only party able to deliver both fairness for the English and stability for the United Kingdom.

■ ■ ■

Another implication of these decentralizing reform processes is the argument that devolution (and the possibility of regional government in England) is a half-way house which will lead inexorably to a federal Britain (favoured by the Liberal Democrats), instead of the traditional unitary British state centralized in Westminster.

7 'A federal Britain'
(*The Economist*, 27 March 1999) abridged

Is the mother of parliaments about to give birth to a litter of legislatures? In a little over a month's time, there will be elections to new parliaments in Scotland and Wales. If the peace deal sticks, power will soon be devolved to a Northern Irish assembly. That will leave the British constitution looking distinctly unbalanced. What about England?

Tony Blair's government will unveil the beginnings of an answer to the English question on April 1st, when regional Development Agencies (RDAS) for eight English regions will be set up. The RDAS are unelected bodies, charged initially with economic development. But the government says that it is 'committed to move to directly-elected regional government in England, where there is demand for it'. And a poll for *The Economist* shows that voters in most English regions are already in favour.

The idea of a network of elected regional assemblies across the United Kingdom has some merits. It would make the position of Scotland, Wales and Northern Ireland seem less anomalous. More important, it would be a significant devolution of power in an over-centralized state. At present, much of England is still governed on the principle that 'the man in **Whitehall** knows best' ... In principle, decentralization would lead to a healthier and more responsive democracy.

All this runs counter to the British tradition that Parliament in Westminster commands all that it surveys. But that tradition has already been substantially eroded by the ceding of legislative and constitutional powers to the European Union; it will have a further bite taken out of it when the Scottish, Welsh and Northern Irish parliaments get going. Setting up regional assemblies in England might allow for a more rational codification of powers between three tiers of government – in Brussels, Westminster and the regions.

Whitehall
The centre of the United Kingdom government ministries and civil service in London.

Why not?

It all sounds good on paper. But before the government plunges into another constitutional convulsion, it needs to meet several conditions.

The first and most important proviso is that regional assemblies in England should not lead to an increase in the overall burden of government. New Labour insists that it is alive to this problem, and would not allow regional assemblies to add to public expenditure . . .

All this sounds encouraging. But the experience of devolution to date is not very reassuring. There is no doubt that setting up the Scottish Parliament, for example, will lead to a net addition of politicians and civil servants. There will be no fewer than 129 MPS in the new parliament in Edinburgh – but the number of Scottish MPs at Westminster will fall by just 15. Replicate that across the United Kingdom and you will have literally thousands of extra politicians.

If the government is to guard against a proliferation of politicians and civil servants, and the inevitable additions in red tape and public spending that they would generate, it must be genuinely committed to devolving power. The worst, (but all too plausible) solution would be to set up regional assemblies to appease the chattering classes in the English regions – but then jealously to guard the powers of Westminster and Whitehall, as well as the privileges of local government.

In the long run, central government in London should envisage setting national standards in areas like education, health and training – but then encourage local experiments . . . But devolution is not simply about creating policy laboratories. In Scotand it happened because there was a clear sense of alienation between the Scottish electorate and a government in London that seemed too remote. A similar, if milder, malaise is evident in much of northern England. Is it sufficient to justify the upheavals involved in setting up regional assemblies? There is an easy way to find out – hold referendums.

Any move towards regional assemblies in England should be judged by three criteria: popular demand, no net addition to the burden of government and a real devolution of power. If – and only if – those conditions are fulfilled, regional assemblies would be worth having.

■ ■ ■

The House of Lords

The debate on how the House of Lords might be reformed continues. The Labour government has followed a two-stage process: first, it removed the right of 750 **hereditary peers** to sit and vote in the House of Lords (but in a compromise to get its Act through Parliament leaving 92 hereditaries elected by fellow hereditaries) and second, it intends to change the House into a different second chamber. But no statutory model for this stage has yet been decided (2000).

In the meantime, the transitional House consists of 524 nominated life peers, 92 elected hereditary peers, the Law Lords and the Lords Spiritual. It seems clear that the Labour government would prefer a future House in which the majority of members would be appointed by an independent appointments commission, with only a small number of elected members. This model would preserve the **bicameral** system but would not detract from the authority of the House of Commons. The next text sets out the original reasons for Labour reforms.

8 *'True peers are made, not born'*
Jack Straw (Home Secretary in the Labour government)
(Author copyright, 25 April 1996) abridged

According to Churchill, the Lords in the early part of the century was 'filled with old doddering peers, cute financial magnates, clever wire-pullers, big brewers with bulbous noses. All the enemies of progress are there – weaklings, sleek, smug, comfortable, self-important individuals'.

Eighty-five years on, after two Parliament Acts have reduced the powers of the Lords, membership of a legislature on the basis of birth remains, in Tony Blair's words, 'a manifest constitutional unfairness'.

There is simply nothing to justify it. An informal committee under the (hereditary) Earl of Carnarvon sought to do so last year and failed. The best argument it could construct was that the 'present House introduces a random element into political life'.

Random? A study of the Lords in 1981 showed that 80 per cent of hereditary peers had been to public school, and well over half (431) had been to Eton. There has been no comparable study since, but precisely because the

hereditary peers
Peers who inherit their titles and seats by birth.

bicameral
A political system in which political power is shared between two chambers
(in Britain the House of Commons and the House of Lords).

Brian Mawhinney
Former chairman of the
Conservative Party.

Upper House is hereditary, the background is unlikely to have changed in the past 15 years . . .

Nor has chance played any greater part in their political loyalties. Today [1996], 328 hereditary peers take the Conservative Whip, 22 are Liberal Democrats and 13 are Labour (another 172 are crossbenchers, and 72 have no affiliation of any kind). In fact the Lords has in recent years become more, not less Tory. Tory peers have increased by 33, while Labour numbers have declined by 28.

The hereditary principle is defended by John Major and **Brian Mawhinney** as though it were the ark of the covenant. Yet whenever the Tories have thought seriously about the position of the Lords in the past, they have concluded that a Second Chamber so dominated by birth and one party is indefensible. In 1948 a party leaders' conference, which included the Conservatives, concluded that a reformed House of Lords should be such that 'a permanent majority is not assumed for any one political party'. More recently, a Conservative review committee in 1978, under the former Prime Minister Lord Home, recommended a Chamber based on a mix of election and appointment. It said: 'The maintenance of the *status quo* is not a prudent policy. Indeed, we are doubtful whether it is a policy at all.'

Labour does have a policy. It is, as a first stage, to remove the right of hereditary peers to sit and vote in the Lords . . .

Some hereditary peers in all parties make an important contribution to the Lords, and as Tony Blair has made clear, some of them could be made life peers . . .[12]

What we will secure is a Second Chamber based on merit – on the attributes of those who hold the title, not on those of their forebears.

Britain is often slow to change its institutions, and the removal of hereditary peers will be an enormous democratic gain. Moreover, a reformed Chamber is likely in practice to be more self-confident and more questioning, precisely because it will have ceased to be dominated perpetually by one party. That will make for better government, if a less comfortable ride for ministers . . . new life peers should be more varied than they are today.

Two arguments are often made against our proposed reforms. The first is that removing hereditaries from the Lords might bring the position of the monarchy into question. This is nonsense. Plenty of Western states have constitutional monarchies, but none has the equivalent of an unreformed Lords.

The second argument is that until there is complete clarity about long-term changes there should be no reform at all. But as with previous constitutional reforms in this country, it is vital that staged changes are made on the basis of a well understood case and wide agreement.

The Constitution Unit's report on the Lords, published today, offers a valuable insight into the process necessary for achieving the second stage of reform, whether it be a Chamber wholly elected or one based partly on election and partly on appointment. The report spells out the need for 'consultation, consensus, inquiry' before a change of such magnitude could, or should, take place. It also has good advice about possible midwives for such a process (such as a royal commission, an all-party parliamentary committee or a party leaders' conference).

It is a strength of Labour's current position that it does not have a dogmatic view about exactly what such a Second Chamber will look like. We are open-minded about the process. As well as being inherently just, our simple reform of removing hereditary peers will stimulate a public debate about the Lords' future . . .

■ ■ ■

Opinions vary considerably about the composition of the House of Lords after the expulsion of the hereditary peers. A Royal Commission (Wakeham) presented a report on the matter in 2000 but none of its various choices have yet been implemented. The next two texts present different viewpoints on the continuing debate, particularly the vexed question of whether a reformed House should be elected or appointed, partly or wholly. Another issue rests on which body should be responsible for any eventual elections and appointments. The first text opts for a mainly elected second chamber.

9 *'The secret enemies of democracy'*
Ivor Richard (former Labour leader in the House of Lords)
(Author copyright, 18 August 1999) abridged

When the Royal Commission on the Reform of the House of Lords starts its detailed work next month, Tony Blair will have an historic opportunity to introduce major reform. It is not clear whether he will grasp it. Although the

crossbench
Independent of a
political party.

Government's own preferred blueprint for a reformed Upper House remains opaque, the Labour Party's stance to date has, unfortunately, leant towards a wholly nominated chamber.

The canard at the heart of the debate is that a second chamber with a substantial elected element would threaten the legitimacy of the House of Commons. Nothing is further from the truth. It is this myth that undermines the expansion of democracy.

We [with Damien Welfare] argue in our new book *Unfinished Business: Reforming the House of Lords*[13] that directly elected politicians should form two thirds of the membership, with **crossbench** life peers making up the remainder. A continuing independent element would widen the debate and contribute, as now, to a less partisan atmosphere. It would also make it very hard for one party to control the second chamber.

The use of PR for those elected to the Upper House would make single-party domination all but impossible.

By mixing democracy and expertise, the House would have sufficient legitimacy to perform its functions, but not too much, and a character which was wholly different from the House of Commons and secondary to it.

To create a non-democratic second chamber would be to miss the basic point of reform. As the rest of Labour's constitutional programme has shown, the key issue is the planned reduction of centralized executive power . . .

The need is no less great within Westminster itself. A second chamber with democratic legitimacy would be a vital check and balance. At a fundamental level, only an Upper House with at least the majority of its members elected would have the legitimacy to make a bicameral system work in the UK. Inevitably, and rightly, a second chamber with legitimacy and credibility would be more troublesome. Otherwise, we might as well do without one altogether.

The real issue is not the balance between the first chamber and the second, but that between Parliament and Executive. Making the second chamber more legitimate strengthens MPs, too, by increasing their ability to make ministers accountable. Arguments against a comprehensive reform have often masqueraded as a defence of the rights of the Commons, when in reality they are a covert defence of executive power.

It is the sole right of the House of Commons to make and unmake governments, to control finance and to have the final say over major legislation under the Parliament Acts. It is the House of Commons which exercises ultimate political control. All that should continue. The second chamber is there to examine the detail, but also to stand back and take the longer view. From time to time it should be able to exercise its power to ask – quite forcefully – the Commons to think again.

As well as revising legislation, a reformed House of Lords should scrutinize the Executive, investigate issues unlikely to interest the Commons (or be too sensitive for them) and debate issues of national importance.

We also suggest special roles in relation to constitutional developments and the human rights legislation [see text 11], as well as enhanced European scrutiny. Underlying all these activities is the important distinction that the fate of the Government does not hang on the result.

That distinction should continue to be reflected in the powers of the two Houses. The second chamber should be able to assert its views but not prevent the Government from proceeding with public business. The **Parliament Acts** should be applied in the event of prolonged disagreement between the two chambers, with a conciliation process to promote consensus.

These rules, expressed in legislation, should be buttressed by the procedures of the two Houses and elaborated over time by conventions.

In all these ways, their relative standing would be reinforced – the second chamber having a secure and clear (if limited) role, but the Commons predominating. In no sense could a member elected to the second chamber claim equal status to that of a Member of the Commons . . .

There is a consensus for a model along the lines of a largely elected membership. It is close to Conservative policy, to Liberal Democrat policy and to Labour's approach when it was in opposition. Opinion polls show consistent support for a wholly or largely elected second chamber.

Some 27 other democracies with bicameral systems have second chambers which are completely or mainly directly elected. Only Canada has an entirely appointed Senate and it is an ineffective body considered ripe for reform.

An approach based on defending the position of the House of Commons is bogus.

The onus is on those who now oppose democracy – which, sadly, seems to include some in the Labour Party – to show how any alternative will produce a second chamber which can make itself felt. So far they have failed.

Parliament Acts
The provision that removes stalemate between the Commons and the Lords. Its use allows government legislation to proceed.

■ ■ ■

White Paper
A government
document setting out
intended legislation
prior to the introduction
of a Bill into Parliament.

The next text argues for a solution whereby members of the Lords would be appointed by a statutory and independent body. This position essentially maintains the traditional expertise of the House and comes down against an elected chamber.

10 'This House is built on solid ground'

Geoffrey Howe (former Conservative Deputy Prime Minister)
(Author copyright, 2 August 1999) abridged

A heart transplant is hazardous enough. Cardiectomy is dramatically more dangerous. Yet that is almost the effect of stage one of the Government's impulsive House of Lords 'reform'. More than half the members of the Upper House will soon be expelled. The Wakeham Royal Commission is still considering how to fill the void. And no one knows when (or even if) their proposals will be implemented.

The case made for this upheaval rests solely on the Lords' 'lack of legitimacy because of its anachronistic composition' – the presence, in other words, of the hereditary element, with its Conservative majority. But in almost every other respect, the Government is ready to retain the advantages of the status quo.

The essential constitutional point is that it is the elected House of Commons alone which disposes of power. The unelected House of Lords, in a strictly advisory role, may propose how that power might be better exercised, may require the Commons to think again. But it is the Commons that has, in the last resort, the power to decide. No change is proposed in that relationship. The Government's **White Paper** acknowledges indeed that 'extreme care would be necessary' to ensure that the present balance between the two Houses is not disturbed.

So, too, there is general acceptance of the present functions and powers of the Upper House, whose performance is described in the White Paper in almost superlative terms. Not one of the proposals now being considered requires the Lords to do things better, only to do more things as well as they do already. How then to maintain these standards for the future? Do the hereditaries need to be replaced? If so, how should the extras and replacements be recruited? Should some be office-holders, such as the law lords or the bishops? Most people seem ready to accept, even extend, the existing categories. Should some or all be nominated; and if so, how and by whom? Here there is also widespread willingness to accept an inflow of nominees alongside existing life peers.

And finally, should some or even all, members of the second chamber be directly elected? And should such elected members be paid a pensionable salary and receive allowances, as the point is often put, 'in line with the arrangements enjoyed by MPs'? These last are by far the most important questions facing the Wakeham commission. Most commentators have been ready to say 'yes' to at least some direct elections. In my own submission to the Wakeham commission, I reluctantly – even if only partially – accepted that.

But the constitutional expert Professor Philip Norton (since 1997 Lord Norton of Louth) takes a different view. In a well argued paper he contends that if the second chamber is to justify its existence, if it is 'to add value to the political process', it should comprise members 'who serve predominantly because of their experience and expertise'. What follows from this, on his analysis, is that the second chamber 'should not be a representative House, an elected House or even a part-elected House' . . .

The qualities which are central to the value of the present chamber are expertise, experience, diversity, independence and availability. This ability to rely upon a wide field of experts, available by self-selection for different topics, is very important.

So is the fact that non-hereditary peers are appointed for life and that membership is unpaid. Peers receive allowances but no salary. This militates against treating membership as a full-time career and enables the House to draw on the knowledge of peers whose expertise is still current. Given the numeric strength of the present House, it is thus able, as Lord Norton points out, 'to function as a full-time chamber with a predominantly part-time membership' – all on the basis of essentially unpaid public service. Each of those features could and should be retained for the new House.

But for elected members (if such there were to be) different presumptions manifestly prevail. The link between election and Commons-type pay and perks now seems to be regarded as virtually unquestionable. The annual cost, including overheads, to the public purse of a Member of Parliament (£366,000) is ten times that of an unpaid peer.

The threat of increasing party discipline and politicisation is clear, as is the risk that the second chamber would seek to compete with, even to challenge, the House of Commons. This would create an entirely fresh threat to constitutional balance.

For all these reasons, I have now been persuaded that Professor Norton is right. The new second chamber should contain no elected members and members should not be salaried. Existing life peers should be significantly reinforced in numbers and topped up from year to year. Nominations would come not from the Prime Minister but from the new, independent and balanced Appointments Commission, of the kind suggested in the Government White Paper.[14]

On this basis, membership is likely closely to resemble the existing chamber, in the diversity of potentially available experience, expertise and independence. The Wakeham commission would have done well, if it thus succeeds in recreating an institution which is in most respects a close reproduction of the original. The wheel having been destroyed, it must be reinvented, just as long as it doesn't look like a wheel.

■   ■   ■

Civil liberties

The Labour government has created a Human Rights Act (passed in 1998 but taking effect in 2000) and a Freedom of Information Act (still passing through Parliament – 2000).

Reformers, such as Charter 88 (an organization devoted to the modernization of Britain's constitution and human rights), have long argued that there is a need for statutory protection of individual civil liberties. A Human Rights Act would be entrenched (ie Parliament either cannot override it or can do so only with great difficulty) and would, as here, entail the formal incorporation of the provisions of the European Convention of Human Rights into British law. The resulting Act allows the judges to rule on individual human rights in cases that are brought before them in the courts.

The main objections to such an Act are that it would increase the 'political' power of the unelected courts; arguably interfere with the sovereignty of Parliament; and encourage an increased and wide range of, possibly frivolous, litigation. But, under the Act, the courts would not in fact be able to overturn an Act of Parliament. In cases of conflict between the Human Rights Act and another Act of Parliament, the courts would make a 'declaration' of the situation. Nevertheless, the roles of judges and the courts under the Act will doubtless continue to be an area of debate and controversy. The next text presents the long-rehearsed arguments in favour of a Human Rights Act.

11 'Why Britain needs a Bill of Rights'
(*The Economist*, 21 October 1995) abridged

Basic human and political rights in Britain enjoy no special legal protection, as they do in most other democratic countries.

Britain invented both the phrase 'a bill of rights' and the concept of one. Yet today [1995] Britain is the only country in Western Europe which either has not incorporated the European Convention on Human Rights into its domestic laws or does not already have ... a bill of rights which provides similar legally enforceable protections for the individual ... Opinion polls by MORI this year and in 1991 for the Joseph Rowntree Reform Trust found that 79 per cent of respondents were in favour of a bill of rights for all of Britain. Labour and the Liberal Democrats now also back the idea.

Given such widespread public support, and Britain's anomalous position among democracies in not having a bill of rights, the argument for introducing one would seem to be an open-and-shut case. Yet it is not, and considerable opposition remains. John Major's government, like its Conservative and Labour predecessors, is hostile to the idea, as are many – on both the right and the left – who see it as a threat to the sovereignty of Parliament (founded on the 1689 Bill of Rights, which enumerated the rights of Parliament, not those of individuals).

An effective bill of rights would, indeed, be an infringment of parliamentary sovereignty; but this would be its principal attraction, not an argument against it. Bills of rights are designed to protect fundamental rights from the actions of transient majorities in the legislature in the longer-term interests of the citizenry as a whole. In most countries, none of the rights thus protected is exempt from revision or abolition by the electorate. But, because they are deemed fundamental, revision is made far more difficult than changes to an ordinary law, through special procedures that require more than simple majorities.

Individual liberties enjoy no such protection in Britain. Governments can eliminate a right, no matter how basic or how long-standing, in a single vote in the House of Commons and have, on some occasions, used their extraordinary powers to do just that.

Traditionalists argue that, in practice, this matters not at all. British liberties, they say, have been better protected by Parliament and the common law built

telephone tapping
Listening in to telephone conversations.

birching
Punishment by whipping with a birch.

law of contempt of court
Punishment by a court of law if an individual refuses to obey an order of the court.

up over centuries by the courts than they would have been by any abstract listing of rights. They often accompany this argument with grandiose proclamations about Britain being a beacon of liberty in a turbulent and uncertain world.

Sadly, this is no longer true, if it ever was. One revealing test is Britain's record before the European Court of Human Rights in Strasbourg. The court has decided 37 cases against the United Kingdom, giving it one of the worst records of any of the 35 signatories to the European Convention. This means that actions in a wide range of areas which British courts, Parliament and successive governments had accepted as perfectly proper were rejected by the Strasbourg court as violations of basic rights.

This is a serious indictment of the state of civil liberties in Britain. The court is not staffed with starry-eyed idealists. In fact the court's judges have tried to interpret the convention as narrowly as possible to avoid overruling elected governments. Nevertheless even this cautious court has found against the British government on issues that include **telephone tapping**, **birching**, discriminatory immigration rules, homosexuality, the **law of contempt of court**, the rights of prisoners and those accused of a crime, the rights of the mentally ill, press freedom, and sexual equality, among other issues – culminating in the celebrated ruling in September [1995] that the killing of three IRA terrorists on Gibraltar was unlawful. Often such findings have forced a revision of British laws.

Britain may not be about to lapse into despotism or tyranny, but that is not the immediate danger facing any established democracy. What British governments have repeatedly failed to do is to meet minimal standards of conduct when it comes to respecting the rights of individuals. It might be argued that the Strasbourg court is sufficient redress against such wrongs. But it is slow and costly. A British bill of rights would make redress easier and cheaper, and thus restore at least some popular respect for Britain's own system of justice.

A stronger objection to a bill of rights is that it is, in many ways, anti-democratic because it transfers power from elected representatives to unelected judges.[15] It does do this, but such a transfer of power is not necessarily anti-democratic. Democracy itself, in all its myriad forms, derives its legitimacy from the consent of the governed, and that consent can only be given freely when certain basic rights – for example, freedom of speech, assembly and the press or the protection from arbitrary arrest – are respected.

British citizens have never had any positive, enforceable legal rights and still do not, except those awarded to them by specific statutes. Instead, liberty in Britain has been essentially negative: citizens have been traditionally free to do anything not specifically prohibited by law.

This may have seemed a reasonable proposition in the 19th century, when governments were tiny and there were far fewer laws. But since then the trickle of legislation has become a flood. The growth of the modern state in Britain, as elsewhere, has meant that government now intrudes into every nook and cranny of life, regulating everything from medical care to buildings to the terms on which employees can be hired or sacked. The purely private sphere has diminished greatly.

■ ■ ■

After long delays, the Labour government produced a draft Freedom of Information Bill in 1999, something that has been demanded by reform groups for many years. This Bill (and eventual Act) is intended to open up official information to public scrutiny, but was still passing through Parliament in 2000. It will allow the public (for a fee) to obtain some official information from schools, local government, central government, hospitals, health authorities, the police and other public bodies.

The government argues that the Bill will result in more open government and give Britons a statutory legal right to information held by public bodies for the first time. An independent information commissioner will regulate the Bill, will be able to impose financial penalties, may overturn decisions taken at local level and can require authorities to release information that is being withheld unreasonably.

But the Bill has been criticized, chiefly on the ground that it preserves the culture of official secrecy in Britain. It is feared that public bodies may prevaricate in their disclosure procedures and some information may be classified as not open to the public. Campaigners and opposition parties claim it is toothless, too restrictive in its powers and lacks openness.[16] It is argued that there are too many exemptions (covering matters of national security, intelligence and defence, policy advice from civil servants to ministers, and other confidential, commercial and personal information). Critics object that public bodies can refuse to provide information that could cause 'prejudice' and to the lengthy time available for such bodies actually to produce data.

As the next text argues, much will depend on demand from the public to make freedom of information effective.

12 'Need to know. It is up to the public to demand access to information'
(*The Times*, leader, 25 May 1999)

At long last a draft Freedom of Information Bill has surfaced from the Home Office. This latest incarnation of the Government's plans to open itself up to scrutiny is by no means perfect. There are numerous exemptions to disclosure upon which public bodies can fall back. And Jack Straw's draft Bill sets out only the general principles for the provision of information. Nonetheless, setting even limited rights to access to information in legislative stone is a step forward. The next step is up to individuals who stand to benefit from improving access to information – they must ask for it. The more often that people ask public bodies to provide information, the more open these institutions will have to become in response. The real accessibility of facts will only become apparent when individuals begin to seek information from public bodies for themselves.

The public will, however, be disappointed if it is expecting this Freedom of Information Bill to strip government bare. This Bill is clearly aimed at patients and pupils rather than litigants and political activists. The institutions which will face the closest examination are schools and hospitals to whom fewer of the exemptions are likely to apply. On the other hand, any government information which falls into the potentially broad band of policy advice can remain under lock and key, regardless of whether it might affect the workings of government. This will not, apparently, include every single Whitehall memo, but it does provide a wide safety net for both political and Civil Service acrobatics. Another apparent bar to the opening-up of government is the lack of extra funds to enable public bodies to meet the new demands for information which the Bill will, if it is successful, generate. Nor will this new information be free. These bodies will be able to charge for part of the marginal cost of providing it – a costly exercise for the sole inquirer. The most common criticism of this Bill, however, is that it is so riddled with tests and exclusions that the Government will not have to reveal any more information than it is already bound to do under the existing Code of Practice.

What is indisputably new, however, is that the public's right of access to information is now protected by law and no longer simply based on governmental goodwill. The public's new, legal, right to access to information will not only be protected by a commissioner, but will be enforceable against public bodies if necessary in the courts. This represents a fundamental shift in the relationship between the public and the Government.

It will now be up to the public to take this relationship further. It is only with the exercise of this new right to information that public bodies will be forced to open up their archives. An occasional request will leave many institutions unchanged. A constant stream of inquiry, however, will force a public body to organise itself to produce information efficiently, rapidly, and importantly, cheaply.

■ ■ ■

Despite the constitutional changes outlined above, Charter 88 in a report in 2000,[17] while acknowledging that some necessary reforms (such as devolution) had been implemented, strongly criticized the Labour government for its alleged failings. It argued that PR had not been established for Westminster and some other elections; official secrecy was still being protected in the Freedom of Information Bill (Act); the House of Lords will probably remain largely unelected; and regional democracy in England was being sidelined after devolution and the London mayoral election.

Charter 88 maintained that constitutional reform was not taken seriously enough by government and there was a growing centralization of power in Downing Street. It alleged that Labour had created an 'elected dictatorship' in which some traditional constitutional checks and balances had been removed but no alternative restraints have been proposed. Charter 88 argued that the Labour government's reforms in some cases conflicted with others and the individual citizen was neglected. It therefore called, as it has done in the past, for a written constitution that would strengthen citizen rights, powers and freedoms.

■ ■ ■

 Exercises

Write short essays on the following topics

1   Why should the British constitution be reformed?

2   What is meant by devolution? Is it different to federalism? If so, how?

3   Examine the argument that devolution will lead to the break-up of the United Kingdom.

4   The House of Lords should be abolished. Discuss.

5   Why does Britain need a Human Rights Act and a Freedom of Information Act?

Explain and examine the following terms

constitution	'elected dictatorship'	conventions
common law	West Lothian question	UK
statute	White Paper	PR/AV
mandate	universal suffrage	judiciary
separatism	hereditaries	bicameral
law lords	House of Commons	Westminster
Whitehall	decentralization	sop

 Further reading

Hazell, Robert (1999) *Constitutional Futures: A History of the Next Ten Years*, Oxford: Oxford University Press.
Hennessy, Peter (1995) *The Hidden Wiring: Unearthing the British Constitution*, London: Victor Gollancz.
Kendle, John (1997) *Federal Britain: A History*, London: Routledge.
Norton, Philip (1988) *The Constitution in Flux*, Oxford: Basil Blackwell.
Mount, Ferdinand (1993) *The British Constitution Now: Recovery or Decline*, London: Mandarin.
Pyper, Robert and Robins, Lynton (eds) (2000) *United Kingdom Governance*, London: Macmillan.
Robertson, Geoffrey (1993) *Freedom, the Individual and the Law*, London: Penguin Books.
Smith, Stanley de and Brazier, Rodney (1998) *Constitutional and Administrative Law*, London: Penguin Books.

 Notes

1. Critics argue today that the Labour government is bypassing Parliament (particularly the House of Commons) and centralizing political power in Downing Street.
2. In July 2000 the Labour government in effect rejected PR. However, there were indications that it and the Liberal Democrats might instead discuss the possibility of the Alternative Vote (AV) system for parliamentary elections. See note 9.
3. In 1999 a referendum of London voters approved the idea of an elected mayor and Assembly for London. The political parties chose their candidates prior to elections (May 2000). The Labour government was criticized for its interference in and manipulation of this process. An Independent candidate (Ken Livingstone) was chosen as the first directly elected mayor of London, together with an elected Assembly.

4. The Labour government seems to have lost its zeal for elected mayors in the big cities following criticism of its handling of the London mayoral election. There has also been no essential reform or improvement of local government

5. This was achieved in 1999, although 92 elected hereditary peers were retained in the new House of Lords.

6. The second stage had not been finalized in 2000.

7. A referendum on the issue has not yet been held (2000).

8. Although PR has been used in elections for the European Parliament, the Scottish Parliament, the Welsh Assembly and the Northern Ireland Assembly, the Labour government is unwilling to extend it to Westminster parliamentary elections.

9. In July 2000, the Labour government ruled out PR. But it and the Liberal Democrats appeared to have agreed on a referendum early in the next Parliament on electoral reform. It seems that an Australian-style voting procedure for Westminster elections might be proposed. This would not be pure PR but the Alternative Vote system (AV) in which electors rank candidates in order of preference. If no candidate won 50 per cent of the first-choice votes, the other preferences of the least popular candidates would be redistributed until someone had the support of more than half of the voters.

10. Even after devolution, the Westminster Parliament still has the sovereign power to abolish the Scottish Parliament and the Welsh and Northern Irish Assemblies.

11. There were signs in 2000 that the Labour government might be actively returning to the idea of elected regional assemblies in England.

12. This has happened.

13. Ivor Richard and Damien Welfare (1999) *Unfinished Business: Reforming the House of Lords* London: Vintage.

14. A statutory independent Appointments Commission was also suggested by the Wakeham Report.

15. The judges' power to rule on cases of individual human rights may bring them into conflict with the government and Parliament.

16. Jill Sherman (1999) 'Information Bill attacked as toothless' London: *The Times* 25 May.

17. Tom Baldwin (2000) 'Charter 88 accuses Blair of dictatorship' London: *The Times* 21 June. *Unlocking Democracy* (2000) London: Charter 88, 21 June.

Britain and the world

Britain's international position as a major colonial, economic and political power was in relative decline by the early decades of the twentieth century. Some large colonies had already achieved self-governing status, and the growth of nationalism in African, Asian and West Indian countries later persuaded Britain to decolonialize further. The additional effects of increasing global competition, two World Wars, the emergence of superpower Cold War politics and domestic economic and social problems gradually forced Britain to recognize its reduced international status. It sought slowly and with difficulty to find a new identity and to establish different priorities, in which traditional unilateral actions were often inappropriate. But, in spite of these fundamental changes, Britain still experiences uncertainties about its potential influence and appropriate role on the world stage.

An unpublished government survey of public opinion commissioned by the Foreign Office in 1998[1] found that Britons appear to be sceptical or unsure about Britain's international standing and the future direction or priorities of the country. Although 25 per cent of respondents to the survey recognized that Britain had historically been a significant power in Europe, 44 per cent saw it now as a 'once great country in decline' and only 30 per cent agreed that Britain is 'a once great country that is now on the way back'.

This chapter examines Britain's foreign policy, its membership of the European Union (EU) and the Commonwealth, its defence strategy and its connection to NATO. These continue to be areas of strongly opposed debate, particularly as Britain moves towards closer cooperation with the EU in the proposed development of common defence and foreign policies and as it is inevitably involved in the processes of EU political and economic integration. A further undecided question is whether Britain will eventually join the euro (the EU common or single currency).

■ ■ ■

Foreign policy

Britain's international position today is that of a medium-sized country dwarfed in size economically by the USA, Japan and Germany and by yet other countries in Gross Domestic Product (GDP) terms. Yet some of its leaders still believe that it can play an important global, as well as a European, role.

The Labour government has been developing a foreign policy with an 'ethical dimension', which might be equated with the 'third way' in the political field. It could apparently be applied to Britain's dealings with other countries, particularly in terms of arms sales, civil wars, aggressive wars, human rights issues and nationalist conflicts. For example, it could be used in connection with British arms sales to another country where such exports would be banned if there was a 'clearly definable' risk that they might be used for internal repression and the abuse of human rights in that country.

The Foreign Secretary (Robin Cook) defines this foreign policy as a strategy of dialogue based on working partnerships with individual countries, rather than either confrontation with other powers or giving in to the demands of a dominant state. Foreign policy had in the past alternated between the opposed formulas of '**rowing** and **kowtowing**'. It might still be necessary on occasions to condemn formally

rowing
Arguing and quarrelling.

kowtowing
Giving in to, showing deference.

Henry Kissinger
Former American
Secretary of State in
the Nixon
administration,
1968–76.

marbles
Brains, intelligence.

and in forthright terms. But the focus of the 'third way' strategy is rather on the promotion of change and real practical improvements (as in human rights) and the construction of proper dialogues in international affairs.[2]

This ethical dimension has been criticized as being too rhetorical, weakening British national self-interest, paying too much attention to packaging or style rather than substance, being ineffectual and self-defeating and ignoring the difficulty of applying consistent standards of human rights to different regions of the world. The government has also been accused of reneging on its own policy by continuing to sell arms and military parts to countries that might misuse them. The following text comments on the question of 'ethics' in foreign policy generally and suggests how foreign relationships might be developed by Britain.

1 'Nudging between Row and Kowtow'
John Lloyd
(Author copyright, 24 April 1998) abridged

Henry Kissinger, that voice which dominated the conduct of postwar foreign affairs, believed that the British had not so much lost an Empire as lost their **marbles**. His book, *Diplomacy*, a combined history of the art he practised and statement of the principle in which he believed, was a long defence of realpolitik combined with an elegant scorn for anything that smacked of ethics in foreign policy.

The British, who had practised realpolitik admirably in the 19th century, lost the knack of it in the 20th century – most of that century being, in Kissinger's view, a history of confused principles and inadequate practice. For realpolitikers such as him all discussion and writing of ethics in foreign policy are a waste of breath and trees; countries do, and should, act according to self-interest.

This is the diplomatic equivalent of the neo-liberal posture in economic matters which holds that firms should concentrate on profits and let the ethics and social effects take care of themselves . . .

The Kissinger doctrine, that diplomacy is not in the human rights business either, accords well with a popular commonsense view that the world is a dangerous place full of foreigners of whom we must beware.

Robin Cook set out to challenge this by proposing an ethical dimension to foreign policy. For a year now, he has moved as jauntily as he could between the despairing pessimism of a Left – which sees a world composed largely of authoritarian torturers to whom Britain toadies in order to get arms orders – and the pessimism of the Right. The latter sees diplomacy as a tool for keeping our patch of the **darkling plain** relatively decent through a credible threat of force. Mr Cook claimed this week to have found a 'third way' between them – between, as he glibly put it, 'row and kowtow'.

Implicit in his words is a critique of the **previous Conservative Government** for doing both. Both the Thatcher and the Major Governments were vigorous in their pursuit of arms sales. An **Oxfam** report, published yesterday, says that both Governments 'appeared willing to allow businessmen to go to jail to hide the extent to which it was breaking its own rules and to use taxpayers' money to underwrite enormous arms deals . . . while cynically misleading Parliament and the public about the extent of the UK's involvement in the arms trade'. This is the kowtow side.

But these governments also had rows. Mr Cook, launching his first human rights report on Tuesday, said that he would not 'trumpet condemnation through a megaphone' . . . Asked about the privileged position given to China in the report's list of achievements, Mr Cook said that 'it is a country where we are making progress through dialogue'. He mentioned the release of the dissident, Wang Dan, as evidence of that dialogue's success.

Is this a 'third way' where one neither picks the fights which one's power allows nor genuflects before the rich and powerful because one is weak or avid for exports, or both? Or is it a 'third way' where one operates in a terrain of 'soft power', in which all actors are careful not to maximise their position in order to accommodate others, especially the weaker powers? Or is it a way where, bit by bit and behind the scenes, one encourages the green shoots of civil society and gently spreads the view that political leadership's first task is to protect the life, freedom and unfettered expressions of its citizens?

Left and Right say 'a third way' is impossible, or at best certainly not achievable by a Government which has barely dented arms sales, toppled no dictators, arrested only a tiny handful of war criminals and kowtows still to unpleasant and bloody leaders who always find money for palaces and guns. But they are wrong.

They are wrong not because Mr Cook's human rights achievements are any more than modest but because a new principle is developing which begins to nudge realpolitik aside. It is a principle which seeks to dethrone principle; to privilege the privatisation of ideology so that those who believe in a fundamentalist vision must do so in their own time, without disturbing the peace and security of others. (The **settlement in Northern Ireland** may – if it holds

darkling plain
A threatening world (from *Dover Beach* by the English poet Matthew Arnold, 1822–88).

previous Conservative Government
1979–97.

Oxfam
A charity formed for the relief of famine.

settlement in Northern Ireland
Peace Agreement, Easter 1998. The structures that allowed eventual devolution in Northern Ireland in May 2000.

East Anglia
Region in south-east
England.

– stand as an exemplar of this.) It is a principle of living with diversity, even when that means living with a great deal of nonsense.

I say 'nudge aside' not replace. Realpolitik still rules much of the time. Mr Cook, after all, clothed himself in it earlier this year when he took a leading role in warning President Saddam Hussein that Britain and the United States could blow his arsenals to bits if he did not co-operate . . .

But the possibility exists of softening down power; of developing a routine of negotiation and accommodation; of replacing order with process. A third way? Not yet; but it is the dim outlines of one, as more and more feet tread it and form a path, trusting it to take them where they wish to go and will be secure.

■ ■ ■

Europe and the European Union

A central and strident debate in Britain continues to centre on British membership of the European Union (EU), the effects of membership and conflicting views about the direction in which the EU is developing. Politicians, businessmen, the trade unions and the general public are divided in their reactions as to whether membership is a good thing or not for Britain. The Labour government leadership wants to play a more central part in Europe; the Liberal Democrats are in favour of a federal and fully integrated EU; and the Conservative Party (while having a Europhile wing) is officially highly sceptical (Eurosceptic) of any further European integration. Public opinion polls have consistently shown that the British people are generally lukewarm about the EU, and frequently negative on specific issues. The next text examines the various perspectives on British membership and the options open to the country.

2 *'Do we need Europe? Do the British have more in common with Americans or Italians? And would anything actually change if we opted out of the EU?'*
John Lichfield
(*The Independent*, 20 May 1996)

Do we need Europe? One might as well ask: 'Do we need **East Anglia**?' We are part of it and it is part of us. Some of us, encouraged by newspapers mostly owned by foreigners, insist that Britain is a continent unto itself. It is not. We are Europeans. There is a simple cultural proof: speak to any Briton who has lived in the US.

They cross the Atlantic assuming that they are more like Americans than, say, Belgians or Italians. Prolonged exposure to American attitudes on guns, sport, religion and health-care persuades them that they are wrong. It is common to hear them utter this sentence: 'I never realised how European I was until I came over here.'

So, do we need Europe? We are Europe. Let's change the question. Do we need European laws and European commissions, councils and parliaments? Would we be better off in a world in which European countries co-operated loosely and had some form of basic free trade agreement? Has not the whole thing spun out of control from the original conception of a common market?

This last complaint – the standard *Daily Mail* bleat – is a lie; or wilful ignorance. The EU, the organization formerly known as the EC, née the EEC, has never disguised its political nature or its political ambitions. The impulse for its creation was not just free trade. Free trade was a means to an end, or two ends: a community of nations so interdependent they could no longer conceive of going to war with each other; a Europe capable of preserving its prosperity and influence in a new world dominated by the US and Russia.

The whole point about the EU, from the very earliest times, was that it was NOT a loose grouping of member states. The Community had its own finances and political identity. It had central institutions and laws, which sometimes took precedence over those of its member states.

In other words it was founded loosely on the F-word, federalism – from the beginning. This is precisely why Britain refused to join in 1958. We have since signed up for the loosely federal principle four times, in three treaties and a **referendum**. One can argue against it but one cannot credibly say, as Lady Thatcher sometimes does, that it was something invented by **Jacques Delors**, or that 'we were never told'.

But why? Why was the EU such an ambitious creation? There is a misconception that free trade – genuinely free trade – is just about scrapping customs tariffs and quotas. The EU, from the beginning, was an attempt to level the entire playing field, to make trade between two member states the same as trade between two cities in one country. This meant going after the whole hidden armoury of trade barriers, such as obscure national regulations, varying safety standards and government subsidies. It also meant trying to help the poorer regions, and poorer sections of society, who might suffer in this newly

Daily Mail
Mid-market daily newspaper, usually having rightist and nationalist political viewpoints.

referendum
The 1975 referendum on whether the British people wanted to continue as members of the EU. Approved by a two-to-one margin.

Jacques Delors
Former President of the European Commission.

The Treaty of Rome
The original treaty signed
in 1957 by six European nations to create the European Economic Community (EEC).

Kenneth Clarke
Pro-European Conservative MP.

competitive world. It also meant making special arrangements for farmers (with famously disastrous consequences, now much reformed[3]). This is why the EU had laws and a budget. The intention, from the beginning, was to make Europe not just one market, but one economy.

That effort, though incomplete, has been remarkably successful. In some respects, the EU is now a more genuine single market than the United States; the trade barriers between its countries are substantially less than those between the Canadian provinces.

After 23 years, the British economy is umbilically connected to the rest of Europe. The EU takes 43 per cent of our exports of goods and services – three times more than all our exports to the US, Japan, China, Hong Kong and South East Asia *combined*. Four of our top five export markets are EU countries. Talk to British businessmen – especially, interestingly, those outside London – and they are in no doubt that Europe is essential to their survival.

Does one economy imply one government? Yes and no. **The Treaty of Rome** speaks of 'ever closer union', which can be read in two ways: a declared intention to merge eventually into a federal super-state; or something vaguer, like railway tracks stretching into the distance, endlessly converging but never meeting.

The ambiguity is deliberate, and creative, but also the source of much of the EU's permanent state of quarrelsomeness.

The truth is that there is minimal support across the EU for going the whole hog to a United States of Europe. In its muddled way, the EU already provides most of the economic advantages, without the political suffering involved in creating a federal government. There is no support at all for the wilder Eurosceptic nightmares of a homogeneous federal monster, determined to stamp out all signs of national character or individuality. Such fears are fed by distortions, or outright lies, about EU policies. The Euro-banana; Euro-hairnets for fishermen; the uniform Euro-Christmas tree – there is no space to go into them all, but 90 per cent of what you read is Euro-nonsense. If the sceptics feel their case is so good, why are so many of their arguments based on distortions?

On the other hand, Euro-enthusiasts in this country are often equally dishonest about the frankly federal implications of what the EU is trying to do, such as the single European currency. A single currency will mean something approaching a common economic policy, whatever **Kenneth Clarke** might say. Operating a single currency with six or seven widely divergent economic policies would be like trying to fly a plane with six or seven pilots. This is not necessarily an argument against a single currency: it is an argument for more honest argument in its favour.

Is the EU a dilution of British sovereignty? Yes, of course. But what is sovereignty? The right of the British people and their representatives to take decisions without interference from foreign forces? Such absolute sovereignty does not exist in the modern world. For over 40 years we have sub-contracted our security – our very survival as a nation – to a **military alliance** whose ultimate political control lies in Washington. There were few bleats about surrender of sovereignty because the arrangement seemed largely to make sense: we were putting our sovereignty into a common pool, the better to defend our real sovereignty and real freedom.

The argument for the EU – for all its occasional idiocies – is broadly the same. The challenges in the post-Soviet world are mostly economic challenges. How to preserve, even advance, our hard-won levels of prosperity and social protection in the face of complex and insistent challenges from new technologies and emergent nations, especially in Asia. How to exert some public control of economic policy in a world in which scores of billions of pounds can pass down a telephone line in a fraction of a second.

The German view is that the EU's federal bandwagon must always roll forward or fall off the road completely. This is silly. Britain sees the likely influx of new members from eastern Europe as a chance to turn the clock back to 1957 and create a looser collection of vaguely co-operative states. This is silly, too. A larger EU will need its supra-national laws and institutional core more than ever. Without them, the whole enterprise will regress to a soggy mass of good intentions and increasingly splintered economies.

In the end, we have to accept that if we are members of the club the decision is not just ours. The EU has been growing for 40 years. Its nature, and its future, also depends on 14 other member states. We cannot say, like the yokel in the *Punch* cartoon: 'If I were you, I wouldn't start from here.'

The most sensible European question is the question asked by the great Franco-British anti-European, **Sir James Goldsmith**. Would Britain be a more prosperous and freer place if the EU carried on but we dropped out?

British economic arguments about the EU have always been shot through with ideology. In the 1960s and 1970s much of the opposition came from the left, on the grounds that free trade would export British jobs to the continent. Now the prevailing anti-EU argument comes from the right. 'We should be more like the fast-growing, rule-free Asian Tiger nations. We need to cut free from the European obsession with social protection and labour rights.'

military alliance
NATO.

Punch
British humorous magazine.

Sir James Goldsmith
Late leader of the former Referendum Party.

Norway
Norway is now a
member of the
European Economic
Area (EEA), ie
cooperation with the
EU short of full
membership.

Just a Minute
BBC Radio quiz game
in which contestants
have to speak on a
topic for one minute
without deviation,
repetition or hesitation.

This argument is – ultimately – an argument for Britain as an offshore industrial park for Asian screw-driver factories and sweatshops, undercutting European competition. It is a wonder the other Europeans let us get away with it inside the EU; there would be small chance of us getting away with it outside it.

A Britain standing alone – in, say, 50 years' time – would be dwarfed politically and economically, not only by the US and Japan but the rest of the EU, by Russia, China and South East Asia. Our economic and political clout in the world – our ability to exert influence over our own destiny, which is as good a definition of sovereignty as any – might be comparable to that of **Norway**. The Norwegians are happy enough with that. Maybe we should be, too.

■ ■ ■

While the Labour government is trying to pursue a more active and positive line in the EU, the following text by William Hague (Leader of the Opposition Conservative Party) indicates the Conservative position on Europe and criticizes that of Labour. It was written prior to the British European Parliament elections in June 1999, in which, despite a very low turnout of voters, the Conservatives increased their share of the seats and Labour did badly.[4] This result was widely interpreted, rightly or wrongly, as a protest vote against Labour policies generally and support for Conservative scepticism on Europe.

3 *'Europe? Oh, don't mention it, Mr Blair'*
William Hague
(Author copyright, 9 June 1999) abridged

Listening to Labour politicians at the moment is a bit like tuning in to *Just a Minute* on the radio. Can they get through a whole interview on the European elections without mentioning the word 'Europe'?

Of course, in their ideal world, Labour would really like tomorrow's elections [for the European Parliament] simply to disappear. Rather than know what you really think about Europe, it would prefer to get on with steadily eroding the independence and freedom of our country in pursuit of outdated dreams of European political union.

But there are European elections tomorrow and you can make your voice heard. Whether or not you normally support my party, by voting Conservative in the European elections you can send an unmistakable signal to the Government that you believe, like me, that Britain's future lies in being in Europe, not run by Europe, and that Britain wants to keep the pound.

The people I meet beyond the Westminster hothouse so often tell me that no one ever listens to their opinions on Europe; now is your chance to speak out.

Vote Conservative tomorrow and you will be voting 'yes' for a Europe that promotes free enterprise and lower taxes, and 'yes' for a Europe that reaches out across the whole continent; in short, a 'yes' for a Europe that does less and does it better.

Vote Conservative and you will be voting 'no' to excessive European regulation, 'no' to the drive for higher and harmonized European taxes, 'no' to the plans for a European army, 'no' to the steady erosion of the British veto, 'no' to government plans to abolish the pound.

Over the past month we have run a real campaign on European issues, presenting our policies in every part of the country openly and honestly. We have put forward detailed proposals to promote free trade through an EU alliance with **NAFTA**, to cut the European budget by tackling waste and mismanagement, to crack down on corruption with an independent anti-fraud office, to give British farmers a fair deal by insisting that foreign food imports meet our high standards, and to reform the disastrous common fisheries policy by returning fishing waters to local or national control.

In Hungary last month I advocated a flexible, expanded Europe in which all countries can sit at the same European table, while not having to order the same things from the menu. What a contrast to a Labour Government which has spent the past four weeks running scared of the issues . . .

So what has become of the Prime Minister's pledge in May that he would lead a national campaign to end British ambivalence about being part of the European drive for ever-closer political union? Some national campaign! He never got beyond **Vauxhall Bridge**.

I suspect his private opinion polls are telling him what I have heard with my own ears all over the country. At these elections the Conservative Party is speaking for the great majority of British people who, like me, want to be part of the European Union, but who also, like me, believe there is a limit to how much power you can hand over to European institutions and that we have reached that limit now.

NAFTA
North American Free Trade Agreement, 1995, between Canada, Mexico and the USA.

Vauxhall Bridge
Bridge across the River Thames in London.

Some fringe parties have argued that we should go further and withdraw from the European Union altogether. That would be a profound mistake. For example, I know from my time as Welsh Secretary when I was negotiating huge Korean and Japanese inward investment projects that businesses come here because we are part of the European Union and because we have not had the same costly employment regulations and social costs that have destroyed jobs on the Continent. That is the right balance to maintain.

Others have argued that the nation state is dead, and that we should be part of a single European state with a single government, single taxes, a single army and a single currency. The Liberal Democrats are the most prominent advocates of this position, but the Labour Party has been pulled along in their wake.

I believe passionately that they, too, are profoundly wrong. Europe can never be a single nation. However many European flags and European national anthems are dreamt up, there will never be a single democratic consciousness that stretches from Portugal to Finland or from the Greek islands to Shetland . . .

The Labour Party does not understand this. It believes that political institutions do not matter. It thinks national identity can be rebranded. That is why the Prime Minister is happy to sign away Britain's independence, to hand over control of our economy and abolish our currency. He is wedded to an outdated notion that in the next century Britain must become part of some great centralized European superstate.

The Conservative Party offers an alternative vision. A vision of Britain as a lightly regulated, low taxed, free and nimble trading nation in control of our destiny and with the self-confidence to thrive in the new millennium – a Britain that can make a success of its own currency if it wishes to do so.

Being in Europe not run by Europe is part of that vision. Vote Conservative tomorrow if you share that vision.

■ ■ ■

Public opinion polls from time to time reveal the British public's attitudes on the EU. But these can sometimes appear to be contradictory and may be variously interpreted. Much depends on how poll and survey questions are actually worded.

An unpublished government survey of public opinion in 1998[5] suggested that a majority of Britons were sceptical about the EU and saw it as a bureaucratic and interfering organization. Commentators argued that the survey did not support the Prime Minister's claim of 'a remarkable shift in public opinion in Britain' in favour of 'constructive engagement' in Europe. Indeed, respondents to the survey did not feel that Britain had a leading role in the EU or that it had great influence. The Franco-German alliance within the organization was seen as much more significant.

Some 42 per cent of respondents to the survey remained highly Euro-sceptical and did not agree that Britain's future lies in Europe. Four in ten maintained that the EU has not worked and that Britain should withdraw from membership. Nevertheless, and despite such opinions, 59 per cent thought that there would in fact be a United States of Europe within 20 years.

Such findings suggest that underlying attitudes towards the EU continue to be sceptical, but that reality and a sense of inevitability are also present in people's minds. For example, a 1996 National Opinion Poll (NOP) for *The Sunday Times*[6] found that 50 per cent of respondents thought EU membership had been bad for Britain and 30 per cent considered it to have been good. But, as in the 1998 figures above, later NOP polls have found that only 22–25 per cent of respondents are actually in favour of withdrawal from the EU. Indeed, a MORI poll in 2000[7] indicated that 62 per cent of respondents wanted to stay in the EU (the highest figure since 1991).

The evidence from public opinion polls seems to suggest that possibly a sizeable majority of the British public see the EU as a fact of life, but not one with which they are overjoyed or satisfied. A minority might prefer a viable alternative if one was available. The same sense of resigned inevitability (or reality) seems to be affecting the continuing euro debate.

■　■　■

The Euro (common currency) debate

A central question in the long-running EU debate is whether Britain should eventually join the euro (the EU common or single currency). Although the euro was adopted by 12 of the 15 EU nations in 1999, Britain did not join the system.

The Labour government's policy towards the euro is 'prepare and then decide'. It insists that the economic indicators for convergence with the other EU currencies must be met and that these should be satisfactory for Britain. But a final decision will be taken only after a referendum of the British people (possibly in the parliament following the next general election if Labour are successful). The government, however, appears to be actively preparing for entry, as part of its policy of closer involvement in the EU, although it argues that entry is not inevitable. Some government ministers are more enthusiastic than others.

Commentators argue that British entry into the euro is now probable.[8] They suggest that the government's case prior to a referendum (and if the economic indicators are met) will probably be based on the arguments that Britain would be isolated outside the euro and lose influence in the EU itself; it would be unable to participate in or influence the policy developments of the euro if it was outside; such policies would nevertheless have a potentially serious and direct impact on Britain; and the British people would consequently suffer economically with risks to investment, jobs and business. According to the commentators, the arguments for joining the euro system will be shown to be part of Britain's evolving participation in the EU, rather than a leap of faith into the unknown, even though the emphasis is clearly on the negative consequences of non-entry.

Nevertheless, the British people must be persuaded before any referendum that the country would actually fit into the euro system; that the euro was a worthwhile development and operating successfully (despite its initial poor performance); that joining would not be against British interests; that the system has positive values of stability and European-wide strength; and that other European countries were successfully reforming their economic and labour markets in the areas of business deregulation, job mobility and competitiveness. Such persuasion might be difficult, particularly in the present climate.

The Conservatives (although split between Eurosceptics and Europhiles) officially rule out membership of the euro in the next Parliament and wish to keep the pound as the national currency. However, although the euro will undoubtedly feature significantly during the next general election campaign, the Conservatives cannot depend on majority support for their position, irrespective of favourable public opinion poll results in the interim. Indeed, commentators question how being part of Europe (which the Conservatives advocate) is consistent with being outside a potentially successful single currency, which many business people want.

The debate has both economic and political arguments. Much could depend on whether people will vote in the referendum on the grounds of personal and national economic interest, in spite of being unable to appreciate all the complexities of the issue. They might also respond in the campaign to the positive economic messages being presented by pro-euro supporters. Some critics, however, argue that the debate is increasingly about the political will of entry (rather than economic factors). Others maintain that entry is inevitable.

It is claimed that, on the basis of various opinion polls, the British people in recent years have been against membership of the euro by a margin of 70–30 per cent.

Such figures have to be treated with caution. For example, the above 1998 poll[9] showed that only 9 per cent of respondents thought Britain should never join, while 73 per cent said that it is right to leave the decision open (at least presumably until the euro has proved itself). Some 48 per cent said they were in favour of eventual membership while 46 per cent were against. Later polls in 1999 and 2000 were interpreted to suggest that public opinion has become less strongly opposed to entry.

What seemed to be happening was that many people in the electorate were open to persuasion either way and there was a general feeling that the result may depend upon economic conditions at the time of the referendum. In a similar fashion to membership of the EU, possibly a majority see entry to the euro as likely or inevitable while a sizeable minority are strongly opposed. But a MORI poll in June 2000[10] showed that there was a 71 to 29 per cent majority against entry and that the percentage of those respondents who strongly oppose entry had risen. *The Sun* newspaper, as in the next text, has led a long campaign against entry and is strongly against.

4 'A big con'
(*The Sun*, leader, 28 March 1998)

The euro is a sham. And a farce.

And a downright menace.

A Bank of England expert admits the single currency will throw millions on the dole unless France and Germany shake-up their labour markets.

Her message is backed up by **CBI** chief Adair Turner, who says Europeans have been conned into thinking the euro will solve all their problems.

That's the problem. We're ALL being conned.

We're told the euro is inevitable: *It isn't*.

We're told it is essential for economic reasons: *It isn't*.

We're told we'll be doomed if we don't join: *We won't*.

We're told it isn't a forerunner of a European superstate: *It is*.

It's time for honesty. Before the big con starts to work.

con
A confidence trick; being cheated.

CBI
Employers' organization: the Confederation of British Industry.

■ ■ ■

TUC
Trade Union
Conference.

The next text examines in somewhat greater detail the political and economic arguments of the euro debate seen from historical and ideological (or party-political) perspectives.

**exchange-rate
mechanism**
The EU system that is
meant to prevent wide
fluctuations in
currencies and stabilize
European economies.
Britain was forced to
withdraw from the ERM
in 1992.

5 'The wrong continent'

Larry Elliott (Economics Editor of *The Guardian*)
(Author copyright, *The Sunday Times*, 12 July 1998)

It was Ron Todd, a trade union baron of the old school, who explained why the left had to rethink its approach to all things European. 'The only card game in town,' said the boss of the Transport and General Workers' Union at the 1988 TUC conference, 'is in a town called Brussels.'

The logic was simple. Margaret Thatcher was in power with a big majority. She was doing things the unions did not care for. She was growing increasingly hostile to Europe. Therefore it made sense for the Labour party and the unions to be nice to Europe. QED. [That which had to be proved.]

The logic may have been simple, but when it came to membership of the **exchange-rate mechanism** it was also fundamentally flawed. It meant that Labour backed British entry into the ERM because it thought it was good politics to be in favour of whatever Thatcher was against. It was not good politics; it was bad politics. And the reason it was bad politics was that it was bad economics. As if to show that it has forgotten everything and learnt nothing from the disasters inflicted on the British economy from 1990–92, the same woolly thinking now informs mainstream Labour thinking on the single currency. If the Conservatives are lining up against the euro, then it makes sense for all progressives to be in favour. Not everybody on the left approaches the single currency in this lazy fashion. But far too many do.

Left-wing fears over the possible impact of a single currency were encapsulated a quarter of a century ago when the party was drawing up its manifesto for the 1974 election. 'We would reject any kind of international agreement which compelled us to accept increased unemployment for the sake of maintaining a fixed parity, as is required by current proposals for a European economic and monetary union.'

This got to the heart of the matter: jobs and living standards. Labour feared that a single currency would be deflationary, leading to higher unemployment.

Looking at the five-fold increase in European unemployment in the intervening 25 years, it was right to be worried.

It is said by supporters of the euro that monetary union will be the key to faster growth, since it will unlock all the hidden treasures of the single market. When inflation seemed to be the big problem a decade ago, it was said that it would keep inflation low. Among the myriad of other contradictory claims are that it will make European companies more efficient, that it will protect the European social model from the forces of globalization, that it will save British manufacturing by reducing the value of the pound, and even that by allowing capital to organize on a pan-European basis it will encourage Europe-wide worker solidarity.

Those not seduced by these arguments are roundly denounced as right-wing bigots, narrow-minded xenophobes and dangerous nationalists. Finally, it is said that British interests will be damaged by remaining outside a project which, in a quasi-Marxist fashion, is predetermined by the forces of history. It's hard to know exactly where to start attacking this ragbag of nonsense, but it's perhaps best to start with the idea that anybody who doesn't like the euro is some sort of antedeluvian Thatcherite. Just as you can like football while loathing Arsenal, so you can be an internationalist while having no time at all for the euro.

The single currency is not the product of Euro-Keynesianism but the fag end of the neo-liberal monetarist revolution in which central bankers will run monetary policy with the sole aim of achieving price stability, and finance ministers will have their hands tied on fiscal policy by the German-inspired stability pact. This alone should be a good enough reason to doubt whether the euro will be the saviour of European-style welfarism. Indeed, to the extent that social democracy has been weakened, it is because of the self-inflicted wounds caused by slow growth and high unemployment over the past 20 years. In the five years 1993–97, the UK economy grew at an average of 3 per cent a year, while the French economy, hobbled by trying to qualify for the single currency, grew at only half that rate.

Nor is it true that workers in England can expect a whole host of new goodies to come their way once monetary union is finally under way. Some unions in Britain have set great store by the **social chapter**, as if it is the modern equivalent of the Domesday Book. In fact, the social chapter remains a volume with very few pages: three, to be precise.

Moreover, the trend is towards labour-market deregulation rather than greater workplace security, and it is folly for the left to believe that the single currency will be a bulwark against globalization. Far from it. One reason why big

social chapter
The part of the Maastricht Treaty, 1992, that seeks to protect European workers' rights, employment and health.

business tends to be so gung ho about the euro is that the explicit aim of monetary union is to reduce wages and public spending. In a single market without any capital controls but with legal ceilings on budget deficits, the upshot will be a drive for lower taxes and lower spending. Once Brussels decided that the scrapping of all controls on capital – both internal and external – was a prerequisite for joining monetary union, the notion that the euro would be a defence against globalization was rendered immediately redundant.

None of these arguments seems to register with those who say that monetary union is a political rather than an economic project.

But as the events of Black Wednesday show, economics does matter. On the afternoon of September 16, 1992, millions of people in Britain were rendered technically insolvent when the Bank of England raised interest rates to 15 per cent as a gambler's last throw to keep Britain in the ERM. Once it was accepted that further resistance was futile, the government changed tack. On September 17 rates were back down to 10 per cent and by the turn of the year they were at 6 per cent. With a 15 per cent devaluation taking the pressure off exporters, a vigorous economic recovery was under way.

The lesson from Black Wednesday is that interest rates and exchange rate are powerful economic weapons that should not be surrendered lightly [by independent nation states]. It would not matter were the European Union really one homogenous economy where monetary policy had the same impact everywhere. Unfortunately, Europe is not one single economy: for cultural, geographic and historical reasons it is a series of diverse economies, a patchwork quilt of regions rich and poor. Of course the same could be said of the United States, where the affluence of Silicon Valley in California contrasts with the industrial decay of heavy industry in West Virginia. But there is a crucial difference. America is what economists call an optimal currency area and Europe is not.

What does this mean? Well, imagine what happens if the economy receives an adverse economic shock, which affects one part of the single-currency area more adversely than the others. If an economy is an optimal currency area there should be mechanisms in place to mitigate the impact of this shock.

First, there should be labour market mobility. In America, for example, it was relatively easy for those Texans affected by the oil-price slump of the mid-1980s to get in their cars and head off to California, where jobs were plentiful during the Reagan defence build-up.

Europe does not enjoy nearly the same levels of labour-market mobility, primarily because it lacks a common language. Bank clerks in Manchester could only move to booming Munich and Milan in the event of a British recession if they spoke German or Italian. In an increasingly service-sector dominated economy, language is likely to become more of a barrier to labour-market flexibility.

But if people can't move to the jobs, what about moving jobs to where the people are? In an optimal currency area, the tax-and-spending system operates so that the taxes paid in regions that are doing well are recycled as benefits for those areas in the doldrums. America has such a system, Europe does not. Indeed, Brussels would need to increase its budget by about 10 times to have the same clout as the authorities in America, and this is not feasible without monetary union being buttressed by fiscal union and – to all intents and purposes – a single European government.

There is a third mechanism for improving productivity and competitiveness, but it is not one that many trade unionists would be keen to embrace. Workers could be forced to take pay cuts, which would lower costs and make run-down parts of the currency area more attractive to business. Interestingly, this very point was made at last year's CBI conference. 'Before the CBI shakes hands with the TUC on a single currency, you should fix them in the eye and ask if they are prepared to tell their members that they may have to take a pay cut.'

The speaker? Not a Labour Minister, nor a trade unionist, but Willliam Hague. Apparently, the leader of the [Conservative] opposition understands what too many on the left do not: that like any card game, the one in Brussels is a gamble, and there is every chance of losing your shirt.

■ ■ ■

The Commonwealth

British attempts to enter Europe since the 1950s have tended to militate against the traditional familial and trading importance to Britain of the Commonwealth (the worldwide organization of mainly former British colonies). But the continuing role of the Commonwealth is a debated aspect of Britain's international standing.

The Labour government apparently feels that the Commonwealth is a success and is committed to raising its profile.[11] Significantly, a large number of countries wish to join the organization, not all of whom have been previous British colonies. But commentators argue that the value of the Commonwealth in the contemporary world should rest on a concrete, realistic and distinctive role for the organization, which would not only appeal to member states but also demonstrate its advantages over existing world bodies. The Labour government's ethical dimension in foreign policy and its modernization project for Britain would appear to have relevance for such an ambition.

The Commonwealth is an ex-colonial association, which claims, despite frequent difficulties, arguments and conflicts, to possess a genuine sense of unity based on fundamental freedoms. Mutual trade, financial aid, investment and economic cooperation continue to be important elements in the organization. But arguably they are not as crucial in today's globalized economy as they have been in the past. Critics consequently argue that the Commonwealth could more fruitfully campaign for accountable government, democratic concerns, anti-corruption reform and civil and human rights.

Such a role would allow a combination of economics and politics, but would importantly allow the Commonwealth to function more persuasively as a political forum, a world-based democratic voice and a guarantor of basic rights. Commonwealth governments in the 1991 Harare Declaration supported 'democracy, the rule of law, just and honest government and human rights' as the goals of the organization. Critics argue that the Commonwealth now needs to demonstrate seriously that these concerns do not become merely rhetorical lip service to ideals. In 2000, for example, Fiji was suspended from the organization, as had happened to other members in the past because of their bad internal conditions. The question is whether such an identity is sufficient to give vitality, influence and status to the Commonwealth. Opinions about the contemporary relevance of the organization, and Britain's relationship to it, therefore vary considerably as the next text demonstrates.

6 'A dysfunctional family?'
Magnus Linklater
(*The Times*, 23 October 1997) abridged

If anyone cast the cold eye of logic over that ramshackle club, the Commonwealth, now gathered in Edinburgh for its biennial conference, he might conclude that its time is up. If the Queen, its head, is no longer welcome in its most populous state [India], what is the point in carrying on as it is? All that seems to be left is an expensive talking shop, an excuse for globetrotting, and a useful boost to the host city every couple of years. Without formal powers, this 'free association' of sovereign states has no economic muscle, offers no collective security to its members, and has little effect on the human rights abuses it is meant to curb. It carries only the flickering memories of empire.

So why not simply declare that this week's Heads of Government Meeting will be the penultimate one, with 1999 a suitable year in which to bring the whole ritual to a close?[12] The Commonwealth has had a decent run, after all. Dreamt up in 1926, it was given legal status in 1931, so it will have reached, roughly speaking, the age of three score years and ten by the millennium. A good excuse, perhaps, for gentle retirement.

And yet the measure of a healthy club is whether it continues to attract new members. For reasons not immediately obvious, this one seems to have become the **Groucho** of the international scene – everyone wants to join. It even has a waiting list. With South Africa back in the fold; Mozambique and Cameroon recent joiners; Fiji, which resigned in 1987, now a member again;[13] and even Ruanda queuing up for entry, it has reached a record 54 members. Its area of influence is steadily extending. On the agenda this week will be applications from the Yemen, and from Yassir Arafat's Palestine National Authority.

One reason for its success, a delegate explained to me, was that it offered small nations a sense of security. There was, he said, no resentment over Britain's colonial past. 'We may have been exploited by Britain, but we would rather be exploited by Britain than anyone else I can think of.'

Compare this to the French equivalent, which seeks to bring together former French colonies, and yet has to dredge up members and bribe them into joining. If there is one overriding reason for continuing the Commonwealth, it is that the French are jealous of it.

The Prime Ministers and Presidents flying into Scotland this weekend seem in no doubt themselves. They are, if anything, more determined than ever that the Commonwealth should continue to expand its activities. A brief look down the agenda shows a plethora of action groups and working panels. A network of organizations, devoted to human, social and economic concerns, now operates throughout the member states. For the first time the United Nations will be joining in, represented in the form of its Human Settlements Centre.

But the Queen's troubled visit to India is a warning that cannot be ignored. If this is indeed a family of nations, it is clearly going through a dysfunctional phase, with some of its children turning nasty. Instead of the affection and respect they have been used to on these trips abroad, the Queen and the Duke of Edinbugh met with a level of ridicule and insult more common to the British tabloid press. If this is to be the pattern for the future, there must be doubts about the role of the British monarch as head of the Commonwealth, and there-

Groucho
American comedian Groucho Marx who said he would not join any club that asked him to be a member.

pall of choking haze
Caused by widespread
forest fires.

fore the whole nature of the organization itself. Her enthusiasm and integrity have, after all, been central to its existence for more than 40 years ...

The row does, however, suggest a theme which could give this weekend's talks some edge: if the Queen were to stand down from her traditional role as head of the Commonwealth and leave it to find its own feet in the harsh climate of the modern economic world, would it still hold together, and, if so, in what form? Looking back over the past twenty years, it has often been defined more by the rows that have divided it than the ethos that is meant to underpin it. Lusaka 1979: Zimbabwe threatens breakaway. Melbourne 1981: outrage over New Zealand's sporting links with South Africa. New Delhi 1983: US invasion of Grenada. Nassau 1985: Britain isolated over South African sanctions. The tensions then were almost palpable ... For a decade, apartheid was the dominating theme. Then, at Auckland in 1995, Nigeria defied the Commonwealth and executed Ken Saro-Wiwa, while the French tested their bomb in the Pacific in the teeth of protests.

Each disagreement has ended with a last-minute compromise of sorts, encouraging the belief that the Commonwealth has genuine cohesion and an independent life of its own. But the political agenda has largely been reactive. This is the first meeting in recent memory with no major dispute to patch up. So what defines its objectives? The nearest we get is the Harare Declaration of 1991 which set out a series of worthy goals such as promoting democracy, the rule of law, sound government and human rights. To those it added a litany of good causes – fighting poverty, disease, drugs and inequality. The only thing lacking was sin.

And yet what progress has been made? No one surveying events in Kenya, Nigeria, Sierra Leone, The Gambia or Zimbabwe, could honestly claim that democracy was universally available in this Commonwealth of Nations, or that human rights were evenly applied ... [Y]et there is no evidence that Commonwealth leaders are prepared to agree on tough collective action, such as the imposition of sanctions. If it cannot even unite on this, what hope is there for the Commonwealth itself?

Even the environment seems to have dropped off the official agenda, despite the crisis in South East Asia, where a **pall of choking haze** pollutes the atmosphere in at least three member states, Malaysia, Singapore and Papua New Guinea. One might have thought that the failure of last year's Earth Summit would offer the Commonwealth, with its highly vulnerable smaller members, the chance to make its voice heard. It could still happen, but the only people holding their breath are the luckless citizens of those countries.

There is, however, a serious new role that Tony Blair, who will chair the proceedings, might consider. He is a constitutional reformer, who has tackled devolution in Scotland and Wales, and is now considering the future of the House of Lords; the Commonwealth should offer a suitable challenge. Here is a body representing a third of the world's population, some 1.7 billion people, united not just by the experience of Empire but by the English language. Hungry for education, for help in sustainable development, and for access to the new technology in which most of its members lag so far behind, it looks to Britain, not for moral leadership, but for practical assistance, skill and investment. It is a massive market, but also a formidable, if hidden, power, where, for once, this country is positively welcome. Bodies like the Commonwealth Development Corporation (now to be partially privatized) provide an infrastructure in the Third World on which to build.

Over the next five years, Mr Blair should begin easing the Commonwealth away from the concept of a large and amiable, if unruly, clan, with the Queen as matriarch, into a modern, dynamic economic organization. It will involve breaking some old links as well as forging new ones. It will mean changing attitudes that have been formed by the conflicts of the past. The reward for success, however, could be to turn it into a club that is genuinely worth joining.

■ ■ ■

Defence policy and NATO

Defence policy is closely tied to foreign policy and both reflect Britain's contemporary international role and identity. The state and future of Britain's armed forces consequently continues to provoke debate and amounts to a balancing act between cost and perceived need. Some critics argue for expansion of the military capacity while others press for cost-cutting reductions and new streamlined defence roles. The debate also involves the question of whether the EU (comprised mainly of countries that are also members of the North Atlantic Treaty Organization – NATO) should have a defence arm that is able to operate separately from NATO in some, if not all, military areas.

British defence policy is based upon government Strategic Defence Reviews, which examine Britain's needs and involve consultations and bargaining with the military. Such reviews may result in cuts in spending, the selling off of military assets (such as property), drives for more efficient use of men and materials and the development of new defence initiatives. These decisions have to take into account global and European developments, Britain's changed world role, its own national defence requirements and its relationships with other organizations such as NATO,

Gulf War
The 1991 Gulf War
against Iraq.

the United Nations and the EU. They have to balance financial costs and security needs and frequently illustrate the tensions between the military that fights for what it considers to be necessary resources and the Treasury that is often intent on cutting costs.

Defence commentators, such as Lawrence Freedman,[14] argue that after 1989, with its dramatic political changes in the Soviet Union and Eastern Europe, it was assumed that there was no longer any danger of a Cold War nuclear and conventional confrontation between NATO and Warsaw Pact countries. The resulting so-called 'peace dividend' strategy encouraged governments to believe that military forces could be 'smaller but better', with significant cuts in defence spending. There could be fewer troops, combat aircraft, ships, nuclear warheads and conventional weapons. But the **Gulf War** showed that events might occur in the contemporary world that still required the large-scale deployment of conventional forces. The British military in recent years have been engaged in the Gulf, the Balkans (Bosnia and Kosovo) and in other United Nations operations around the world.

Defence experts maintain that British defence policy has to consider not only national security but also the European and the global dimensions of any potential problem. Serious instability in one area may quickly affect others and agreed international intervention may be necessary. It is argued that Britain must therefore improve its ability to operate overseas if it is to contribute internationally on an active, responsive basis. Air-lifting and naval transport mobility, which can be costly, has to be improved so that equipment, supplies and trained manpower can be moved quickly to wherever they are needed.

Such international contributions could easily strain British finances and military capacity. Lawrence Freedman argues that this burden can be justified only if it is successful, effectual and frequently operational at a low risk. Otherwise, the British government could be criticized for amassing expensive and unnecessary provisions for no positive purpose.

Yet problems have started to emerge with these policies, particularly following action in Kosovo 1999, where aircraft were unable to function properly, high-technology equipment failed and the infantry operated with defective weapons and supplies. Critics argue that military hardware is still inadequate and out of date and troop numbers are insufficient. The following text illustrates these problems and asks whether Britain can really afford its international role.

7 'The army: over-stretched and over there. Is Britain taking on more military commitments than it can cope with?'
(*The Economist*, 17 July 1999)

Cross your fingers and hope there will be no new fires for the British army to fight over the next six months. Even as Britain basks in the international lime-light as leader of the peacekeeping effort in Kosovo, its top brass is uneasily aware that the thin red line of troops deployed on foreign operations is about as thin as it can get without snapping. General Sir Peter de Billière, who led British forces in the Gulf War in 1991, has warned that the services are 'dangerously and unacceptably overstretched'. The Ministry of Defence, for its part, admits being 'heavily committed'. Over 47 per cent of Britain's 110,000-strong army is now engaged in overseas operations or on duty in Northern Ireland[15] – the biggest commitment anyone can remember in peacetime.

Not that all the news from the Balkans is bad, from the military planners' point of view. In some ways, the crisis there has provided a neat vindication of the philosophy that underpinned last year's Strategic Defence Review. It highlights the way in which a medium-sized country can turn its military tradi-tions into a diplomatic ace, by keeping at the ready a modicum of well-trained, mobile forces with experience of inter-communal peacekeeping as well as wars. Given the American electorate's aversion to casualties, and the continental European armies' domination by conscripts, the total number of effective peacekeepers available to western governments is surprisingly low. At NATO headquarters, all contributions are gratefully received.

With that in mind, the Strategic Defence Review envisaged a force structure which (in addition to Northern Ireland) can cope with one stable peacekeeping effort and one 'active operation', which might involve fighting. That is exactly what the British army now faces: a 4,500-strong contingent building schools and arresting the occasional war criminal in the quietish environment of Bosnia, plus the 10,500 or so who are either in Kosovo or just over the border in Macedonia.

For the moment, the military can cope; but it leaves virtually no slack. In an ideal world, the Ministry of Defence likes to keep at least two brigades, say, 10,000 soldiers, ready to go almost anywhere for six months at virtually no notice. In a recent burst of internationalist enthusiasm, George Robertson, the [former] defence secretary, proposed a more formal arrangement to keep 8,000

Martin Bell
Independent MP for
Tatton.

British troops on standby for UN peacekeeping. But as long as commitments to south-eastern Europe remain at their current level, don't expect much help from Britain in the event of, say, another crisis in the Gulf.

Whether this poses a really serious problem should be clear by the end of the year. Mr Robertson has said he expects a significant reduction in the British military commitment to Kosovo over the next six months: but this is based on the optimistic assumption that Kosovo (and other places in the neighbourhood) will remain relatively manageable; and that other NATO countries will send peacekeepers in decent numbers. Although he has not said so, the minister must also be chafing to reduce the commitment to Bosnia.

Overstretch, as the Strategic Review acknowledged, is a vicious circle. Because the demands on soldiers are so high, the services often find it hard to hold on to people they have trained at huge expense. The divorce rate in the army is horribly high. A regiment which goes on a six-month tour of the Balkans can expect 10 per cent of soldiers' marriages to fail in consequence, according to **Martin Bell**, a war reporter turned politician. In theory, soldiers are supposed to get a two-year break between 'emergency tours' in trouble spots where they cannot bring their families. In practice, the interval is much shorter, especially for signallers and engineers who are heavily in demand. Although the government claims a 20 per cent improvement in recruiting levels over the past year, the army remains about 5,000 under strength – without counting the extra 3,000 which it is supposed to hire by 2004 under the Strategic Defence Review.

Does all this mean that the assembly of a 150,000-strong ground force to attack Serbia – widely mooted at the height of the war,[16] with Britain assumed to be providing about a third of the invaders – was never more than a fantasy? The answer is that in a national emergency, almost anything is possible: leave can be cancelled, reservists called up, garrisons in odd places like Brunei and Gibraltar closed down. But there is a limit to how long such a crisis footing can be maintained, unless national survival is at stake.

The defence ministry says that to sustain a long-term operation, with a proper rotation system, it ideally likes to have at its disposal three or four ships or aircraft, and up to five army units, for every one deployed at any given moment. But of course, it stresses, all such guidelines would be discarded in the event of war or even a sudden increase in peacekeeping demands on more than one front. So far, the government has managed to display Britain's military prowess in the Balkans without acknowledging the existence of a crisis. But if things took a turn for the worse in, say, Northern Ireland and Kosovo simultaneously, it might have some hard choices to make.

■ ■ ■

Although Britain is committed to NATO, the Labour government, after initial scepticism, is considering the development of plans for a European defence identity and
a force within NATO under the aegis of the EU. This could sometimes operate in
future without the USA, but should not develop a defence posture that was a rival
to NATO. However, the EU has not in recent years shown a united competence
in defence and foreign policy matters when faced with international crises. The next
text draws attention to the alleged shortcomings of such plans and the continued
importance of NATO and an American presence.

8 'Nato is still our sword and shield. The Cold War may be over – but an American-based defence alliance remains vital to Europe's safety'
William Rees-Mogg
(Author copyright, *The Times*, 2 February 1998)

Before I went to America to gauge the reaction to the latest Clinton scandal,
I had paid a visit to Brussels. I went across to visit the Nato headquarters,
and was indeed able to have very informative discussions about current Nato
issues, including Bosnia and enlargement. When I was there I stumbled across
another issue I had not gone across to discuss. That is the relationship between
Nato and the European Union.

Both Nato and the EU have their headquarters in Brussels, only a few miles
away from each other. Yet there is little direct official contact between the
two organizations. As I was told, the only real link between them is that the
Secretary General of Nato and the President of the Commission have an
informal breakfast together once a month. These breakfasts sometimes have
to be cancelled, because both men have very full diaries.

This is surprising; it is as though, in Whitehall, the only contact between the
Ministry of Defence and the Treasury was that the Secretary of State for
Defence and the Chancellor of the Exchequer had a monthly breakfast
together. This must reflect some deeper unease about Nato in the minds of
the Commission: otherwise it would be natural for it to want the closest
possible liaison with the body charged with the security of Europe.

There is a potential conflict of jurisdiction. Article V of the Treaty of
Maastricht commits the EU nations to a 'common foreign and security policy'.

It provides that 'the common foreign and security policy shall include all questions relating to the security of the Union, including the central framing of a common defence policy, which might in time lead to a common defence'. This is part of the treaty, but from the British legal point of view it is only an intergovernmental agreement; it was not included as part of the 1993 Maastricht Act, and does not, therefore, form part of United Kingdom law.

The Maastricht treaty was agreed in 1992, and signed in 1993. In their Berlin meeting of June 1996, the foreign ministers of the Nato countries agreed that European security and defence should continue to be organized under Nato. The key phrase was that the Nato forces should be 'separable but not separate'. The Berlin decision is not in conflict with Article V of the Maastricht Treaty, but it must have been a setback for those who wanted to organize 'a common defence' on a separate European basis. There could not be a United States of Europe without responsibility for the defence function.

Nato is not one of the 'pillars' of the Maastricht Union, but is an independent alliance. Eleven European countries do, indeed, belong both to Nato and to the EU, but five Nato countries are outside the EU, and four EU countries are outside Nato. The five are the United States, Canada, Norway, Iceland and Turkey; the four are Ireland, Austria, Sweden and Finland. The important difference between the two memberships is the relationship with the United States. Nato is not only based on co-operation with the United States, but is dependent on American power and technology. The European Union is independent of the United States, and has some tendency to trade conflict.

Nato is much bigger than the EU because of its broader membership. Last July Nato formally invited Poland, the Czech Republic and Hungary to join; when ratification of their membership has been completed, that will give Nato a population base of more than 700 million. In defence technology Nato is by far the strongest defence system on earth; in population, it comes third to the 1.2 billion of China and the 935 million of India.

Russian attitudes to the enlargement of Nato seem to be changing. Russia would still be sensitive to the Baltic states joining Nato, because they are near home, but probably welcomes a stable western front, and is far more worried about security relations with the Islamic countries and China.

The disintegration of the Soviet Union and the end of the Cold War seemed for a time to be leaving Nato without a role; Bosnia has already shown that the organization is essential to deal with European problems. Bosnia could not be solved, or even be contained, without Nato force and the United States. Yet the proliferation threat goes much wider than that, and may well force Nato to reconsider its doctrine of operating only inside its own theatre; that doctrine has already been stretched both by Bosnia and the Gulf War.[17] The threat, exemplified by Saddam Hussein, is the proliferation of nuclear and biological weapons of mass destruction. Long-range missiles carrying these weapons mean that every security system has to be concerned with a wide periphery from which terrible attacks could be launched.

One cannot defend Europe without regard to its peripheral areas. The Russian defence relationship is now stable, from our point of view as well as theirs. The Mediterranean and the Middle East are not. Even if the Nato alliance did not include Turkey – and it does – Iraq would have the capacity to hit targets well into Nato's southern flank. Athens is not all that far from Baghdad as the missile flies. In the event of major conflict in the Middle East, Nato would almost inevitably become involved.

In 1992, it may have seemed possible that Nato, deprived of the justification of the Cold War, would simply fade away, and be replaced by the common foreign and security policy envisaged in Article V of the Maastricht Treaty. That now seems very unlikely to happen. The EU failed in Bosnia, and Nato has done well. The 1996 Berlin doctrine that European security will remain under Nato is itself a decision of historic importance, however little attention has been paid to it. Most important of all, the technology of defence has been moving Nato's way.

This is true of the proliferation threat, which requires a broad rather than a narrow security alliance. It is also true of modern defence systems. American information technology is as much the master of war communications as it is of business communications. The modern Nato doctrine is that of 'the transparent battlefield', in which communications systems give both the individual tank commander and the commander of his division a complete picture of what is happening. At present, any defence forces which lack American technology are condemned to fighting blind. The new technology allows the soldier and the general to see what is happening the other side of the hill.

Such technological development has great political importance for Europe. Both the technology of the external threat and of advance defence systems make American defence leadership unavoidable. The Americans have the technology and Europe on its own does not. There is no possibility of building a European defence industry which would provide an alternative. Yet American information technology dominates the economic as much as it dominates the world of security. In the global village, you cannot defend one hut, or trade in one shop. The same technology that has made Nato the inevitable provider of security applies in the world of trade and economics. In the next century, a little Europe will not be a valid structure for defence, for foreign affairs, or for economic affairs.

■ ■ ■

Exercises

Write short essays on the following topics

1   Discuss whether countries should always pursue self-interest in foreign policy. Is Britain's 'third way' valid?

2   Critically assess the Conservative Party's position on the EU (text 3). What does William Hague mean by 'being in Europe, not run by Europe'?

3   Analyse the political and economic considerations of the British debate on joining the euro.

4   Is there any future for the Commonwealth?

5   Should Britain cut down on its defence commitments and spend the money on domestic needs?

Explain and examine the following terms

'ethical dimension'	realpolitik	common market
free trade	federalism	referendum
neo-liberal (economics)	Cold War	(British) veto
'ever closer union'	Eurosceptic	exchange rate
inward investment	euroland	supra-national
sweatshops	tariffs	Foreign Office

Further reading

Bayliss, J. (1989) *British Defence Policy: Striking the Right Balance*, London: Macmillan.
Black, Jeremy (2000) *Modern British History since 1900*, London: Macmillan.
Bulmer, Simon *et al.* (ed.) (1992) *The United Kingdom and EC Membership Evaluated*, London: Pinter Publishers.
George, Stephen (1991) *Britain and European Integration since 1945*, Oxford: Blackwell.
Holland, Martin (1994) *European Integration: from Community to Union*, London: Pinter Publishers.
Warner, G. (1994) *British Foreign Policy since 1945*, Oxford: Blackwell.

Notes

1.   Andrew Price and David Smith (1998) 'Blair "cool" fails to catch fire in poll' London: *The Sunday Times* 12 April.
2.   Michael Evans (1998) 'Cook claims success for strategy of dialogue' London: *The Times* 22 April.

3. The Common Agricultural Policy (CAP) that attempts to regulate agriculture in the EU and to provide farmers with a reasonable income.
4. European Parliament Election results, June 1999:

> Conservative 36 seats
> Labour 29 seats
> Liberal Democrat 10 seats
> UK Independence Party 3 seats
> Green 2 seats
> Plaid Cymru (Wales) 2 seats
> Scottish National Party 2 seats
> Democratic Unionist Party (Northern Ireland) 1 seat
> Ulster Unionist Party (Northern Ireland) 1 seat
> Social Democratic and Labour Party (Northern Ireland) 1 seat

5. See note 1.
6. See note 1.
7. Philip Webster and Peter Riddell (2000) 'Cook pushes for early euro poll' London: *The Times* 30 June.
8. Peter Riddell (1999) 'Blair books his ticket to euroland' London: *The Times* 1 March.
9. See note 1.
10. Philip Webster and Peter Riddell (2000) 'Cook pushes for early euro poll' London: *The Times* 30 June.
11. Leader, (1997) 'Blair's Commonwealth' London: *The Times* 24 October.
12. The Commonwealth still continues.
13. Suspended 2000.
14. Lawrence Freedman (1998) 'Britannia returns to the waves. The Forces' future is global' London: *The Times* 7 July.
15. The army in Northern Ireland is being gradually reduced as the effect of devolution continues.
16. 1999.
17. And Kosovo, 1999.

Chapter 7

Central social institutions

This chapter examines the condition of those central social institutions that are of primary concern to people in contemporary Britain, namely the welfare state in general (including questions of poverty and inequality), social security, the National Health Service (NHS) and education.

The NHS, education and social security have been at the forefront of political and public debates in recent years. There continues to be a feeling (reflected in opinion polls) that the Labour government has not yet delivered on its 1997 election promises to reform and improve these areas (except partly in education). The government in 2000 announced substantial spending plans on education and health (among other areas) for the next ten years. But its actual structural intentions for improvement have still been criticized as insufficient and ill-defined. The government, for its part, argues that successful reform will take time.

The issue of devoting more resources and attention to public or state services has to be placed within the context of the national economy (costs) and social expectations (demand). Britain is supposed to have a market economy, in which over two-thirds of its services and production are in the private sector. Yet governments continue to spend public money on state services up to some 40 per cent of GDP. The debate centres on whether this figure can or should be reduced and still leave an adequate balance between the free market and a strong public services demand. Most of the texts in this chapter are concerned with the cost and necessity of state services, how to manage them more efficiently and how to raise the necessary funding to support them.

The welfare state is sometimes defined narrowly to include only those social security benefits and payments that are disbursed by the state to people who have earned them through lifetime contributions (eg state pensions) and to those (often non-contributors) who are in need. At other times it is defined to include all the public services that are organized by the state and that Britons expect governments to provide. The first text, which tends to see the welfare state in social security terms, illustrates the Labour government's attitudes, policies and intended reforms in these areas.

■ ■ ■

The welfare state

1 'Why Britain needs a new welfare state'
Tony Blair
(Author copyright, 15 January 1998)

Today at a meeting in the West Midlands I want to begin a national debate about how we modernize the welfare state. Not whether; but how.

£3.5 billion from the utilities
A one-off tax in 1998 on the profits of the privatized utilities, such as water and electricity, which was invested in employment programmes (the New Deal).

childcare
Funds, either from individual private sources or limited state help, to cover childcare provision while the mother is at work.

benefits
Social security benefits such as income support, which provide financial help to the needy.

income support
State funds for those in financial need. Very often elderly people do not claim their rightful benefits, either because of ignorance or because they regard such help as charity.

focus files
Information based on small sample opinions of British citizens.

benefit fraud
Estimated at £7 billion a year in 2000.

Beveridge
The Beveridge Report in 1942 made proposals for a universal and free welfare state.

My aim is to build a consensus behind the need for reform. It will mean tough decisions, like taking **£3.5 billion from the utilities** to tackle structural long-term unemployment – an indication of how serious we are.

Some say the task is too difficult, so why risk the unpopularity? I say that the human cost of the failings in the current system is too high to do nothing. Why should a mother have to stay at home when she wants to work, simply because she has no **childcare** and is trapped on **benefits**? Why should more than one million poor pensioners, entitled to **income support**, not get it? What kind of system leaves four million children living in poverty [see texts 2 and 3].

Welfare is not working. There is more poverty and social division as well as a growing cost to ordinary taxpayers. Today we are publishing a set of **focus files** that spell out the facts and underline the need for reform. The welfare state costs each family about £80 a week. We spend more on social security than we do on education, employment, health and law and order combined. We spend more on disability and incapacity benefits than we do on the entire school system in the UK. **Benefit fraud**, estimated at £4 billion a year, is enough to build 100 new hospitals.

For too many the system is simply not doing the job it was set up to do. And it's not surprising. You don't expect to buy the same model of TV or car as 50 years ago. You don't expect to take as long to fly across the world. Why should you expect a welfare state created 50 years ago to be tailored to your needs today? More women now work. Most people change jobs at least six or seven times in their career. People live longer, in some cases for 30 years after retirement. More marriages end in divorce. These are big changes in the way we live. The welfare state must adapt to them.

I want to build a new architecture for a system that, like **Beveridge**'s in 1945, successfully tackles poverty, and provides security and opportunity at points in your life when you need it most. Our changes will be based on principles, and though the system of 1945 is not working as we would like in 1997, the principles are the same. Just as new Labour in opposition was about putting traditional values in a modern setting, so is the reform of welfare in government.

First, those in genuine need will always be helped and supported by a Labour government. That is my guarantee. Second, anyone of working age who can work should work. Work, for those that can work, is in our view the best form of welfare. It provides financial independence, a network of contacts, and dignity. So those who have in the past been excluded from job opportunities, such as lone parents or the disabled, many of whom can work and want to work, will be given the chance to do so. Third, we believe in the responsibility of individuals to help provide for themselves where they can do so.

And we will build on these principles. Our welfare state will root out fraud wherever it is found. It will be based on a partnership between public and private sectors. It will be about providing services and not just cash. That is behind the New Deal **welfare to work programme**, the biggest ever attack on long term and youth unemployment. The **pilots** have begun. It will go nationwide in April [1998]. It is the key building block of our welfare reform plans for this Parliament. I am determined to make it work.

But I am beginning to see why most politicians tend to stay clear of welfare. Most of the changes are long-term. On pensions any reforms will take two Parliaments and more to come into effect. Other reforms, even if begun soon, will only yield savings in several years' time. Most politicians are fonder of measures that prove instant successes, preferably attached to votes.

I am acutely aware that this is a very sensitive area. To many people benefits are a lifeline and work is not an option. That is why any changes will be made in consultation with those who rely on benefits so that we can ensure support and protection for those most in need. I will not be put off by scare stories in the papers. The reason for going out as I am today, to talk to the people, is to make sure they see the scare stories for what they are. A government that is working on policy options combined with journalists sometimes unwilling to wait for the outcome is always going to be a recipe for wild press speculation. There is nothing I can do about that other than promise that when we put forward our plans they will be the result of serious work, consideration and consultation.

This Government will listen. But let nobody underestimate my determination to see this through. I am embarking on this programme of reform because I believe it is central to the **modernization of Britain** and the building of a decent society in which everyone has the chance to play their part, no matter what their background. If the rewards come in the next century, with the welfare state put on a sound, modern footing for future generations, then it will have been worth the controversy.

When I look at the welfare state I don't see a pathway out of poverty, a route into work or a gateway to dignity in retirement. I see a dead end for too many people. I want to clear the way to a new system. The status quo is not an option. Long-term, thought-out, principled reform is the way forward. The aim is to relieve poverty, narrow social division, extend opportunity and security and spend taxpayers' money wisely. I believe that the people I meet tonight and in the rest of the country will be able to sign up to those objectives and help us to carry them out for the benefit of Britain.

■ ■ ■

welfare to work programme
Encouraging young people to move off benefits and into training, education and jobs.

pilots
Initial schemes in selected parts of the country.

modernization of Britain
The reform of the welfare state is allied to the general modernization project of the Labour government (see texts in Chapter 2).

Social security

universal state benefits
The social security system that provides for state pensions on retirement for all and a range of cash payments for those in need. Some people will have contributed to these schemes over a lifetime of work, while others (because of individual circumstances) will have been unable to do so.

accommodation needs
Provision for care needs and housing.

state retirement pension
The state pension is the basic pension, to which employees make lifetime contributions while in work. It will be equalized at 65 for both men and women and is relatively low at some £66 per week for a single person.

means-testing
Benefits given only after an examination of a person's means or income.

child benefit
Payable to the mother for each child, tax-free.

Social security covers state financial benefits such as the basic old age pension, child benefit, income support for those in great need, a family tax credit that in effect supplements the low wages of those in work, a jobseeker's allowance for the unemployed, housing benefit to pay the rent of housing for needy people who qualify, maternity benefit, incapacity benefit and disability benefit. Social security is very complicated, hugely expensive (£100 billion a year), amounts to one-third of public spending by the government and suffers from some £7 billion worth of fraudulent claims a year.

Successive governments (Conservative and Labour) have pledged to reduce these figures and to cut the so-called 'dependency culture' in which people rely on the state to help them when in difficulty. But reform has been piecemeal and critics argue that more radical measures to cut costs substantially are needed. One side of the debate argues that the state has a duty to supply social security for its needy citizens out of taxation. The other side maintains that individuals have a responsibility to provide for themselves in as many areas as possible, unless absolutely incapable.

Public opinion is divided about the pace and nature of proposed reforms. Britons are concerned about the changes that the Labour government is trying to implement. A 1998 MORI poll[1] was undertaken after Tony Blair had begun his series of welfare speeches [see text 1], with conflicting findings. But it did indicate that, although more people now accept that they will have to take out private provision for an increasing number of needs such as pensions and health insurance, there is still strong support for **universal state benefits**.

Some 42 per cent of respondents to the poll agreed (and 46 per cent significantly disagreed) that 'people in employment should be required by law to take out insurance to provide for their **accommodation needs** in old age'. The question of old-age residential and nursing provision (and who should pay for it) is a controversial part of current social debate in Britain. The latest developments suggest that individuals (rather than the state) will have to pay more.

But 63 per cent of respondents to the poll (including higher-income voters) opposed any proposal to limit the **state retirement pension** only to those without an adequate private pension. The public was also against any **means-testing** of child or maternity benefits. Some 49 per cent agreed (46 per cent disagreeing) that **child benefit** should be universally available to all mothers irrespective of their or their family's income. Some 57 per cent believed (35 per cent disagreeing) that maternity benefit should be available to all. However, support for tax concessions for women who stay at home to look after their young children had decreased from 74 to 70 per cent since 1996, and opposition rose from 14 to 19 per cent.

The Labour government has restricted some social security benefits, such as single parents' additional allowances, increased the requirements on others, such as specifying compulsory independent medical examinations for those on disability and incapacity benefits, and tried to move people off benefits and into work. But the next text points to continuing weakness in, and concern about, social security.

2 'Darling's anniversary'
(*The Economist*, 31 July 1999) abridged

Listen to government ministers, and you might think that social security policy was designed from scratch every year. After the general election [1997], **Harriet Harman and Frank Field** were told to 'think the unthinkable' on welfare. A year later, they were replaced by Alistair Darling, who promised 'action not words'. But on Mr Darling's own anniversary in office, he is promising Labour's national policy forum 'a national debate on the future of the welfare state from first principles.'

In fact, the relaunches have been less drastic than these soundbites suggest. Many of the big decisions on welfare are now taken by Gordon Brown, the chancellor [of the Exchequer]. Behind their hands, Labour officials downplay the importance of the new national debate, which seems to have been offered largely as a sop to internal party critics. No changes are planned to Mr Darling's welfare bill, which Parliament is currently considering.

Even so, there have been some significant shifts in Labour's welfare thinking. The most significant concerns money. In opposition, Tony Blair led Labour spokesmen in promising to 'cut the bills of social and economic failure' – code for the social security budget – to finance bigger spending on health and education. In office, Labour has dropped this pledge. The government's annual report . . . says only that the rise in the social security budget is being curbed. Over the current five-year parliament, ministers crow, benefit spending will rise more slowly than under the Tories.

But even this claim is misleading. First, the government's spending figures are dodgy. It counts the new **Working Families Tax Credit** (WFTC), a low-wage benefit, as a tax cut. Adding back the WFTC to the social security budget would pile another £5 billion onto welfare bills. Nor is this all. The annual report boasts that the government's New Deal – a **workfare** scheme – has taken on 284,000 young people. The New Deal offers youngsters training,

Darling
Labour government Secretary of State for Social Security.

Harriet Harman and Frank Field
Former Social Security ministers.

Working Families Tax Credit
Families with children and in work obtain in effect extra cash through taxation to increase their low wages.

workfare
Welfare-to-work.

employer of the last resort
That is, the state itself creating jobs (rather than the market) and subsidizing them.

make-work schemes or subsidised jobs. Getting New Dealers off welfare cuts benefit bills; but lopsidedly, the New Deal's £5 billion cost will not show up on the social security budget.

The government's choice of dates is even more dubious than its accounting. Taking over social security is like becoming captain of a super-tanker in mid-ocean – it takes a long time to make much difference. So the first year of this parliament, when real social-security spending actually fell, was the result of measures taken in the last years of the previous Tory government. But from now until the end of the parliament, as the Labour government's measures take effect, social security spending (including WFTC) is set to grow faster than the economy.

In part, these figures reflect the government's lack of stomach for a fight. The government suffered its two biggest backbench rebellions of this parliament over plans to make quite modest savings in benefits for lone parents and disabled people.

But the figures also reflect changes in philosophy. The Tory government's welfare reforms aimed to target benefits to people according to their circumstances. Incapacity benefits, for example, were restricted to those really incapable of work. The present government, by contrast, prefers to target benefits based on people's incomes. So far, there has been little reform of the structure of benefits, but bigger means-tested handouts to poorer pensioners and disabled people.

The other difference concerns the attitude to work. Under the Tories, only people available for work, and actively seeking it, could claim unemployment benefits. But the Tories avoided forcing people to work because it meant making the state the **employer of last resort**. The present government has no such qualms. Youngsters either join the New Deal or lose benefit. Figures released by the government on July 29th [1999] showed that 69,000 New Dealers had found lasting unsubsidised jobs by the end of May. How many would have found jobs without the help of the New Deal is, and will remain, anybody's guess.

■ ■ ■

Poverty

The existence of poverty and inequality in Britain is a contentious matter, since definitions of what constitutes poverty vary widely. It is also tied into the workings of the social security and taxation systems.

According to a Labour government report (*Opportunity for All, Tackling Poverty and Social Exclusion*)[2] in 1999, poverty indicators have increased since 1979. A quarter of the population now live in households with incomes below the poverty line of £132 a week (usually defined as half the national average income). A third of all children, or 4.5 million, live in poverty and one-fifth of them live in households with no working adult. Over half the 5.6 million people claiming income support, jobseeker's allowance and incapacity benefit are on long-term benefits.

According to the report, the gap between rich and poor in Britain has increased since the late 1970s and is worse than in other developed countries, such as France, Germany and Italy. A decline in male employment rates (despite a total growth of jobs in the national economy) and an increase in lone-parent households have increased the number of households where no one person is in work. The proportion of families with lone parents and dependent children increased to 21 per cent in 1996 and lone parents are often unemployed and on benefits or else on low incomes. Britain's rate of teenage (under 18) pregnancy is 46.5 per 1,000 girls and frequently contributes to poverty and social exclusion. Many children leave school without basic skills and qualifications and are thus unable to get on to the employment ladder, which demands an information and skill base.

Poverty in Britain is considerable according to a United Nations report in 2000,[3] which ranked the country as 16th out of 18 industrialized nations. Determining factors were low incomes, short life expectancy, long-term unemployment and illiteracy. But the report found that the number of people living in poverty had actually fallen from 13.5 per cent to 10.6 per cent, and long-term unemployment had decreased from 3.3 per cent to 2.1 per cent. But inequality in Britain is one of the highest among industrialized countries, with 20 per cent of the population owning 43 per cent of the nation's wealth and the poorest 20 per cent having 6.6 per cent.

The Labour government argues that poverty and inequality cannot be solved merely by spending more money on them. Combined action is needed across all government departments since the problems allegedly stem from a mixture of poor housing, poor health, poor education, lack of childhood opportunity, unemployment and social exclusion.

Some commentators argue that the Labour government's current reforms of social security and allowances/credits within the tax system are in fact making a significant inroad into the poverty figures.[4] But others maintain that of the poorest tenth of the population, some 28 per cent continue to lose out.[5] The statistics for and evaluation of poverty in Britain have been challenged as the next text illustrates.

3 'Labour's crusade'
(*The Economist*, 25 September 1999) abridged

[The government's report on poverty – see above] sets out what the government thinks needs to be done, and what its approach will be. There are, in fact, no new policies in the document: the 'key initiatives' listed in it (all 49 of them) have been announced before. What is new is that Mr Darling [Social Security Secretary] has set out 40 indicators of poverty against which the government says it will measure its progress.

The sheer number of indicators demonstrates the difficulty of answering an apparently simple question: how many Britons live in poverty? Researchers have used a host of definitions. The most cited, by both academics and politicians, is the number of people living on less than half average income. This yields figures that are alarming to some and incredible to others. On this measure, almost one quarter of Britons were poor in 1995–96, the latest period for which data are available. No fewer than 4.6 million children, or 34 per cent of the total, lived below the poverty line. And far more Britons are poor, on this definition, than in 1979 . . .

Ministers are fond of this measure. Mr Darling said yet again this week that one child in three was living in poverty . . .

Nonetheless, many Britons find it hard to believe that so many people are truly poor, and that poverty has increased so dramatically. Even some eminent New Labour academics think the notion that one in four Britons is living in poverty is so counter-intuitive that it discredits the very notion of poverty. The doubters have a point. The definition measures inequality, which has certainly increased, rather than poverty. If someone on above average income gets more money, pushing the average up, 'poverty' rises even if the real incomes of the poor are unchanged. This, in essence, was what happened in the economic boom of the late 1980s, when most of the rise in relative poverty under the Conservatives took place. Similarly, if a rich person loses some income, 'poverty' falls.

An alternative is to try and fix a poverty line which does not change as economies get richer – enough to meet a generally acceptable definition of basic necessities, say. However, the only survey to measure poverty in this way has not been updated since 1990. But it is possible to look at the real (inflation-adjusted) incomes of the bottom 10 per cent of the population in 1979 and now.

These figures paint a less dramatic picture. Still, they scarcely justify complacency. The incomes of the poorest 10 per cent of the population in 1995–96 were slightly lower, after housing costs, than those of their counterparts in 1979; their income before housing costs rose a bit. 'During the 1980s, despite a 40 per cent overall increase in living standards, the absolute standards [of poverty] didn't fall,' asserts John Hills, director of the Centre for Analysis of Social Exclusion at the London School of Economics (LSE) . . .

In its report, the government promises to be assessed on both relative and absolute measures. Its own rhetoric and the practice of the anti-poverty campaigners mean that the more demanding relative measures are likely to be given more prominence. However, the government's 40 indicators include much more than just income levels. Ministers expect to be judged on, among other things, the length of time that households spend on low incomes, the proportion of children living in poor housing, educational standards, babies' birth weights, the numbers sleeping rough and suicide rates.

This splurge of measures reflects two things. The first is that it is impossible to find a single measure of poverty. It has many facets, and so it makes sense to collect plenty of information, most of which will be relevant most of the time. 'The search for the definition of poverty is missing the point,' says Andrew Dilnot, director of the Institute for Fiscal Studies, a research body. 'Just as a rough index of price changes isn't going to tell you everything about inflation, a single measure isn't going to tell you everything about poverty.'

Second, the government is concerned as much with the future levels of poverty as with current ones. So although it is redistributing money from rich to poor, through measures such as the Working Families Tax Credit (WFTC) . . . and some increases in pensioners' benefits, it is setting more store by policies which, it thinks, will have long-term effects. In particular, it emphasises the importance of work as a route out of poverty, both for parents on low incomes and for their children once they leave school . . .

■ ■ ■

The National Health Service (NHS)

The NHS, funded mainly by taxation, has historically provided a largely free health service at primary (local doctors) and hospital levels for the British population. Yet its services and funding have been heavily criticized in recent years and people are very concerned about the present state of the NHS.

The Labour government has outlined its aims for the NHS in 1997,[6] 1999[7] and in a Ten-Year Plan in 2000. It initially blamed the previous Conservative government for a legacy of record hospital waiting lists, financial deficits and structural inadequacies. It argues for modernization of the NHS without increases in taxation, charges for medical services or rationing of care. It maintains that the NHS is a resilient organization that can cope with new diseases, increased numbers of operations, the introduction of expensive medicine and the needs of an elderly population. It believes that technological advances will allow cheaper treatments; more day surgery could reduce expensive in-patient care; and further improvement can result from better public health and the tackling of social inequalities.

Britain spends 5–6 per cent of GDP on the NHS. But increasing demand requires further resources. The Labour government says it will raise spending in real terms every year without raising taxes, up to the European GDP average.

However, the government stresses that the NHS needs to spend its funds more effectively and efficiently in order to provide a fair, modern and dependable service. It aims to reduce expensive bureaucracy and management weaknesses within the NHS for investment in frontline or primary patient care. It wants doctors and nurses to work with their local health authorities on controlling resources so that NHS money is spent on effective and cost-efficient treatments. It plans to introduce ways of raising standards and spreading best practice for care and treatment, so that wide regional variations in the cost of medicine, appropriate treatments, operations and screenings for diseases would be eliminated. It intends to provide clearer statements of how services should be delivered and more rigorous assessment of clinical and cost-effective treatments. The government's aim is to improve the relative healthcare position of Britain globally.

But the latest World Health Organization figures in 2000 placed Britain in 18th place worldwide for the efficiency of its healthcare based on the money spent on it and in 9th place for its quality.[8] Critics argue that a close reading of these complicated statistics shows that Britain has a third-rate health service that is failing in its purpose.[9] The public are also not apparently convinced by government arguments and see little substantial improvement since 1997.

The next text looks at the NHS 50 years after its creation and addresses the possible ways in which it might be better funded and organized in order to satisfy demand.

4 'The Health Service at 50'
(*The Economist*, 4 July 1998) abridged

Depending on how you examine it, the National Health Service appears to be either in fine form for its age – lean, fit and adaptable – or chronically malnourished, in poor physical shape and verging on senility.

On the one hand, the NHS seems remarkably cost-effective compared with America's obese health-care system: by the rough-and-ready measures of average life expectancy and infant mortality, the health of the two countries' populations is much the same, even though America spends twice as much of its national income on health than Britain does. Dollar for dollar, America spends three times as much on each person as Britain. In general, it is hard to discern any link between a country's health spending and how long its people survive.

On the other hand, the NHS does have some worrying symptoms: a queue of almost 1.5m patients waiting for hospital treatment; old and often shabby buildings; and a lack of assessment and accountability among doctors that can lead to spectacular failures . . .

Those who are concerned for the future health of the middle-aged NHS fear that, as a service almost entirely funded from taxes, it will be especially difficult for it to cope with the ever-rising expectations of the public at a time when the population is ageing (and therefore more likely to need medical care) and when expensive new treatments are appearing by the day. Under its current funding arrangements, extra cash to meet such growing needs must be found through higher taxes or big spending cuts elsewhere – and these have proved extremely difficult for politicians to sell to the voters, for all their professed enthusiasm for a better-funded NHS.

Despite all this, the NHS's 50th birthday should be a cause for celebration, not gloom. No longer does one child in 15 die before the age of 11, as was the case before the health service was invented. A boy born today in an NHS hospital is expected, on average, to live for 75 years, compared with just 66 years in 1948. And, whereas poor people once feared the knock of the 'doctor's man' (ie, his **debt collector**) at their doors, they can now call on the services of a doctor, round the clock, without ever thinking of the cost.

debt collector
Payment had to be made for doctors' services.

Until the late 1960s, there was only one NHS. Since then, many other rich countries have moved towards a similar system, offering universal access to health care and funded largely through taxes. Though still young, these children of the NHS can teach it a thing or two . . .

Medical myths

In its early years, the NHS greatly overshot its budget. Spending hit £276m in its first nine months, compared with the expected £198m . . . Throughout its fifty years, the queue for hospital treatment has got steadily longer, despite the ever larger sums of money the NHS has swallowed up. This week, in a fresh attempt to turn the tide of history and bring waiting lists down, the government gave strong hints that it was preparing to give a big boost to the NHS's annual budget, currently £44 billion ($73 billion).

This idea, that demand for health care is finite, and that some sum of money would therefore clear the NHS's backlog, is one of the central myths on which the service was built. Another is that its creation separated medicine from money, allowing doctors to offer treatments based entirely on their judgement of the patient's need, not their cost. In fact, the lack of medical knowledge of most patients has, throughout the NHS's history, made it easy for doctors to clothe essentially financial decisions in clinical justifications.

A third myth is that the NHS can offer equal service to all, regardless of who or where they happen to be. In fact it was founded with most of its best facilities close to richer people who, being healthier, needed them less. It was not until the 1960s that ministers realised they ought to be distributing health funding to different parts of the country according to medical priorities rather than historical precedent. It took until the mid-1970s to come up with a formula, and until the late 1980s to phase in the funding changes resulting from this formula. Even now, great variations persist from one district to the next in whether treatments, from new cancer drugs to fertility treatments, are available on the NHS, and after how long a wait.

Perhaps the most important lesson from successive governments' struggles to make the NHS live up to these myths is that the 'backlog' model of demand for health care must be wrong. The NHS has used its extra cash over the years to treat ever more patients, but the queue at the door persists. And evidence from abroad suggests that, if there ever is a limit to be reached to demand for treatments, it is still some way off. Other rich countries manage to spend an even higher share of their national income on health than Britain and yet there are no signs that the demand for health care in these countries is sated.

Take Australia, for example, which created an NHS-style health service in 1984. Even though the country spends 8.3 per cent of its national income on health – rather more than does Britain – it still has a hospital waiting list of 100,000.

If demand for treatment is, apparently, endless and therefore fails to reveal what is the 'right' amount to spend on health, what about the outcomes of treatment? Does America's vastly expensive health system, for example, actually make the American people healthier than the British? Life-expectancy rates and similar broad measures suggest not, though it is extremely hard to separate the effects of either country's health system from the effects of different diet, lifestyles, the quality of housing and other such factors.

More specific evidence suggests that Americans are at least getting something for all the extra money they spend. Survival rates for cancer patients and for those treated in intensive-care units seem to be higher than in Britain. And Americans with kidney failure are more likely than Britons to get dialysis treatment, which both prolongs and improves the quality of their lives. Another piece of evidence suggesting that extra health spending achieves something comes from surveys of public satisfaction with their country's health service. A 1996 study of public opinion across the European Union found that the more of its income that a country spends per person on health, the more content they are about the health service.

Won't pay, must pay

Though survey evidence shows that the British are less satisfied with their health service than other nations are with theirs, and want more money spent on it, come election time they vote with their wallets and choose governments that promise not to put taxes up. One way around this might be to separate and label (or 'hypothecate') a proportion of income tax as a special tax devoted to the NHS. The public might then be prepared to see this tax rising, because it would know that its extra contributions were heading in the direction it wanted them to, and not to other, less popular areas of state spending.

The other obvious solution to the conundrum of public demand for more spending but opposition to greater taxation lies in the fact that much of the extra slice of national income that other rich countries spend on health comes not from taxes but from private contributions. One way of boosting such private spending on health would be to get more people to take out private insurance. It is widely assumed that this is already happening, as dissatisfaction with the NHS drives more people to the private sector. In fact only 10 per cent of the population have private medical insurance, a proportion which has hardly changed since the mid-1980s.

Perhaps, then, a more promising way of increasing the level of spending on health without raising taxes is to introduce more charges for NHS treatment. At its inauguration in 1948 the NHS levied virtually no charges on its patients – who could request limitless quantities of medicine and bandages. Within three years, huge cost over-runs had forced a rethink. Now, patients (other than those judged most needy) have to pay a small share of the cost of prescriptions and a rather larger share of dental treatment. Overall, though, such charges raise only about 2 per cent of the NHS's budget.

In many other countries, such direct contributions by the public to the national health system account for a larger share of total health spending. This is even true in egalitarian Sweden, where in addition to paying for the health service through their taxes, people pay small fees to see a doctor or nurse, and small daily charges for hospital stays. Altogether, such charges raise about 10 per cent of the Swedish NHS's budget.

In a new book[10] on the options for financing the NHS, John Willman weighs up the evidence for and against direct charges, and finds on balance that they could provide a significant source of new money, without undermining its core objective of offering equal access to health care. A package of fees, he suggests, such as £10 to see a doctor and £50 a day for hospital stays, could raise £5 billion a year, raising the share of NHS spending from charges approximately to Swedish levels.

Of course there are arguments against such fees. Unless they are carefully designed, with exemptions for the poorest, they may discourage those most in need of medical help from seeking it. But such worries may be overdone. Mr Willman quotes the results of a study in America – the only known scientific experiment to measure the impact of charges on patients' health. Patients were offered a range of health plans in which the charges varied from zero to 95 per cent of the full cost, subject to an annual limit. The study found that while those charged most tended to make less frequent demands for treatment, it did not seem to affect their health. The only exception was for poor people with chronic ailments, who could be exempted from such charges.

Furthermore, despite Sweden's system of charges, studies have shown that health inequalities between rich and poor are smaller there than in Britain. Closer to home, despite the imposition of dental charges in Britain since the 1950s, there has been a steady rise in the proportion of people with a healthy set of teeth. And the introduction of charges for eye tests in 1989 led to only a temporary drop in the number of tests taken, which is now higher than before the charges were levied.

But, even if such money is found through charges, the lesson of history is that demand for health care will never be entirely satisfied. Some form of rationing will still be needed, and it would be better if this were an open form of rationing in which clear priorities were set. New Zealand has recently moved towards such a system: patients get points for such things as their operation's chance of success, the number of dependants affected by the patient's illness, and the time they have already waited. Those with the most points are operated on first. While it is not without its critics (as is inevitable – there will always be a debate on exactly what the priorities should be), at least such a system means that the most urgent cases should get treated first. Under the present British system, hospitals are set targets for the length of wait regardless of the urgency of treatment.

Imposing such a priorities system across the whole of the NHS would also highlight, and thereby create pressure to reduce, the great disparities in the availability of treatment from one area to another. If so, at least one of the NHS's founding myths – equal access for all – might come a little closer to reality.

In all, there are grounds for optimism that the NHS can adapt itself to a less egalitarian and more consumerist society than the one it was born into in 1948. And that there are ways of raising more money to pay for it, given that this is what people seem to want and that there is evidence that the money will do at least some good. The talk of a crisis in the NHS, which seems to have been a constant feature of its first 50 years, will no doubt continue. But, most likely, it will struggle through, as ever.

■ ■ ■

Medical professionals (nurses and doctors) have responded critically to the state of the NHS and government policies,[11] particularly at a time when increased violence and abuse is being directed at them in their work.

Although nurses are held in high public esteem, many of them feel that they are underpaid, over-worked, under pressure, unappreciated and undervalued. They leave the NHS because of staff shortages and because they feel that they cannot do a professional job. The Royal College of Nursing argues that nurses, patients, management and government must understand the need for a mixture of nursing skills and the central role of nurses in healthcare. It maintains that safe staffing levels, extra nurses and performance indicators improve the quality of patient care and reduce death rates.

Higher salaries for some grades of nurses, which the Labour government have implemented and which have resulted in increased recruitment, are an improvement and an important factor in halting declining standards. But nurses feel that, while salaries are important, the real healthcare challenge is in realizing the actual value of nursing.

Commentators also argue that nurses should be able to take over some of the clinical jobs done exclusively by doctors. They maintain that the strict division of labour between doctors and nurses should be eliminated, that doctors should be made more accountable for their actions and that the 'consultant culture', whereby specialist doctors have an all-powerful role, should be reduced. Recent medical scandals involving doctors, consultants and surgeons have led to a demand that the self-regulating doctors' profession should be independently controlled. But doctors also see themselves as under pressure in the NHS, as the next text demonstrates.

5 'Blair is driving us out of the NHS, says doctors' chief'
Jenny Hope
(*Daily Mail*, 6 July 1999) abridged

The leader of Britain's doctors yesterday launched an astonishing attack on Tony Blair, accusing him of alienating the entire medical profession.

Dr Ian Bogle claimed the Government had deliberately attempted to undervalue and undermine doctors.

He blamed Labour's spin-doctors for working against the medical profession through leaks and off-the-record briefings to turn the public against them.

The extraordinary outburst comes as Britain's hospitals face accusations of providing a service which is sometimes no better than in the third world.

Dr Bogle, head of the British Medical Association's [BMA's] council, said the profession was being ignored and denigrated at a time when patients are being put at risk by the 'frightening pace' of NHS reforms and the Government's obsession with waiting list targets.

He told the BMA's annual conference in Belfast that doctors were being forced to quit the NHS by the intolerable pressures of excessive bureaucracy, stress and uncertainty caused by 'one organizational upheaval after another'.

'Doctors are working at a pace which is, at times, contrary to safe medical practice,' he said. 'They are demoralised and driven out of the NHS by the workload and its intensity.

'Congratulations, Mr Blair. You have managed to alienate the whole profession.

'For too long, Governments have exploited our dedication and our goodwill to keep a sinking service afloat. Sooner or later, the well will run dry.' ...

It was the strongest, most direct attack on Government policy for many years from the BMA which initially welcomed the new Labour administration ...

'I believe there is a drive to undervalue what we do and undermine the public's confidence in us,' [Dr Bogle] said.

'The adverse publicity the profession is receiving – some of it whipped up by Government spin-doctors – is confusing patients into believing poor practice is far more common than it actually is.

'The vast majority of doctors practising in this country deliver high quality care, often under exceedingly difficult circumstances.' ...

A spokesman for the Department of Health said: 'Everything we have proposed has been introduced in consultation with the BMA.'

Representatives overwhelmingly rejected calls for the introduction of fees such as a £10 charge to see a GP to bring in new money into the NHS.

■ ■ ■

The contemporary NHS and the Labour government's attempts to revitalize it have been subjected to a good deal of scrutiny and criticism by the media, as the next text illustrates.

6 'An unhealthy state'

(*The Sunday Times*, leader, 11 July 1999) abridged

Labour paraded its devotion to the National Health Service during the general election [1997] in a way its pioneers would have admired. Tony Blair knew it was a vote winner and committed himself wholeheartedly to its historic principle of universal health care. He pledged to save and modernise the NHS by pruning its costly bureaucracy and spending money where it was most needed – in frontline care. Access to healthcare would depend on need alone, said the party's manifesto, 'not on your ability to pay, or who your GP [General Practitioner or non-specialist doctor] happens to be or where you live'. Two years later, the facts show otherwise. Labour, like the Tories in power before them, is on the rack over the NHS. It is failing to meet the expectations it aroused. Its failure to bridge the gap between limitless demand and finite resources has forced it to take refuge in the rhetoric of frustration, the politics of denial and crisis management.

Mr Blair's attack on the public sector last week derived from his irritation with its failure to meet his expectations. The feeling is mutual. He accuses NHS hospitals of failing to take proper care and maintain their facilities. The British Medical Association accuses him of alienating the entire medical profession. The prime minister's subsequent praise for the public services has been forced out of him by the uproar caused by his original assault on their obstructiveness and resistance to change. Labour's honeymoon with the public sector unions and professions is over. The battle lines are much the same as they were when the Tories struggled against public dissatisfaction with basic public services. In health, as in education and transport, Labour promised much but is finding it hard to deliver.

For many people with a life-threatening illness, the widely held view that the NHS offers a world-class service is tragically untrue. For those whose condition requires surgery, the shock of discovery is acutely distressing. International comparisons show the discrepancies clearly. British sufferers from breast and colon cancer have a lower chance of survival than in most of western Europe. Anyone with heart, respiratory or kidney disease is also at a disadvantage in Britain. Patients generally can wait up to nine months for an outpatient appointment with a consultant. True, waiting lists for hospital admission have fallen to 1.1m. But these people are comparatively lucky; another 456,000 have still to see a consultant before their name goes on a waiting list for a hospital bed. That is 200,000 more than at the general election. For them, Mr Blair's trumpeting of the government's record has a hollow ring.

Downing Street's response to this first outbreak of deep discontent over its performance has been to say: 'We're working on it, give us time.' But that is what thousands of sufferers do not have. They will want to know why a 58-year-old German can be diagnosed for lung cancer and operated on in 76 hours and why someone needing a heart bypass in Spain can have one within 93 days on average – yet Britain lags far behind. Why does Britain have only 83 renal units when Italy has 654? . . . Pilot walk-in centres for minor ailments are fine: receiving telephone advice from NHS Direct is a good idea. But Mr Blair's celebration of the birth of the NHS 51 years ago last week was lost in the uproar created by the BMA's declaration of war and **John Prescott**'s rebellious defence of the public sector ... For the sake of the NHS ... the health secretary ... should stop playing party politics and come clean with the public.

First, ministers should admit what we all know – that rationing exists in the NHS. How could it be otherwise? Britain is so far behind in the international stakes, and its health needs are so great, that even the extra £21 billion the government has allocated to health over the next three years will not solve its basic problems ... [W]e should begin an urgent national debate about our health priorities and be prepared to think the previously unthinkable about how we are going to make ends meet.

Britain's population profile is changing fast. Medical technology and new drugs are enabling us to live longer. Yet we are three times more prosperous than we were when the NHS was founded. So where do we draw the line at citizen's rights to a free, tax-funded health service? Do we muddle on, watching an institution that was a world-beater half a century ago coming apart at the seams? Or do we face up to the challenge of adapting it to fit the needs of a society almost totally unlike the one it was originally founded to serve?

[There is a] need for radical change. [The] priority of improving the health of 'the least healthy' was calculated to go down well in Labour heartlands. [Such] policies will play less well in the middle England Mr Blair cultivates. The NHS needs to be put on a new footing, not used as a political plaything. The next stage of development needs the support of the middle classes, [who take up a] disproportionate [share] of free health services ...

Some health experts would like people who can afford it to pay for their NHS care through a private insurance system; others advocate an annual charge for basic NHS services, covering prescriptions, visits to the GP and non-emergency hospital treatment. Either of these developments would enhance patient power. The problem with health insurance schemes is their tendency to exclude high-risk applicants. But private insurance is growing and there is no good reason why the NHS should not cooperate with the private sector. The government does so in financing new hospitals; it should do so on a much bigger scale.

Charges look a better option of funding the NHS without raising taxation. As a new Social Market Foundation paper says, a 'season ticket' of, say, £150 for an individual – £3 a week – or £400 for a family, could provide GPs with most of their income. No inviolable principle is at stake; the NHS has imposed charges for prescriptions, spectacles and dental treatment for 47 years. With or without charges, **GPs' individual fundholding** should be restored. It was working well and has been foolishly undermined. Hospitals should be spared

John Prescott
Labour deputy Prime Minister.

GPs' individual fundholding
Doctors (GPs) had their own individual budget that they could direct to specific patient care and medicine.

Hackney LEA
Hackney Local
Education Authority,
east London.

Ofsted
Independent Office for
Standards in Education
that inspects schools
and their performance.

GCSE
National examination
(General Certificate of
Secondary Education)
taken by pupils at
15–16, outside
Scotland.

further organizational turmoil, but the present lottery in treatment must be ended. This requires a negotiated peace between ministers and the professions. Nobody benefits from an NHS in strife. There is an enormous task ahead. The NHS has much to be proud of, but it is overburdened and plagued by party politics. It deserves better; so do we.

■ ■ ■

Education

The debate on state school education in Britain has been, and continues to be, heated. There are widespread concerns about standards and the kind of pupils that the system is producing. The Labour government says it is committed to reform and improvement, is taking action to turn around underperforming and failing schools, and is dealing with incompetent teachers, as the next text illustrates.

7 'Why schools must do better'
Tony Blair
(Author copyright, 7 July 1997)

Three years ago, in my first week as Leader of the Opposition, my first press conference was about education. I said then that education was central to my ambitions for Britain, and I vowed that quality of teaching and learning would be at the heart of Labour's agenda for government.

Since I stood on the steps of 10 Downing Street [London] on May 2 [1997] and said 'it is time now to do', the Government has placed education first. Improvement teams are going into failing schools. **Hackney LEA** has been opened up to **Ofsted**, the schools inspectorate. And last week in the Budget, we announced major new funding of £1.3 billion for capital investment as well as £1 billion of revenue spending. Today we take a major step towards the other side of the bargain – reforming our school system so every penny is well used.

There are many good schools in Britain, but not enough; many good teachers, but not enough; many well-educated children, but not enough.

After primary school, more than 40 per cent of children have not reached the expected standard in English and Maths. At **GCSE**, two-thirds of 16-year-olds do not achieve a grade C in Maths or English. Ofsted estimates that 2 to 3 per cent of schools are failing, one in ten has a serious weakness, and a further third are not as good as they should be.

Today's White Paper, 'Excellence in Schools', is founded on six principles. The first is to put education at the heart of government. I have said that my three priorities for government are education, education and education. I mean it. Unless we get our education system right, our children will not be prosperous and our country will not be just. Just as during the 1980s a spirit of enterprise was needed for the economy to become more competitive, so now an improvement in educational standards is a prerequisite for Britain's success as we prepare to enter the new millennium.

This is why education throughout life is central to our economic and social policy. Skills are the key to our ambitious Welfare to Work programme for the young and long-term unemployed, designed to reduce the bills and misery of mass unemployment. Meanwhile, the University for Industry will create new opportunities for people in work.

Secondly, we will design our system to benefit the many, not the few. That is the justification for modernising the **comprehensive principle** to take account of children's different abilities without returning to the failed **11-plus**, which meant that 80 per cent of our children were consigned to **secondary moderns**. Children do have different talents and different abilities and we should recognise them, stretching children to progress as far and as fast as they can. We thereby favour **setting**, rather than mixed-ability teaching, in comprehensive schools, with accelerated learning for the most able. And we support, too, the development of specialist schools – focusing on languages, technology, sports or arts – helping children with interest and talent, but also acting as a resource for all pupils in an area.

Thirdly, we say that standards matter more than structures. The last government tried to use structural reforms to raise standards. They failed because what counts is what goes on in the classroom – above all the skill of the teacher, the way they teach and how they are supported.

For example, there is a proven best practice for the teaching of literacy and numeracy, based on the use of phonics to teach children words and whole-class teaching for Maths. To meet our targets of 80 per cent of 11-year-olds reaching the expected standards in English, and 75 per cent in Maths, a national programme will direct the training of existing teachers and the spreading of best practice. Our literacy and numeracy initiatives will have first call on resources.

comprehensive principle
All children educated in the same local schools, irrespective of ability, class or background.

11-plus
Former examination taken at the age of 11 that divided children into those who passed and went to academic grammar schools and the majority who failed and went to secondary modern schools.

secondary moderns
The alternative school for those children who failed their 11-plus. Regarded as academically and socially inferior to grammar schools.

setting
Children placed in classes according to their ability, earlier known as 'streaming'.

revised code
Sacking incompetent
teachers.

LEA
Local Education
Authority.

lottery money
The National Lottery.

Similarly, we know that a head teacher is the key to a successful school. So we will ensure that every new head displays the necessary skills and is qualified to be a head teacher, and we will set up new fast-track procedures to identify heads of the future.

Fourthly, intervention should be directed at what is wrong, not what is working well. Where there is success, let us celebrate it. Where teachers are excelling, let us give them scope for promotion without leaving the classroom. Schools achieving good results, and improving, will be left to get on with their work.

Government, local and national, should focus on the problems. That requires regular external inspection, to which we are firmly committed, with rigorous systems for improvement within schools. Inspection will take place at least once every six years, but more often for schools shown to be underperforming. Every school will have clear targets based on information about the progress of similar schools, national targets and recent inspection evidence. Where there are problems, action will be fast and focused.

Fifthly, there will be zero tolerance of failure. Children have only one chance. That is why we are seeking to draw up a **revised code** to ensure that poor teachers are dealt with more quickly. It is why we will establish Education Action Zones to encourage local initiative where traditional structures have not delivered. It is why we will order a 'fresh start' – closure or the reopening of the school under new management – where schools have been unable to improve.

Zero tolerance of failure applies to local education authorities, too. Their role is to support, not to control. Every **LEA** will produce an Education Development Plan, detailing its contribution to raising standards, and agreed with central government. Then, all LEAs will be inspected by Ofsted. Where failure is deep-seated, the relevant powers of the local authority will be suspended and improvement teams sent in.

Sixthly, we are committed to work in partnership with all those able to help us to raise standards. Government can lead, but there is a shared responsibility on teachers, parents, governors, LEAs, churches and businesses to help us to deliver. Home–school contracts between schools and parents will detail the responsibilities of each. We will use **lottery money** to support after-school clubs. And we will develop the use of information technology through a public–private partnership to create a new National Grid for Learning.

I see the Government's education crusade as something in which we all have a stake, and in which we all have a part to play. Get it right, and our children will learn more and earn more. The world of learning is the passport to fulfilment in the 21st century, and all our children must have that passport.

■ ■ ■

The following text addresses the Labour government's policies to deal with those schools that are adjudged to be failing or under-performing.

8 *'Time's up for schools that fail'*
David Blunkett (Secretary of State for Education and Employment)
(Author copyright, 20 May 1997) abridged

The [Labour] Government was elected on a manifesto with education at its heart. The Prime Minister has repeatedly made it clear that our priorities are 'education, education and education'. Having been given this important brief, my priorities are standards, standards and standards. The aim is to infuse everyone connected with education – teachers, parents, governors and business people – with ambition and purpose. We want schools that match the best in the world. This is the background to my announcement today about failing schools.

We shall always draw attention to the many successes of good schools. We shall search for best practices, celebrate them and seek to spread them across the country. But we absolutely will not tolerate underperformance. This may sound harsh, but if we are genuinely committed to success for every child – and each gets only one chance – then nothing less will do.

Our inheritance from the Conservatives includes almost 300 schools which have been inspected and found to be failing. Of these, the vast majority are improving, some steadily and some at an impressive rate. Those involved at every level deserve congratulations for this achievement. A hard core have been closed, enabling their pupils to transfer to more successful neighbouring schools.

But there are about 15 where progress is limited 18 months and even two years after an inspection, and where the evidence suggests that more might have been done by the school and the local authority to ensure that the pupils receive the education they deserve. The last Government was prepared to let things drift in this way. We are not.

window-dressing
Elaborate furnishing or
decoration that
disguises a lack of
substance.

From today, the Government will be calling in the local authorities and schools concerned to meet the Minister of School Standards . . . We have targeted the local education authorities and schools without political favour. Our concern is for the pupils, regardless of which party controls the local authority in which they live.

We recognize that by doing so we risk provoking controversy, but we have no intention of getting bogged down in sectional conflict with local government or anyone else. Yesterday *The Times* published its list of 38 long-term failing schools. Today we defend those which are making the necessary effort, but we shall be intervening in the other cases.

At the meeting, [we] will want to hear from the local authorities and schools concerned what they have been doing to put things right and what they plan to do next. No one pretends that it is easy to turn around a long-standing failure, but it is right to expect that everything that can be done is at least tried.

There is now extensive knowledge of what works in such cases. Many successful turnarounds have involved a change of head. Where a new head with high expectations and determined and astute management skills is appointed, success usually follows. Finding a suitable candidate for some of the failing schools has proved difficult. This is what prompted Tony Blair's suggestion in a speech last December that it might sometimes make sense to allow the head of an already successful school to take over a failing one . . .

Success has often involved dealing firmly with a small number of incompetent teachers. The Government is committed to streamlining the procedures for doing so. In the meantime, what matters is that heads and governors have the will, and that education authorities provide the back-up to ensure speedy progress.

Above all, progress has been associated with the development in each case of a clear action plan, which sets targets and is then monitored. This plan must focus on bringing change in the classroom and must deal with more than just **window-dressing**. The clearer the plan is in the first place, the more likely it is that success will follow.

The Government will want to hear from those involved in reviving schools how far they have sought and followed advice based on this good practice. We shall urge that where progress is inadequate, the idea of a 'fresh start' – closing a school and reopening it with new leadership and a new mission – is considered. This has worked well in a number of instances.

No blueprint can be imposed in every school, but we should expect to see improvement quickly. What matters is that in each case no stone is left unturned in the search for improvement. Our starting point is that responsibility for improvement lies firmly with the school and the education authority concerned. We commend the efforts that many are making. If we find either schools or authorities dragging their feet, we will as a last resort use our powers to send in an improvement team to take over.

It may be said that concentrating so much attention on a handful of schools is not the main issue. I disagree. Of course the main thrust ... will be the improvement of all the nation's 25,000 schools, but it is vital to establish at the outset that this Government means what it says about standards. The central message of today's announcement is that every child matters and that we want to work with teachers and parents to give every one of them a good start in life.

■ ■ ■

The Labour party said in 1997 that it would spend more money on schools, reduce class sizes to 30 or under for all five- to seven-year olds, and raise standards. The government has achieved significant reductions in primary school class size. But secondary school levels still remain high with a quarter of classes now having 31 or more pupils.

Standards, when judged by national examination results, seem to have risen. These are reflected in league tables, which publicize the examination performances of all schools. But primary school children are still failing to meet targets in writing skills; many children leave school with no or inadequate qualifications; functional illiteracy (22 per cent of the population) and innumeracy continue to be of concern; and there are weaknesses in some school subjects. Critics argue that bright but poor children have suffered since Labour abolished the assisted places scheme that helped the less well-off to benefit from independent school education and has also opened the way for the abolition of the remaining academic grammar schools.

Teacher shortages, particularly in some subjects, remain. But offers of financially rewarding golden hellos to attract new teachers, performance-related pay to encourage better teaching and 'Oscars' for the best teachers are apparently beginning to help the situation. On the other hand, government policies, frequent inspections, constant scrutiny through reports, increased workloads, the burden of management and added bureaucracy have been unpopular with the teachers' trade unions. Teachers feel that success seems to be measured only by sets of figures, leading to some 38,500 teachers leaving the profession in 1997–98. Some failing schools have not been turned around and indiscipline, violence and low standards are still present in a number of schools. But commentators, as in the next text, urge the government to be more radical by promoting diversity in schools.

link pay to performance
Teachers paid according to the quality of their performance.

progressive teaching methods
Liberal methods of teaching in which pupils are encouraged to develop their abilities freely, creatively and subjectively.

streaming
The Labour government refers to this as setting: pupils are placed in classes and subjects according to their ability.

9   'Education, education, education'

(*The Economist*, 10 April 1999) abridged

David Blunkett [Secretary of State for Education and Employment] could well, on the face of it, be the cabinet minister least likely to provoke a fight with the Labour Party's traditional supporters in the public sector. Having worked his way up through the trade union movement and local government ... the education secretary is sometimes portrayed as the voice of the left.

For all this, Mr Blunkett's reforms may provoke the first real confrontation between New Labour and the public sector. At their Easter conferences the teachers' unions threatened to strike over the government's plans to close failing schools and to **link pay to performance**. In response, the government promised to delay implementing its pay plans. Delay is all it should be. Taken together with the reforms introduced by the Conservatives, Mr Blunkett's latest proposals are an important stage in tackling the endemic failings in the school system.

Britain's education reforms are best understood as a concerted attack on the mushier version of the 'comprehensive ideal' of the 1960s and 70s. In the name of egalitarianism this held that all pupils, all teachers and all schools should be treated identically. Any comparisons were invidious. The idea was that standards would rise for everybody. But the current system has failed. A recent study revealed that 19 per cent of British adults in their mid-thirties have problems with basic reading.

In response to these problems, Britain's education reforms have tried to be much tougher about discriminating between successful and failing schools. League tables of schools, based on exam results, are published every year. The government has begun to close failing schools and is encouraging private-sector management to get involved. Within schools **'progressive' teaching methods** are being discouraged, and there is more of a focus on basic literacy and numeracy. Mixed-ability teaching is being discouraged in favour of **streaming** by ability. Measurable progress is being made.

The next step

The introduction of performance-related pay for teachers is part of this trend. But the government should go even further. 'One-size-fits-all' is not a philosophy that satisfies consumers in any other walk of life. It should be ditched in education. The government should continue to insist that schools meet certain basic educational targets, and should inspect them, and publish their exam results. But within that basic framework schools should be given much more latitude to specialise and experiment, and parents should be given much more choice over where to send their children. Successful schools will be over-subscribed and this will mean allowing them to select their pupils on any fair and open criteria they choose – including academic ability. But it will also mean allowing popular schools to expand and to take over failing and unpopular schools. The best mechanism for this would be to attach funding to pupils, not schools, so giving successful schools the money and the incentive to expand.

Proposals such as these will meet a storm of protest. The first line of attack will be that they are impracticable. But elements of such schemes are already in place. An under-performing school in Guildford in southern England has already been taken over by the private-sector arm of a successful west Midlands school. The government has also advertised for other private companies to bid to take over failing schools. The hope will be that, as with private schools, successful institutions will develop brands which inspire confidence and attract parents.

Getting private firms to manage schools under contract to the state should just be a start. Attaching funding to pupils, not schools, is the next stage . . . The last government made a start by introducing vouchers for nursery schools – a move regrettably scrapped by Labour. Alternatively schools could be given a per-capita grant, as in Ireland. This process has the virtue of having a natural correction mechanism built in. If schools expand too fast, they will lose popularity and pupils and be forced to shrink.

Another criticism is that this would be socially divisive. The rich would peel off into their own schools, leaving the poor to fail in **'sink' schools**. But sink schools exist already. The rich already opt out, by going private or moving to the suburbs. As Andrew Adonis, now a Downing Street adviser, has written: 'The comprehensive revolution has not removed the link between education and class, it has strengthened it.' School choice would expand opportunity for all.

■ ■ ■

Higher education is another source of controversial debate in Britain. The university sector, currently consisting of 108 universities, has been expanded since 1992 by upgrading the old polytechnics and other colleges to university status. Government policies to increase the number of young people in higher education (one-third of 18-year-olds) have resulted in a very large growth in the student population. But critics argue that the government has not increased its university

sink schools
Disadvantaged and often failing schools, usually in poor inner city areas.

A-level
A-levels are the national
exams (outside
Scotland) taken usually
at 18 and passes are
needed for entry to
universities.

**examination
standards**
One side of this debate
argues that better
examination marks are
due to pupils and
teachers working
harder; the other side
says that the so-called
improvement is due to
lower standards and
expectations.

funding (which is supposedly dependent on student numbers) to cope with such expansion.

Academic resources have been squeezed and university teachers are claiming higher salaries. They argue that they are underpaid, their pay scales have long been neglected and they have slipped behind comparable groups by up to a third. A graduate entering school teaching is paid £1,000 more than the starting salary for university lecturers and British academics are paid half the salaries obtainable in the USA. A lack of qualified academics could seriously threaten the expansion and quality of higher education. A 'brain drain' would operate as graduates move to better jobs in other countries.[12]

Additionally, students must now pay tuition fees for their education (which used to be free) in order to help pay for university costs and must also provide for their own maintenance while studying. Indications are that tuition fees could rise considerably in the future.

Universities face the choice of either trying to finance themselves or pressurizing the government for more state aid. Some commentators feel that British universities should be free to raise private finances to pay their costs, attract high-quality academics and improve degree courses. But others argue that the government needs to address the consequences of the expansion of higher education and seriously consider the issue of public funding for the universities. In fact, the government surprisingly increased its funding in 2000. It remains to be seen whether this will be sufficient and will be directed to the real problem areas.

Against this background, employers continue to criticize the quality of university graduates and the relevance of their courses to the contemporary job market. Critics argue that expansion and funding squeezes have resulted in reduced university standards, with some dubious degree courses and a division between élite universities and the rest. The quality of British higher education is examined in the next text.

10 *'Higher education – a fraud or worth every penny?'*
John O'Leary
(*The Times*, 20 August 1999) abridged

The **A-level** results are in; the celebrations and commiserations are almost over. We have had the inquest into whether **examination standards** are falling. Now begins the annual heart-searching about whether modern higher education courses are worth the candle.

Expect a rash of features about surfing studies and universities that will take candidates with barely a **GCSE** to their names just to **fill up their places**. The message will be that the expansion of higher education was a waste of taxpayers' money, and only traditional degrees are worth three years' study.

Over the next few days, thousands of teenagers and their parents will be poring over **clearing lists** in *The Times* and elsewhere, wondering whether that verdict is correct. Most of the available places are in new universities and colleges of higher education and many are in subjects that hardly fit the label of 'traditional'.

As usual in higher education, as in so many other areas, America went through the same process and had all the arguments long ago. Next week a book[13] is published by an academic who has seen British and US universities at close quarters and who addresses the question of what should legitimately be recognized as higher education.

Not one to beat about the bush, Alan Ryan, Warden of New College, Oxford, asks: 'Is higher education a fraud?' Unlike some of his academic colleagues, he does not pretend that universities have maintained standards absolutely. Most will concede privately, he says, that less is these days expected of students, even in traditional disciplines.

Dr Ryan's concern is for the state of liberal education, by which he means a broad general education, rather than the vocational equivalent. But he does not see the two as mutually exclusive, and is not one to dismiss the newer subjects, which are the lifeblood of the new universities. In his ideal university system, all students would acquire 'the skills they require to earn a living, and to possess the sense of cultural ownership that was once the prerogative of the few'.

Any university would surely hope to give its students that much, but Dr Ryan says that some courses do neither effectively. He argues that the answer is not for the universities to abandon the new style of higher education, but to improve it. That may only be possible with better funding – through higher fees in the case of the top universities and increased government support elsewhere – although he shares the critics' concern that the recent expansion has been questionable in terms of economic returns.

Many traditionalists would have the new universities ape their older cousins, but Dr Ryan is more pragmatic. 'Golf studies may or may not be a good foun-

GCSE
National exams (except for Scotland) taken usually at 16.

fill up their places
University funding from the government is dependent upon the number of students they recruit to their courses.

clearing lists
If students obtain the required A-level passes, they are normally able to take up offers already made by the universities. If they do not obtain the required grades, they must go into the clearing system. This consists of university places that are not already taken up by students.

dation for intellectual exploration, but a degree in golf-course management from a former polytechnic is more likely to make its holders employable than is a degree in English.'

In purely educational terms, Dr Ryan's message is not entirely discouraging for the doubters in clearing, although there are plenty of conventional degrees to choose from in the listings. But, while he sees American undergraduate education as generally superior to the British model, he argues that much of the criticism of the new universities is unfair. They cannot be expected to be innovative and responsive to students' and employers' needs while maintaining an unchanging standard . . .

■ ■ ■

Exercises

Write short essays on the following topics

1   What are the advantages and disadvantages of a welfare state?

2   Discuss whether state social security systems should be replaced by individual self-help.

3   What are meant by the concepts of poverty and inequality in British society?

4   The National Health Service: is it just a matter of more money being spent on the provision of medical care?

5   Examine the texts written by politicians in this chapter (texts 1, 7 and 8). What is significant about their style and content?

6   Explain what the Labour government is doing to raise standards in British state schools.

Explain and examine the following terms

welfare state	childcare	WFTC
pensioner	workfare	handouts
universal benefits	sleeping rough	lone parents
tax concessions	public sector	GP
(medical) charges	registered nurse	LEA
league tables	comprehensives	BMA
A-level	cost-effectiveness	brain drain
primary school	zero tolerance	best practice

Further reading

Black, Jeremy (2000) *Modern British History since 1900*, chapters on education, health, work and social welfare, London: Macmillan.

Gladstone, David (1999) *The Twentieth-Century Welfare State*, London: Macmillan.

Johnson, Norman (1990) *Reconstructing the Welfare State: A Decade of Change 1980–1990*, London: Harvester/Wheatsheaf.

Ludlam, Steve and Smith, Martin J. (eds) (2000) *New Labour in Government*, chapters on education, health, work and social welfare, London: Macmillan.

Mullard, Maurice (1995) *Policy-making in Britain*, London: Routledge.

Pilkington, Colin (1998) *Issues in British Politics*, chapters on education, health, work and social welfare, London: Macmillan.

Savage, Stephen P. and Robins, Lynton (eds) (1990) *Public Policy under Thatcher*, London: Macmillan.

 Notes

1. Peter Riddell (1998) 'Voters cautious in support for welfare reforms' London: *The Times* 30 January.
2. Alexandra Frean (1999) 'A third of Britain's young live in poverty' London: *The Times* 22 September.
3. Jenny Booth (2000) 'Britain "now less equal"' London: *The Times* 30 June.
4. Robin Marris (2000) 'The shocking truth about Britain's poor children' London: *The Times* 27 June.
5. Alexandra Frean (2000) 'Middle classes gain most from help for poor' London: *The Times* 26 June.
6. Alan Milburn (1997) 'Getting the NHS off its sickbed' London: *The Times* 26 November.
7. Frank Dobson (1999) 'Modernizing Britain's National Health Service' *Health Affairs* Volume 18, Number 3.
8. David Smith (2000) 'If only we felt as good as we looked' London: *The Sunday Times* 25 June.
9. Leader (2000) 'Radical medicine' London: *The Sunday Times* 25 June.
10. John Willman (1998) *A Better State of Health* London: Profile Books.
11. Ian Murray (1999) ''As bad as it gets' in the NHS' London: *The Times* March 11.
12. Leader (1999) 'Why dons are angry. University teachers have paid too high a price for expansion' London: *The Times* 16 August.
13. Alan Ryan (1999) *Liberal Anxieties and Liberal Education* London: Profile Books.

Chapter 8

Social behaviour and 'moral panics'

Britain occasionally experiences 'moral panics' about the alleged state of its society. These may sometimes appear to be deliberately created and exaggerated by the media but can, more genuinely, be based on the real anxieties of politicians, commentators and ordinary British people.

They often centre on the behaviour of the disadvantaged and the young, such as drugs, crime and teenage pregnancies. However, some concerns (including drug abuse and crime) have a wider social and age application, such as marriage, religion and racism. All reflect seemingly widespread worries about the moral state of contemporary Britain. But there may be no large statistical relationship between such fears of a morally decaying country and their actual manifestation in society. Nevertheless, there are moral tensions in Britain between those people who exemplify new patterns of behaviour/thinking and those who believe in more traditional values.

Teenage pregnancies and drugs

The increase in illegitimate (non-marital) births generally in Britain, but particularly among teenage girls, is a concern. The country now has the highest rate of teenage pregnancy in Europe (46.5 per thousand under-18-year-old girls and 90 per thousand 18 to 19-year-olds). This situation raises questions about school sex education, sexual behaviour generally and the resulting state of marriage as an institution. Some critics strongly object in principle to any sex instruction in the classroom, feeling that this matter is the province of family and home. Others argue that there is too little such teaching and that which exists is either inadequate or confusing. They feel that a culture of British reticence and prudish moral values results in sexual behaviour not being properly handled or discussed openly.[1]

A survey by **Brook Advisory Centres** in 1999[2] found that 14 to 18-year-olds (both heterosexual and homosexual) were worried, when seeking advice and help, that they would be subjected to awkward questions, treated as irresponsible, ridiculed for their ignorance or would be judged, belittled or condemned. They felt that **GPs** and counsellors did not respect their legal confidentiality and that parents would be notified of their personal lives. Such fears illustrated a lack of openness, communication on sexual matters and acceptance of teenage sex in Britain. Gay and lesbian youngsters felt isolated and were even more cautious in seeking help and advice from parents or professionals.

The Brook argued in its report that advice centres need to be more encouraging and inviting to young people in order to be effective and to reduce the environment of secrecy and ignorance. They should emphasize privacy and be more aware of teenagers' anxieties and apprehensions in a complex world. It pointed out that international research confirmed that satisfactory access to confidential contraceptive services and reliable information about contraception is essential in reducing teenage pregnancy.

The use and abuse of so-called hard, soft and recreational drugs is also a growing problem in Britain, is closely allied to many forms of crime, such as theft, burglary and assaults and involves all age groups and classes. But it has increasingly affected young people and provoked calls for action, as in the next text.

Brook Advisory Centres
An organization with centres around Britain that gives free advice on sexual and personal matters.

GPs
General Practitioners are local doctors.

1 *'Drug-taking Britain is "worst in Europe"'*
Victoria Fletcher and Ian Brodie
(*The Times*, 2 January 1999) abridged

Young Britons are much more likely to take drugs than any of their European neighbours, with 'soft' drugs proving the most popular.[3]

A recent survey by the European Monitoring Centre for Drugs found that 35 per cent of British teenagers regularly took cannabis compared with 25.7 per cent in France and 21 per cent in Germany.

The 'recreational' drug ecstasy has been tried by 9 per cent of young Britons but by only 2.8 per cent of Germans, 3.1 per cent of French and 1 per cent of Swedes.

For the past decade, schools and politicians have struggled to find a successful approach to slow the increasing number of young people taking drugs. Campaigners have divided between those arguing for a tough, straightforward message that all drugs are dangerous – typified by the 'Just Say No' adverts – and those arguing that children need to be given more information to inform their decisions.

Two years ago, the Government showed its commitment to tackle the drugs problem when it ploughed £1.6 million into a range of innovative educational projects . . .

However, Britain has become aware that the drugs education has so far not worked and that the problem is escalating. Exactly one year ago, the Prime Minister decided that the only way to co-ordinate drugs education was by appointing a 'drugs czar' . . . Keith Hellawell took up the position with a mission to draw up a detailed and clear drugs education policy for schools.

The British and American drugs czars are responsible for co-ordinating national drug control policy and have direct access to their heads of government.

America's drug czar, Barry McCaffrey, takes the same hard line as his British counterpart in saying there should be no distinction between hard and soft drugs.

His spokesman, Bob Weiner, [said that] marijuana ... cannot be called soft when it is second only to alcohol as a substance implicated in car crashes. Similarly, marijuana disrupts productivity in schools and the workplace ...

In the official American view, those in favour of legalising soft drugs always maintain that increased use is irrelevant. According to Mr McCaffrey ... it is the most important reason against legalisation.

According to his staff, the point was proved in Alaska, which recriminalised marijuana after several years of reducing it to the level of a parking ticket. The switch was prompted by a surge in use and increase in traffic accidents and overdose cases taken to hospital emergency rooms ...

■ ■ ■

Crime and the fear of crime

Discussions about crime in Britain are hindered by the inadequacy of statistics and their varying interpretations. But the fear of becoming a crime victim is a concern for many Britons, even though some statistics purport to show that the reality of individuals actually being affected is remote. A further concern is the amount of crime committed by young people (particularly men) in the 18–24 age group, and the increasing number of offences perpetrated by youngsters under 18. While crime may proportionally mostly affect deprived and inner city urban centres, the countryside and affluent areas are by no means immune. Commentators argue that the Labour government's policy of being 'tough on crime and tough on the causes of crime' has not worked, that there need to be many more police on the streets, and that stricter treatment of offenders is needed. The next text is as relevant now as in 1996. It draws attention to the reporting of criminal offences and analyses the causes of crime and proposals to prevent it.

2   'Bolt-down Britain'
Tim Rayment
(*The Sunday Times*, 7 January 1996) abridged

A boy of 19 is kicked to death on his doorstep while trying to save his father from the taunts of a gang of youths. Four people seeking work are stabbed by a stranger at a **JobCentre** in suburban London. Ten shoppers suffer stab

JobCentre
Shops or offices in major cities and towns where the unemployed may seek advice about jobs.

999
Emergency telephone
service.

Michael Howard
Home Secretary in the
last Conservative
government.

wounds in a supermarket in the West Midlands. A boy of 15 . . . is charged with the murder of Philip Lawrence, the headmaster whose killing last month shocked the nation.

Sir Ronald Hadfield, the West Midlands Chief Constable, calls for police to be armed with CS or pepper sprays after a young woman constable on a **999** call is left by burglars with a fractured skull. If he does not get them, Hadfield says, his next option is firearms.

A death in a front garden, panic in a JobCentre, a call for American-style police sprays: is anywhere safe in violent Britain? Or, with our fears that sudden, random violence is on the increase, are we over-reacting to the cumulative effects of a few isolated incidents, unusual but widely reported?

One disquieting feature is the age of some recent assailants, illustrated by pictures of Edith Pedder, 78, recovering in hospital after being knocked to the ground by a gang of muggers apparently aged between 10 and 14.

Yet fear of crime, which reflects actual neighbourhood experience as well as media images, is not getting worse, according to the Home Office. Figures to be released this week show that our anxieties, and particularly fears for our personal safety, have not grown in a decade.

Worries about car theft have risen, and fear of burglary is up a little, but the fear of attack is static at a fairly high level. For many people, caution has become a way of life. About a third of us (including one in two women) feel unsafe walking alone after dark; and 11 per cent, even those living behind multiple door locks, feel 'very' or 'fairly' unsafe at home at night.

For those who live in fear in bolt-down Britain, the official crime figures, as recorded by the police, seem to be from another planet. Last September . . . the home secretary trumpeted 'a real turning of the tide against crime'. **Michael Howard** was able to announce a fall in the crime rate for the second year in succession, including the first recorded fall in violent crime for 49 years – by 2 per cent, to 301,000 offences in England and Wales, equivalent to an attack on each of us once every 171 years.

After the apparent 'crime wave' of the 1970s and 1980s, the upward spiral was over. However, the statistics were widely challenged.[4]

The decision to report a crime depends partly on whether the victim thinks the police will solve it. The Home Office's own British Crime Survey suggests that only one incident in four is reported. Even this survey, which charts crime from what people say rather than police files, probably underestimates offences such as sexual assault.

This week a team of academics . . . will publish their own analysis [Options for Britain] of how and why crime has risen 'substantially' since the 1950s . . .[5] 'Despite an approximate doubling (in real terms) of spending on law and order since 1979, crime has continued to increase,' they say.

Within the increase, national statistics disguise real problems. In some areas, if you draw a line round a few streets you will find that the chances of being robbed are one in two every year.

Women worry more about safety than men, and with reason. They suffer aggravation that is potentially serious and yet too trivial to record. One criminologist likens the sexual harassment of women at night to a man who is invited to fight every time he steps from the house.

'People say these attacks are random and therefore nothing to worry about,' said Jock Young, professor of criminology at Middlesex University. 'The Home Office and people on the left have been playing down the level of crime for years. It is a peculiar alliance. The crime rate obviously has gone up.' The question is: why? And what can be done?

'I am an emotionally volatile, unpredictable and aggressive young man: I come from a large family and live in the back streets of Birmingham. I have left school, and don't have enough money to move very far from the streets where my family and their friends live.

'I got drunk one night, fell out with a mate and beat him senseless. The trouble is that in the pub and out of it, lots of people know me and my family. My chances of a job depend on their goodwill.'

That was what happened in the 1930s, and the voice belongs to Barrie Irving, director of the Police Foundation, a charity that researches policing. The words are fiction; Irving is describing the social constraints that once discouraged violence. People in the Midlands of his childhood were 'put on' (put forward) for jobs by their families. 'This was considered to be hugely unfair nepotism, but it offered a form of indirect social control,' Irving said.

Today, society is more mobile. Irving's volatile, unpredictable and aggressive young man probably drives a car in a fragmented community where few would know his name.

There are other forces at work, too. The Options for Britain team . . . says that among the influences driving crime are increases in affluence and goods to steal, changes in the nature and strength of informal constraints, and 'socio-economic and aspirational factors'. Criminal justice policy has been based too often on short-term political needs, they say, and is hindered by the view that 'nothing works'.

Others claim we are raising a generation of problem children. 'I have been taunted, attacked, spat at and verbally abused,' said one Warwickshire teacher, quitting because she cannot cope with what she sees as the violence of four- and five-year-olds. 'Infants behave like vicious thugs. They are hard. We cannot even smack them, and they know it.'

Then there are the weapons. After the death of Philip Lawrence, I visited the Tabernacle community centre in west London, a supportive place for young people in Notting Hill. 'Do you carry a knife?' one teenager asked, wondering why I should bother to go there if all I wanted was to interview people with knives. I said no.

'Well, don't your friends carry any?' He carried a small blade because it made him feel safer. He could not understand why a white, middle-class 35-year-old in a good job should not do so too.

'We no longer provide employment for a huge band of rather poorly educated youth in the inner cities,' Irving said. 'All the conditions for frustration, which is part of sudden, unbridled aggression, are going up.'

The good news is that there is much that can be done. The Options for Britain team conclude that it is time to [see] . . . local authorities, in collaboration with the police, as the natural bodies to coordinate measures to improve community safety.

. . . there is evidence that the theory can work. For example, the Pepys Estate in Deptford, southeast London, which had an exceptionally high crime rate in the 1980s, introduced changes including security improvements to flats and lighting, and closed-circuit television (CCTV).

There was a new estate-based community policing unit and a full-time presence by the local housing management. Tenants and community associations were involved throughout. Recorded crime dropped 57 per cent in two years, before rising slightly. The one caveat is that, as always with anti-crime measures, further research might show that criminal activity has merely been displaced elsewhere.

The focus of some work – notably by John Braithwaite at the Australian National University in Canberra – is to bolster the shaming system that kept Irving's aggressive young men in the 1930s in check. The idea is to embarrass offenders, then reintegrate them into society . . .

Criminologists are also interested in Home Office projects designed to promote fellow-feeling in troubled communities, leading to greater cooperation in the prevention and investigation of crime ...

As for the police, the desire for sprays was given fresh impetus after a woman police constable was stabbed in the face during a siege at a house in Bradford on Friday night. Lisa Sharpe, 23, needed six stitches in her cheek after attempting to disarm a man who was threatening a woman with a 10in blade.

The manufacturers of pepper spray claim the acute stinging and burning it causes to eyes and throats lasts no longer than 45 minutes, leaves no permanent damage and results in fewer complaints of excessive force against the police. Its use in New York almost tripled last year to 603 spraying incidents, from 217 in 1994. At the same time, arrests where truncheons were swung declined from 158 to 118 ...

However, American civil liberties groups say that for asthmatics exposure can be lethal. The National Coalition on Police Accountability claims 41 people in the United States, 27 in California, have died from police use of pepper spray since 1992.

The American experience shows that get-tough policing can have results. Willliam Bratton, commisioner of police for New York, achieved a 37.3 per cent drop in the murder rate in 20 months, with serious crime down 27 per cent over the same period. Steps included 7,000 new officers and an approach borrowed from business.

... To the government's critics, however, deeper measures are needed.

'You can't keep going with a society where many are excluded unless you have gated communities,' said Jock Young. 'You cannot have them watching the **glittering prizes** on television and staying in and being happy. People say, "We have heard all that before." Probably we have, but it's true.'

■ ■ ■

Marriage

Changing social attitudes, lifestyles and forms of morality are reflected in new relationship patterns in Britain. The institution of marriage has been in decline in recent years and has been replaced by alternatives, such as cohabitation, single people living alone, lone-parent families and same-gender relationships. A central question in Britain today is whether schoolchildren should be taught these realities or whether marriage and traditional values should be emphasized and reinforced.

glittering prizes
Consumer products.

The political parties have made the family a central point of their policies, although their approaches differ. The Conservatives support marriage and the family unit but are being forced by demographic changes to widen their perspective on alternative relationships. The Labour party seemed at one stage to be embracing an inclusion of all types of family groupings and other lifestyles, but has been forced by protests to give greater weight to marriage and the traditional nuclear family.

Government statisticians reported in 1999[6] that, for the first time since centralized marriage records began in 1801, married couples will in future be outnumbered by the unmarried. The decrease is caused both by an increase in the divorce rate and, more significantly, by a rise in the number of people who will never marry. These will be either single or enter non-marital relationships. It is predicted that the number of married adults will fall from 55 per cent at present to 48 per cent by 2011 and to 45 per cent by 2021. The proportion of men who will never marry is predicted to rise to 39 per cent by 2011 and to 41 per cent by 2021. For women, the proportion will rise to 31 per cent in 2011 and 33 per cent in 2021. The divorce rate is expected to decrease for the younger male and female age groups (increasing numbers of whom will never marry) and to rise only for those married persons over 45.

The number of people who will be living together without being married (cohabitation) is predicted to rise. But this increase in cohabiting couples over the next 25 years to 2.93 million will not, in all probability, compensate for the decrease in married couples. It is expected that the marriage rate will continue to decline, but will level out over time. These figures suggest that many more adults will be living alone in the future.

Such demographic changes will obviously influence Britain's social environment and its future housing and welfare provisions. They also raise concern as to how young children can be accommodated to these shifts and what attitudes they should be taught in the schools, as the next text illustrates.

3 'Pupils taught marriage is "just one option" for family life'
Judith O'Reilly
(*The Sunday Times*, 10 January 1999) abridged

A new moral code proposed for Britain's schools has upset traditionalists by telling pupils that marriage is just one of a number of routes to a happy family life, and that cohabitation and single parenthood can be equally valid.

The code is already being piloted in 150 schools and could be introduced nationwide from this year. It tells teachers that they must prepare youngsters not only for marriage but also for the potentially much wider range of relationships that exists nowadays.

It coincides with last week's figures from the government actuary, which showed that within 12 years more than half the adult population will be unmarried. It will be the first time since records began in 1801 that those who are single, cohabiting, widowed or divorced have been in a majority. In the next 25 years the number of cohabiting couples is expected to double from 1.5m to 3m and about half of all adult men between 30 and 44 will be single.

Under the new code teachers will have to recognize that: 'The love and commitment required for a secure and happy childhood can be found in different forms of family and there are marriages in which there is neither love nor commitment.'

The code adds that teachers must recognize that many pupils already come from non-traditional families. 'Schools will want to give careful thought to this issue.'

The guidance continues: 'One way forward is to explain that values are ideals, something we try, but sometimes fail, to live up to. Pupils need to understand that difficulty in living up to our values does not give us a reason to revise our values downwards.' . . .

Once the code has been approved schools will be expected to dedicate about 5 per cent of the school week to preparation for life. Within two to three years, the government will change the statutory requirements to make it a compulsory part of the [national] **curriculum**.

Such moves have, however, been criticized by Chris Woodhead, chief inspector of schools. He has argued that [by] expanding the curriculum, issues such as citizenship and personal finance will take too much time away from basic literacy and numeracy lessons.

The guidance seems certain to prompt complaints from traditionalists over what children should be taught about marriage. Nick Seaton, of the Campaign for Real Education, said: 'Most parents and many teachers will be deeply disappointed that the guidance isn't more clearly in support of marriage, two-parent families and absolute commitment.' [See text 7 for the Labour government's position.]

national curriculum
The centrally devised national curriculum containing those subjects to be taught in British schools and to children at various stages of their school education.

■ ■ ■

Racism

It had been generally assumed in recent years that Britain's multicultural society had seen a substantial decrease in racism and racial disturbances. Racism no longer seemed to be a central issue and race relations were thought to be generally healthy.

But the murder of black student Stephen Lawrence in 1993, allegedly by white racists, was followed by the criminal court acquittal of those accused, a private civil prosecution, considerable media comment and attempts by the Lawrence family to obtain justice. The Macpherson inquiry (1998–99) into the matter provoked a significant debate about the state of race relations in Britain. Its report recommended sweeping changes, which in part were heavily criticized. The next text asks whether the report's conclusions and the assumption of widespread racism in British society are justified.

4 'Is Britain really a nation of racists?'
Stephen Bevan and Nicholas Rufford
(*The Sunday Times*, 28 February 1999) abridged

It started a month ago with a few white children hurling names, then stones. Last Thursday, the Somali man was found prostrate in the street in central Manchester, blood oozing from his mouth and skull. Eyewitnesses said he had been beaten by a gang of four or five white youths.

'They set about him with bricks, leaving him with head injuries, broken teeth and extensive bruising,' said Tony Simpson, the detective sergeant in charge of the investigation. 'At first we thought he had spinal injuries. He could have been killed.'

Simpson, 34, is head of one of Britain's first racial incident units. Set up three weeks ago, its beat is a densely populated inner-city area of four square miles covering the Longsight, Gorton and Levenshulme areas of Manchester. Black and Asian ethnic minorities comprise up to 30 per cent of the population.

The unit's brief is to seek out and solve racist crime. 'Our first priority is to make sure all racial incidents are reported to us,' said Simpson. 'We suspect there is massive under-reporting and we need to change that.'

Since the unit was set up, 15 racial crimes have been reported – more than half as many as were reported last year. They include assaults, verbal abuse, stone and egg throwing, vandalism and, in one case, a white youth urinating through a black family's letter box ... 'It's racism and it's widespread,' Simpson said.

There are racists in Britain. But is Britain racist? Last week, the inquiry into the murder of Stephen Lawrence implied that racism has infected much of society. Is it right?

In the southeast London suburb [Eltham] where Lawrence died, armoured police vans were parked on street corners. Metal barriers and tape sealed off the roads. Scores of officers were stationed along the thoroughfare and side streets, some on guard, some conducting door-to-door inquiries. Last Thursday afternoon Eltham looked as if it had been hit by a national emergency. In a sense it had: someone had thrown a pot of paint, desecrating the memorial to Lawrence, and Jack Straw, the home secretary, was investigating.

On the pavement at the spot where Lawrence bled to death in April 1993, stabbed by a gang of white youths, lies a granite slab inlaid with gold lettering. When the Macpherson report was published, white paint was splashed over the memorial. A childish gesture by a stupid youth, or further evidence of a deep-seated culture of racism?

As he studied the damage, Tek Anim, a 19-year-old black student of business and marketing at Greenwich University, was unequivocal. 'Yes, it's a racist area,' he said. 'Before I started at the university, my brother warned me not to walk around Eltham, but I didn't think he was serious. I soon learnt after a certain hour at night not to walk through the place.'

Many black residents describe an atmosphere of violence and intimidation. Anim said a black friend of his had been attacked recently. He himself had suffered an unpleasant incident last November when he was making his way home through the area ...

But others report a very different kind of experience. Down at the Eltham Kebab restaurant, outside which two youths have been stabbed, the view was the opposite. 'There have been two incidents in the 12 years I have been here. It's not as bad as they say,' said the manager. He is Turkish, but does not feel threatened by race hate.

A Sri Lankan man, who moved with his family to Eltham in 1993, painted a similar picture. 'All our neighbours have been very helpful,' said the man, who lives on the Brook estate, home to some of those suspected of killing Lawrence. 'We haven't had any problems.'

bail
Freedom from
imprisonment while
awaiting trial for a
criminal offence.

If they cannot agree on whether they are racist, the residents seem to agree that the police are racist. In Greenwich, the local police received about 400 complaints of racial offences last year. One of the local community organizations received more than 1,000. A discrepancy explained, according to one community worker, by local distrust of the police.

Dr Tom Butler, the Bishop of Southwark, said: 'The police need a lot of help on building links with the black community.' In his conversations with black youngsters, they almost invariably raise difficulties with apparent racism in the police.

Around Britain, ethnic minorities complain of prejudice at the hands of the police. Throughout the country, blacks are more likely to be charged than whites, more likely to be jailed if convicted, more likely to be denied **bail**. Stop-and-search figures show that blacks are far more likely to be pulled over than whites – and this experience, too, holds true across much of the country.

In London, 37 per cent of those stopped are black or Asian; in the West Midlands 31 per cent and in Bedfordshire 19.8 per cent.

The Lawrence inquiry reached this conclusion: 'Institutional racism . . . exists both in the Metropolitan police service and in other police services and institutions countrywide.'

The institutional racism with which the police are charged is not an overt prejudice. It can be 'unwitting', a pernicious attitude of mind. The report explains: 'It can be seen as detected in processes, attitudes and behaviour which amount to discrimination through unwitting prejudice, ignorance, thoughtlessness and racist stereotyping which disadvantage minority ethnic people.' It has aroused controversy. How can such a thing be detected? How can one man know what is in the mind of another?

Macpherson goes much further than Lord Scarman in his report following the Brixton riots in 1981, who said he found no evidence of institutional racism. Instead he said there were racists and there was racial discrimination.

Macpherson justifies his much more sweeping conclusions in a detailed and shocking account of the Lawrence murder and the extraordinary, unbelievable degree of incompetence and mismanagement shown by the officers in charge of its investigation. This was not just blundering. Macpherson says it reflected something more sinister: racism.

Sir Paul Condon, commissioner of the Met, has refused to accept that his force is racist, but on the grounds that prejudice may be 'unwitting', he was prepared to back the report last week. Condon has already launched a series of initiatives to improve race relations, including the establishment of a special racial and violent crime taskforce ...

Last week, other measures were also announced to curb racism inside the force, including the use of undercover black officers to test racist attitudes.

But Macpherson's report has been condemned as over the top and unworkable by some of the brightest and most liberal officers in the force. In its recommendations, it calls for a range of changes to the criminal law and police practice. It calls, for instance, for the police immunity to prosecution under the Race Relations Act to end. One senior officer said that the move would bring a flood of bogus claims, leaving the police hamstrung with paperwork. 'It would be all too easy for a suspect about whom we were making legitimate inquiries to accuse us of racism,' said one senior officer ...

There are other profound reservations. There was almost universal criticism of the suggestion that the double-jeopardy system under which a person cannot be tried twice for the same offence be reviewed. It is almost certain not to be adopted by the government.[7] But another reform which appears superficially to be a positive step forward – to fix quotas for ethnic recruitment – has also prompted concern.

In America, the experience of such quotas was that they lowered standards and increased corruption. In the 1970s and 1980s the New York police department lowered its standards in order to increase the recruitment of minorities. In other forces, the ethnic quota has led to an increase, rather than a decrease, in the amount paid out in compensation for police brutality. There is no guarantee that a force which is demographically more like the local community will act with any greater sensitivity towards it.

Tackling racism in the police is only one part of Macpherson's purpose: he calls for broad and radical changes throughout society. Most important, the report says, is to quell racism in the playground ...

'Racism exists within all organizations,' the report states. 'It infiltrates the community and starts among the very young.' On this basis, Macpherson calls for a number of wide-ranging reforms in education, including the establishment of league tables showing the level of racial incidents in schools and a broadening of the national curriculum to improve ethnic awareness.

But are British schools a seedbed of institutional racism? The report cites one piece of evidence: a research project undertaken by the Racial Equality Council in Wales. It examined 407 cases of racial abuse and violence reported last year. Of these 50 per cent were committed by children under the age of 16 and 24 per cent between the age of six and 10.

Can any national conclusion be drawn from this?

The picture is confused. Michael Marland, headmaster of North Westminster community college, warned of mounting youth gang violence. The gangs were both black and white and as likely to attack rivals of their own colour as each other.

'It is about gratuitous violence,' he said. It is not so much a problem of racism, he warned, but about the creation of a youth underclass.

Meanwhile teachers' unions warn of increasing violence against their members. One black teacher was recently beaten up by white pupils in her class at a school in Lewisham, south London.

The experience at Kidbrooke school ... is inconsistent. [In 1991 there were] only four black children out of 120 in [a] year. Now 42 per cent of the pupils have parents who were born overseas. One student said last week: 'I do feel there's been a lot of bad press around. People's first impression is that we are all racists. But that's not been my experience.'

Multiracial schooling seems to work for her.

Macpherson maintains that racism is not just endemic in the police or schools but in 'institutions countrywide'. But is that fair? There is ample evidence of individual outrages of racism ...

But a cursory inspection of available statistics contradicts the simple view expounded in the report that the black Briton is a victim of institutional racism. In fact, in many areas, the black and Asian community have performed far better than the white.

Darcus Howe, the black writer and broadcaster, said: 'At times I could barely recognize the Britain that was being described in the report and the reportage that surrounded it – this rampant, crazy, racist place – I have a little difficulty with that.'

Tariq Modood, professor of sociology at Bristol University and author of the 1997 report *Ethnic Minorities in Britain* for the Policy Studies Institute agreed. 'There has been movement. There is a growth in self-employment, in non-manual occupations and managerial posts,' he said. 'Most ethnic minorities now are getting very well-educated. Even young black men are much more likely to stay on in education after the age of 16 than their white peers. Taken as a whole, ethnic minorities are now twice as likely to go to university as whites.'

In London, where there are 20 per cent blacks and Asians in the population, 29 per cent of nurses, 31 per cent of doctors and more than 20 per cent of civil servants come from the ethnic minorities.

Although there are still no black High Court judges, blacks are relatively well-represented within the legal profession. Last year 15.8 per cent of all new solicitors were black, as were 25 per cent of those enrolling on the bar vocational course to become barristers.

In medicine the picture is the same: 23 per cent of those studying medicine at university are black.

In the media, 7.4 per cent of BBC staff are black; at **Channel 4** the figure rises to 9.5 per cent.

Among leading employers, British Airways employs 13 per cent blacks and Marks and Spencer 9.5 per cent.

This not to deny that there are institutions which are racist, in Macpherson's definition. The armed services, plagued with complaints of racism, still only employ 1 per cent from ethnic minorities. But they have a policy in place for boosting this to 5 per cent by 2002.

Ruby Spolia is a successful Asian businesswoman . . . 'Second and third generations have prospered here. They have been allowed to prosper, allowed to develop their potential, even if it wasn't a deliberate decision to let them do so,' she said.

There were no black faces around the Downing Street table last Thursday morning when Tony Blair . . . convened a lengthy debate on race.

Straw opened with a summary of the Macpherson report. 'It was a serious debate,' recalled one minister present. 'We debated what we could do as a government to fight racism, and what the limits of government action should be. We did not want to go totally politically correct.'

Indeed, Straw welcomed much in the report, including the plan to extend the scope of the Race Relations Act. But this was balanced by scepticism about other recommendations.

Many cabinet ministers feel uneasy about legally defining a racist offence as any where the victim feels this was so. David Blunkett believes school league tables of racist incidents would be counter-productive.

Channel 4
Independent television station.

And Straw, as he outlined the report to cabinet, highlighted Macpherson's suggestion that using racist language, even in private, should be an offence . . .

'If we were to go all the way with Macpherson, that would mean making what people say within the family in the privacy of their own homes a possible criminal offence. Many of us were uncomfortable with that,' said a cabinet minister.

In an article in tomorrow's *New Nation* newspaper, Blair will write of his intention to make 'Britain a beacon to the world of racial equality' . . .

[That is a] laudable ambition: but is the Macpherson report going to bring [it] about? And is Blair missing the point? Matthew Griffiths, editor of the Brixton-based *The Voice*, said he welcomed the report and what it stood for but added: 'Still nobody has lost their job over it. And still nobody has ended up behind bars.'

In all the racial uproar, the real point may have been obscured. The more important reason that Lawrence's killers are still at liberty is that the Metropolitan police was grossly incompetent . . .

It should be remembered that other white victims of thuggery by the suspects in the Lawrence murder have also been failed by the judicial system. The case of one white youth who was stabbed in the arm by one of them . . . never went to trial.

Perhaps more vital to the operational credibility of the Metropolitan police are reforms inspired by Condon, not Macpherson, to establish rapid-response teams to descend on murders during the 'golden hour' after they are first reported. This is as important as race relations in improving the performance of the police . . .

The report has not helped to bring her son's killers to justice and Doreen Lawrence is pessimistic that it will be the 'watershed' in race relations predicted by Straw. Institutional racism or not, the reality is that racists like those who killed her son are not going to go away. 'My feelings about the future remain the same. Black youngsters will never be safe on the streets,' she said.

Others are more optimistic. Nina Wadia, 29, star of *Goodness Gracious Me*, the hugely successful Asian BBC television comedy, says there has been a marked improvement in race relations. 'There is a very positive trend happening,' she said. 'Six years ago there would just be myself and two other black girls who would meet at every audition. Now when I go to auditions, there are 20 other new faces.'

She is about to play a non-Indian girl in a new television sitcom.

'That will be a break-through character,' she said. 'She will just be a character, and her race will be completely ignored – that is when we will know that something has been done.'

■ ■ ■

Commentators have varying views on the question of whether British society is generally racist or not, and on the state of race relations. There are also different views on how to counter that racism which undoubtedly exists.

The Macpherson report could result in the reform of police operations. But commentators question whether other proposed changes will contribute to social harmony. They find that some of the report's recommendations are unfortunately prescriptive; its proposals for the criminal justice system are problematic; and its suggested reforms of the education system are highly debatable and allegedly divisive and counter-productive (see above text).[8]

For example, in order to promote an understanding of diversity at a young age, the report said that schools can stress education and example and an attitude of zero tolerance of racism. It recommended that such aims could be incorporated into the school national curriculum; records of racial incidents in schools could be maintained; and racial league tables could be drawn up for all schools and the results published.

Critics argue that such recommendations would be detrimental to that work which is already being done in schools to encourage inclusiveness and toleration in the classroom. It is argued that teachers have worked hard to promote a healthy spirit of mutual respect among children. In this view, harmony is best promoted by emphasizing the value of each individual and downplaying surface differences. The emphasis should be on respect for individuals, rather than categories. Children should be taught more constructively to think beyond all stereotypes, distorting lobby interests and awareness campaigns.

The road to better race relations followed by some race relations institutions and radical multiculturalist activists in Britain has long been criticized, in a similar manner to the above arguments. The next text discusses whether such vested interests do more harm than good in their emphases on racism, discrimination and a separatist agenda.

5 'We should shut down the race industry'
Melanie Phillips
(Author copyright, 20 December 1998)

A few weeks ago I happened to take part in a television show about race relations. The attitude of the mainly black audience was unsettling. They were angry; they saw British society as universally racist. Anyone who did not subscribe to this view was hissed. They accepted no responsibility for anything that happened to them. Their only role was to demand the 'rights' denied to them by a malevolent white society.

Equally disturbing were comments made by Sir Herman Ouseley, [former] chairman of the Commission for Racial Equality (CRE). He rejected, he told the audience, the validity of a common culture. Black children needed to be taught black culture. Yet this approach spells disaster for black children in Britain. Without access to English culture, without command of its language, appreciation of its literature or a grasp of the history of its institutions, black children will be unable to play an equal part in a society which assumes such access as a given.

Ouseley's premise was that British society and English culture are racist. This view is as tendentious as it is dangerous. Of course there are alarming pockets of prejudice; the police have given a warning that language used recently by some newspapers about refugees amounted to incitement to racial hatred. The Stephen Lawrence inquiry exposed lethal racial stereotyping by the police themselves, which causes black people to be viewed as suspects rather than victims. Certain areas populated by disaffected white working class people are potent breeding grounds for racially motivated thuggery.

But all this should not be exaggerated. According to Ouseley, British racism is running at such a high level that shock tactics are needed. Accordingly, the CRE ran a poster campaign deliberately displaying deeply offensive racial stereotypes. These were intended to cause such disgust that we would get the message that we were all rotten with racial hatred. Instead, the CRE itself was hauled before the Advertising Standards Authority for promoting racial hatred.

In general, Britain is a fair and tolerant place – remarkably so if you recall the vicious racial divisions in America or the rise of racist political parties in mainland Europe. Not only has this fact been all but obscured, but racism itself has been redefined by American-inspired political correctness. This holds that racism is not just prejudice, but prejudice plus power. By this definition, only white people can be racist. This is not only untrue but is the kind of lie that stirs up racial hatred. It was one of the many dangerous fallacies exposed in a devastating critique of the CRE by Blondel Cluff, one of its former comissioners.

Cluff, who was backed by at least one other commissioner, revealed what has long been the CRE's unspoken secret: the destructive dislike that divides its Asian and Afro-Caribbean commissioners.

She accused the commission of perpetuating its own existence rather than doing anything useful. She also questioned its active promotion of court cases, a 'dangerous approach' which failed to take into account the 'harmonious relationship' between different ethnic groups and which introduced instead a 'litigious and aggressive attitude towards race relations'.

Everyone, black or white, is potentially prejudiced against people unlike themselves. It does not follow, however, that these prejudices become active. Prejudice tends to explode when a particular group feels its identity has become fragile or is threatened. People turn nasty, essentially, out of fear. Failing to recognize this fuels hatred and strife – which is what the CRE does. It pays scant attention, for example, to the way white working-class racial prejudice is fomented by the destruction of collective pride. This in turn is often caused by a combination of multicultural education and the wipe-out of local industries, with unemployed young men following their fathers and grandfathers onto the scrap-heap.

The outcome, as a remarkable report by Greenwich council revealed two years ago in the wake of the murders of Stephen Lawrence and other local black students, is white youths for whom 'the celebration of cultural variety' seems to include all cultures but their own.

Political correctness takes a palpable wrong such as racism and uses it as a stick to beat liberal culture. This is what happened in social work, where training manuals in the early 1990s required the teaching of propaganda that every British institution was racist, sexist, ageist and all the rest of it. There was no room in this illiberal analysis for white individuals to be innocent of racist behaviour. This attitude still prevails in the public and voluntary sectors. And it results in no more than counter-productive gesture politics.

The only way to tackle racial prejudice is to recognize the realities of human nature. Thus, instead of being subjected to multicultural propaganda in the classroom, neo-Nazi thugs should be thrown out of the public housing from where they terrorize black families.

**Equal Opportunities
Commission**
An independent body
charged with
monitoring employment
and discrimination in
the job market.

The way to tackle racism among police officers is not to browbeat them with
the awfulness of racism or toss them a few facts about other cultures. It is
surely to recognize that the kind of people who join the police will always
have prejudices which need to be actively managed, controlled and contained.

On a deeper level, racial prejudice cannot be damped down unless people are
secure both in their attachments to their own tribal traditions and to a common
culture which they share with everyone else. That is also the only way to
achieve equality for minorities. It is possible and desirable to be attached to
both an ethnic and a common, or majority, culture. Yet the latter is derided
as racist.

Black people rightly perceive that the schools have failed them – but many
get the reason wrong. Multicultural education is, after all, the norm among
teachers. Many history teachers think teaching British history to black children is racist. Yet it is such teachers who are racist by excluding these children
from the culture to which they are entitled to belong.

Like the **Equal Opportunities Commission** (EOC), the CRE is an architect of
the grievance culture which produces racial strife. These commissions bathe
society in a glow of virtue about their commitment to equality, yet they have
made few things better and have made some things worse. Prominent among
their originators were lawyers committed to the codification of human rights.
This idea is embedded in the constitution of America and most European countries – yet it has not made these nations conspicuous for their racial harmony.

Local initiatives, where people talk to each other and find common cause
rather than the nearest lawyer, are much more effective. It is time to shut
down both the CRE and the EOC and move on.

■　■　■

Moral concern

The above images of drug abuse, teenage pregnancies, crime, racism and changing
social attitudes suggest for many concerned commentators that Britain is in
moral decay and fearful. Some, as in the next text, argue that this is due to moral
relativity and a lack of firm or accepted standards. Yet it is difficult to assess just
how widespread and representative this alleged social and moral deterioration actually is.

6 'Our moral wasteland. In a Britain ruled by evasion and cynicism, few dare to speak of right and wrong'[9]

David Selbourne
(Author copyright, 30 December 1998)

It is often argued that there is 'no new thing under the sun', as **Ecclesiastes** puts it. But where, until now, has there been anything like the observation in *The Guardian* by a spokesman for Castle Morpeth council that **residents of private care homes** are 'income-producing raw material' and the dead represent 'the waste produced by the business'?

Is it a new moral thing, or an old, that a lesbian couple practising self-insemination should, before breaking up their partnership, have had two **DIY** babies using a pickle jar and syringe? Or that another similar couple should purchase the frozen sperm of a stranger via the Internet?

And when, until now, would a distinguished surgeon, describing 'the prospect of taking a dead person's face and draping it over the skull of a living man or woman', declare, as *The Times* reported, that 'it is simply like changing the cloth of an armchair'?

Is it an old moral thing, or a new moral thing, that there is now an arson attack in at least three schools every day? Or that one in three churches can expect to be the target of an attack of some kind – theft, vandalism, arson – each year? Or that malicious vandalism is now the biggest cause of railway accidents? Or that 86 per cent of alarm calls in the Metropolitan Police [London] area are shown to be false? Or that trees and shrubs planted in memory of the **Dunblane victims** were stolen within days from the local cemetery?

Has there ever before been such violence directed in a time of peace by youth against the frailest and most elderly, so that even women in their eighties come to be raped? Is it an old thing under the sun, or a new, that doctors – it is estimated that 1,000 of them are assaulted each year – teachers and priests should feel themselves at risk from those for whom they care? When, before, could nursing be regarded as Britain's 'most dangerous profession' with one nurse in three, compared with one policeman in four, suffering an act of violence in accident and emergency units?

The temptation to retreat into the safety of unknowing denial and disbelief is strong. Yet into this moral quagmire the Office for National Statistics and

Ecclesiastes
Philosophical biblical work in the Old Testament traditionally attributed to Solomon.

The Guardian
British left-of-centre daily quality newspaper.

residents of private care homes
Usually elderly people and pensioners.

DIY
Do-It-Yourself.

The Times
British independent daily quality newspaper.

Dunblane victims
Schoolchildren who were shot dead at their school in Dunblane, Scotland, in March 1996.

nuclear families
Married mother and
father with children
living together.

stepfamilies
Subsequent marriages
after divorce.

hubris
The ancient Greek flaw
of pride, leading to
disaster and tragedy.

Ark
Noah's Ark, therefore
ancient.

other bodies continue to pour their data on the composition of households, population changes, marriage and divorce rates, drug abuse and much else.

As early as the year 2000, **nuclear families** could be outnumbered by **step-families**. By the year 2020, with present trends, one in three people in Britain will be living alone and most women will be single, only 48 per cent of them being wives as such. Married couples will be a minority.

In this whirlpool, the intensifying corruption of our sensibilities, the **hubris** of technological experiments with the human body, the genetic abuse of the natural order, the disrespect for the carer, the aggression of the impatient, the self-harming of the young, and the accelerating fragmentation and dissolution of the old familial bond are all ethically conjoined. They are, in combination, lethal in their effects, each element intricately, and sometimes causally, linked to another.

And yet there are, everywhere, evasions. These seek to show, and have us believe, that nothing can any longer be done about our moral condition, or that nothing *needs* to be done about it, since there is nothing much at fault with it in the first place. The cynicism and amorality with which some address our moral and social confusions are a further cause of our ills.

'The moral issue is dead,' declares Hugo Young in *The Guardian*. 'The family has had it,' says Sara Maitland, again in *The Guardian*, seeming to gloat over its 'terminal sickness'. 'When politicians talk about strengthening the family, liberals reach for their revolvers,' says Polly Toynbee, also in *The Guardian*. 'Families are by their nature Darwinian units,' argues Simon Jenkins, demeaningly, in *The Times*.

And marriage? The cynic and the amoralist are hard at work on it, once more with women to the fore. Here is Tania Kindersley in *The Times*: 'Nobody seems able to tell me why we're still doing it . . . Surely we have the imagination to come up with something better . . . than an institution that came in with the **Ark**?'

This is a mere glimpse into a small part of the moral wasteland being made for us – or, it seems, being in some cases sedulously striven for – by our fellows, and to which the media give an ever enlarging and unwarranted space.

It is a cynicism which saps commitment by attrition, amorally rearing its head in every field of debate. Are you concerned, for example about the increasing incidence of violence reported to be committed by young girls? You may well be. But replies a 'professor of gender relations' in *The Times*, 'Young women are much more positive about themselves and are likely to be more assertive

... If women are becoming more active in society, their behaviour is more likely to be like men's.' And, says a woman academic researcher in *The Guardian*: 'If, to prove their equality, they have to punch someone, then so be it.'

We are continually being given sight of a cynicism which dwells in moral darkness, and deepens it. The common link with all these commentators is that an important ethical issue generally lies latent within their arguments, and that, seemingly in consequence, a destructive urge is aroused to desecrate a moral truth or civic principle.

'The first thing you notice, as you plead to get out of **jury service**,' noted Catherine Bennett in *The Guardian*, 'is how many others are doing the same thing.' This is to dump ordure on a civic duty.

There is no shame shown in this denial, or amoral rubbishing, of belief and value. Its reach is now far and wide, even getting at the very core and crux of the idea of principle itself. Consider John Lloyd in *The Times*: 'If one does not stand for policies in the old sense ... then you are free and can set others free ... in these merry, piping times of peace, a Prime Minister (Blair) who stands for nothing is the best leader to have ... for that is the way the times must move and "isms" would stop it.'

You would be wrong to look for irony in this last sentiment, as for principle. It is a nadir of its kind. It emanates from a moral wasteland made bleaker by the evasion of moral responsibility and engagement.

There are many types of such evasion, but 11 arguments recur when a moral problem confronts us. There is the notion that 'there is nothing you can do about it, or not much'; the idea that 'it has never been any different'; the proposition that 'there is no quick fix' for a given ethical dilemma; the excuse that 'this is the price of a free society'; the call that 'everything is changing and you must move with the tide'; the cliché that 'it is no use turning the clock back'; the insistence that a problem is 'much more complex than you think'; the alibi that a problem is 'beyond the reach of law'; the smear that 'you are focusing on the wrong issue'; the defence that '**people in glass houses shouldn't. . .**' and the base evasion that, since 'everyone does it', how can you object?

The cumulative effect of these evasions is often to paralyse debate itself. And when all other argument fails, the objector is dismissed as a 'moral crusader'; a 'puritan' or – the old standby – 'right-wing'. One ends with a situation in which even a church leader, the Bishop of Edinburgh, can pronounce 'moralising' to be 'one of the least attractive of human characteristics'.

jury service
The citizen's duty, when selected, to serve on a criminal jury in the Crown Court.

people in glass houses shouldn't . . .
'throw stones'.

Evasion and falsehood are widely employed to give the slip to the idea that common moral rules can and should exist. There has not been, since the French Revolution, a greater concern for, and insistence upon, the promotion and expansion of individual rights in an already deeply free society. Yet this culture of rights coexists with a cynicism about the distinctions between right and wrong. There seems to be no doubt about the former and every doubt, assiduously promoted, about the latter. It is a drastic combination.

■ ■ ■

The Labour government's programme of modernization and social inclusion has also had to acknowledge that many British people are worried about what they perceive to be the moral decay of their society and are anxious for standards. The next text argues that politicians need to respond to voters' concerns, that standards still count in society and that an emphasis on rights also involves a consideration of responsibilities.

7 *'Teenage mums are all our business: government should not be indifferent'*
Tony Blair
(Author copyright, 8 September 1999)

A few days ago I said that the country needed a new sense of moral purpose for today's young generation. It came after publicity about two 12-year-old mothers. The reaction has been predictable. One part of the media says that it is all about '**back to basics**' and who sleeps with whom, desperate for a repeat performance of what they visited on John Major. From parts of the Left come cries of outrage about moral preaching.

Let us start from first principles. Does it matter that we have more teenage mothers than any other West European country – twice as high as Germany, three times as high as France and six times as high as The Netherlands? I say yes. Not just because 12 is too young to be a mother, but because the issue of teenage pregnancy is one part of a far bigger picture.

It's not simply that they become mothers too young. It is indicative of a way of life that harms them and their children. A significant minority of children, often in **sink estates**, grow up amid deep family instability, poor education, endemic crime, drug abuse and few decent job opportunities. They are the ones most likely to become the teenage mothers and fathers.

It is simply not acceptable for young children to be left without supervision, parental or otherwise, free to **truant**, vandalize and roam the streets at all hours. And it is morally wrong for us to stand aside and to be indifferent to it. Of course, the Government can't solve it all. But we have a role. The answer is neither the traditional right-wing cry of 'preach responsibility but leave them to it' nor the old left solution of 'keep silent but sign the cheques'.

Our ambition is to improve the quality of people's lives but to demand responsibility in return, whether from those who live on benefit, those running away from their duties to children or people who commit crimes.

None of this remotely means government controlling people's private lives or sexuality or turning the clock back to some Victorian moral order. Most people have no difficulty in distinguishing between trying to impose a moral code on an adult's private life and 12-year-old girls becoming pregnant, which is part of a much wider social problem.

That's why I set up the **Social Exclusion Unit** soon after taking office. It reported on teenage pregnancies months ago and its recommendations for better prevention and support, including a hard-edged national campaign to change teenage behaviour, are now being implemented.

The unit has also reported on **school exclusions**, sink estates and **rough sleeping**. Truancy is an issue for schools and parents: hence our new targets and funding to reduce truancy and school exclusions – now falling for the first time in years – but also the new home–school agreements to secure proper parental support for teachers. We have also been unashamed about encouraging parents to read to their young children and later to oversee homework, as part of our drive to raise standards, and the signs are that this is having a positive impact.

Education is our number one priority because nothing does more to reduce exclusion than confidence and achievement at school. But schools are not value-free zones. They are an integral part of society and shape its character. That is why the **curriculum** reforms to be announced tomorrow emphasize personal, social and health education, including the importance of marriage;[10] and why citizenship education is to be given a firm place in the curriculum. Surveys indicate that these reforms have overwhelming support among teachers and parents.

Our dual approach – opportunity for all, responsibility from all – is equally strong in work and welfare. Life on benefit is not an option. The **working**

truant
Repeatedly fail to attend school.

Social Exclusion Unit
A body set up to examine why some groups in society are excluded from the general society.

school exclusions
Expulsion from school because of bad behaviour.

rough sleeping
The homeless.

curriculum
The national curriculum.

working families' tax credit
An attempt to get people off benefits and into work. Rather than losing money by leaving benefits and entering low-paid work, the government guarantees an income of £200 per week.

families' tax credit, which I launched with **Gordon Brown** yesterday, makes work pay as never before. No longer can the prospect of a better life on benefit dissuade people from taking up jobs to support themselves and their families. About 1.5 million families, mainly low-paid but in some cases with incomes up to £30,000 a year, will be on average £24 a week better off through the credit. Every parent with children to support will be guaranteed a minimum income of £200 a week in full-time work. The ethic of work is vital to a modern Britain of rights and responsibilities.

As for antisocial behaviour, we will not hesitate to bring home to young people and their parents both their duties and the consequences of ignoring them, and we look to local authorities and other local agencies to play their part. All my adult life in politics I have fought against the battle between out-of-date right and left ideologies. On this issue, both end up in much the same place: social indifference. The Right says that society doesn't matter; the old Left says we have no right to interfere: it matters only what society can do for you, rather than the responsibilities we each have for ourselves and our dependants. The result, for a minority, is exclusion – from opportunity, from prospects, from achievement. It is a waste and morally wrong.

I've been reminded in recent days of some of the reaction when, in Opposition, I shifted Labour's emphasis on crime to take greater account of the victim as well as the social causes. I was told that we were deserting our principles; but public support was overwhelming, not least on the **estates.** I believe now that it is the decent majority, who play by the rules, who want us to take a lead in defining a new moral purpose. We were elected to start putting Britain right, and we will not be deflected.

■ ■ ■

Religious behaviour

The above text does not define in detail (beyond some political action) what is meant by 'a new moral purpose'. It is therefore legitimate to question whether traditional religion and its moral concerns any longer have a part to play in Britain. There is conflicting evidence about the level of religious values and observation. Formal attendance is falling for some faiths but there is growth in other areas. Public opinion polls also consistently show that there is a moral or religious sense among British people (such as belief in God, heaven and a soul), which is manifested in their personal lives, but outside organized or institutional religion. The next text examines the condition of one of the largest churches, the established Church of England, and compares it with Catholicism and Islam.

8 'O go all ye faithful'
Rebecca Fowler
(*The Sunday Times*, 5 December 1993) abridged

'Where is God?' read the brightly coloured children's painting, facing the congregation of St Peter's, **Ealing**, as members trickled in through the brittle autumn sunshine. They arrived to the ringing of a single bell shortly before 10am, convinced that if the Creator is anywhere, it is here, at the heart of the Church of England.

An amplified piano rang out, and the worshippers burst into a warbling rendition of Sing Hosannah at breakneck speed. The building was almost full, members varying from the youngest babies to the elderly, and the scene conjured up almost forgotten images of faithful Britain.

This is the established church of the land, open for business in the 1990s, bringing God to the people. As the fanfare of trumpets subsided and two clowns arrived to give a children's sermon to the younger members of the congregation, it seemed dramatically removed from the dismal shadow hanging over Anglicanism.

Yet St Peter's is also part of a church which, at national level, is perceived to be embroiled in the biggest crisis in its history. Not since Henry VIII broke the country's papal ties 450 years ago has the church been riddled with so many doctrinal disputes, from the debates over women priests and homosexuality to the wording of its liturgies, and most recently claims at government level that it has failed in its primary purpose, by not giving the nation the moral guidance it is starving for.[11]

These conflicts have led to a mood of 'absolute desperation', according to the most disenchanted insiders. They see a church of discontent, schism and bitterness, confronting the potential exodus of hundreds of members to the Roman Catholic faith when women are ordained for the first time in March [1994]. 'All the dreams I had for the Church of England have gone, and it is quite terrible,' says the Rev John Broadhurst, chairman of Forward in Faith, the body opposed to women priests.

'It is not just one issue any more. Once I would have said the church's two greatest assets were its great clergy and its financial strength, but the clergy have lost their nerve, because of this desperate mood, and the accounts are in a mess.'[12]

Ealing
West London.

The ordination of women has ripped open the church and exposed all the other layers of internal discord . . .

. . . And . . . the number of regular worshippers has dropped to 2.4 per cent of the population, with only 1,137,000 people regularly attending services.[13]

On the ground, vicars such as the Rev William Taylor, at St Peter's, believe the church has as much to offer the nation as it always had. 'The church as I know it is thriving,' he says. 'There is nothing anachronistic about it. We are not avoiding the issues, we're not retreating into a private world of piety. We are very much a serious contribution to society.'

Although the church's annual statistics, published last week, show that the attendance figures appear to have stabilised,[14] it is still a fact that they are at the lowest in the church's history . . . [T]he question hanging over it is not so much 'Where is God?', but 'Where is the Church of England and where is it going?' . . .

'There was a time when the bishop could make a pronouncement on anything and it would be news,' says the Rt Rev Peter Dawes, Bishop of Derby. 'But, at the same time, people are still searching, worrying about the world and looking for answers to questions which the church is addressing.'

If Britain is unchurched, there is no doubt that it is certainly not ungodly. Nearly 79 per cent claim a belief in God. So why has the church failed to galvanise the spiritual vivacity of the nation?

'What concerns me is that every time there is a comment in support of the Church of England, it is not heard,' says Peter Bottomley, the Tory MP and a committed Anglican . . .

Undoubtedly Anglicanism has been relentlessly exposed as a ramshackle mess. The intricacies of its theological debates seem increasingly remote from everyday Britain, and, in the context of the enormous problems it is facing, appear on occasions similar to arranging deckchairs on the Titanic . . .

In the meantime, the Roman Catholic Church [demonstrates] a moral conviction, however controversial, in the form of an encyclical earlier this year that was clearly the papal A–Z of rights and wrongs, just at the time when Anglicanism seemed incapable of offering a committed moral position on anything . . .

'There is no doubt Catholicism is moving towards the centre stage in this country again,' says the Rev Broadhurst. There are currently more church-going Catholics than church-going Anglicans in Britain. The only other contender to match Catholicism worldwide is Islam, with each faith having about 1 billion adherents, compared to 70m in the Anglican community . . .

Yet as the liberal bishops clamour to win back the church's street credibility, moving with the times, the traditionalists insist it must hold on to the values that it has been accused of losing. 'Perhaps the church has let the people eat cake instead of bread too long,' says the Rt Rev Noel Jones, Bishop of **Sodor and Man**. 'Of course we must have a firm line and strict teaching, and there are fundamental Christian truths that should not be played around with.'

But how can the church win? A return to something more akin to Victorian morality will alienate the vast majority of the people. At the same time it needs a religious package that is convincing and does not compromise the faith. The Rt Rev David Hope, Bishop of London, one of the dioceses most deeply divided over women priests, says: 'I do come back ultimately to the fact that we must not lose sight of the purpose of the church, its mission to bring the Gospels to bear on people's lives. There must be a recovery of that vision at the end of the day, otherwise we're lost.'

If it is going to come from anywhere, it must be **Lambeth Palace**, where the head of the church presides [George Carey, 103rd Archbishop of Canterbury and primate of all England] . . .

But none of his predecessors can have received more criticism in the course of their reigns from within and outside the church, and none can have overseen the church at a more difficult period in its history. If he succeeds in pulling the church out of its trough, say even his most outspoken critics, he will have proved that miracles can happen.

Meanwhile, the people of St Peter's hold on to the belief that the church is not the grey men in suits at Whitehall and Lambeth, but the congregations in the parishes. They must be a symbol of hope . . .

■ ■ ■

At a time when the Church of England appears to be languishing (and attracting only 25 per cent of those people identifying themselves as belonging to a particular denomination), evangelical Christianity and other faiths have shown their vitality, to which individuals have responded out of personal needs, as in the next text.

Sodor and Man
Isle of Man.

Lambeth Palace
London headquarters of the Archbishop of Canterbury.

9 *'All God's children'*
Rebecca Fowler
(*The Sunday Times*, 7 November 1993) abridged

Every morning, Rupert Fisher climbs out of his bed in Fulham, west London, at 7am for the first prayers of the day. They might be for a friend who is ill, or someone who is unhappy in their job, or perhaps a general plea for peace in Bosnia, but whoever they are for, they are passionately felt.

Ten months ago, the 22-year-old estate agent found God. Before images of sandals, nylon shirts and heavy spectacles come to mind, think again. Fisher is part of the growing ranks of the young 1990s God-squad – a trendy, street-wise, successful individual who is turning to religion.

Ever since the 1950s, the main faiths in Britain, such as Christianity and Judaism, have lamented their gradually declining numbers.

Last week, a survey by the Christian Research Association (CRA) suggested that 1,500 people were falling away from Christian churches – including 600 from the Church of England, the established faith of the land – each week. Although Anglicans are already questioning the figures, there is no doubt that mainstream congregations have dwindled. Most worryingly for church leaders, it is estimated that more than half of last year's 6.7m churchgoers will have died by 2005.

Within the Jewish faith, the numbers of orthodox members, the majority, have dropped from nearly 500,000 at the end of the second world war to 300,000.

And yet, every weekend and many weekday evenings, Christian evangelical services, across the board from C of E to Methodism, are packed with congregations of which half the members are under 30. Around 120 new recruits join this wing of Christianity each week, according to the most recent English Church census. Local 'raves in the nave' – church-held discos as lively as any in private clubs – [are] thriving . . .

As for Islam, its youth groups are also growing across the country – Manchester, Bradford, Rochdale, Crawley and parts of London have seen particularly vigorous attendance.

Within Judaism, there is a boom in temples of learning – where youngsters study, outside school or college, the rules and language of their faith. 'Young people are definitely coming back. Probably fewer than those who are moving away,' admits Rabbi Shlomo Levin of the south Hampstead synagogue in London, a magnet for young people. 'But it is a hopeful sign.'

What the young believers seem to have in common is the zeal normally associated with the convert – it could, in some cases, loosely be termed fundamentalism, a strict adherence to the tenets of the faith. But what is less clear as yet, in these early stages of religious revival, is why.

While the acquisitiveness of the Me generation does not seem to have satisfied Thatcher's children, neither is conventional, mainstream religion always able to supply their need.

Instead, Britain's embryonic congregations of the future are seeking moral certainty and a faith that appears to offer 'value for money', with rules and guidelines that are a rebellion in their own right against the anything-goes legacy of their parents.

Rupert Fisher, like the majority of his fellow Christian returnees, has turned to evangelism. It is at once modern in its services, typified by tambourines, twanging guitars and one-line songs, and fundamentalist in its teaching, adherring to the word of the Bible in the most literal way . . .

The phenomenon is far from confined to Christianity. While Fisher is reaching for his Bible each morning, Raheed Mohmood, also 22, climbs out of his bed in Crawley, in Sussex, at sunrise and faces in the direction of Mecca for the first of five prayer sessions of the day. A photocopier engineer, he also rediscovered his faith earlier this year, after a period in the wilderness.

. . . But the questions began and the conversion came. 'I was aware of how many wars were going on, and how much of it seemed to be everyone teaming up against the Muslims, either in the Gulf or Bosnia,' he says.

For such young people, the tension between the secular world, which has brought liberalisation, and powerful religious backgrounds is not an easy one. Many, notably women, believe secularisation has brought freedom from the oppressions of strict faith. A large number still believe the challenge to their culture should allow them to maintain their religious identities while still enjoying the spoils of modern society.

For hundreds of other young Muslims, however, recent political events have driven them back to the faith without compromise. The Muslim community in Britain claims women are as enthusiastic as men. 'Girls of my daughter's generation, who are at London University with her, are proud to wear the veil,' claims Kalim Siddiqui . . .

**Salman Rushdie
issue**
Muslim communities in
Britain protested about
the publication in 1988
of Salman Rushdie's
novel *The Satanic
Verses*, which they
regarded as
blasphemous.

It is these politics of Islam that have provided the biggest incentive to such returnees, according to Jamil Mohammad, currently studying the Muslim community for his doctorate at Salford University. 'Young people, 16 to 25, are into Islamic politics – the **Salman Rushdie issue** and the Iran–Iraq war help them focus on themselves even more. The extended Muslim family helps, too. Even parents who have become less devout themselves do everything to encourage their children when they show an interest in the faith.'

Despite more conservative figures from government sources, he claims there are currently 2.2m Muslims under the age of 20 who are potential soldiers for the growing army of zealous worshippers . . .

Observers of this across-the-faiths revival sceptically refer to the F-word (for fundamentalism). The mainstream Student Christian Movement, for example, has prepared a guide to its seductive quality in a new pamphlet to be published later this month. It claims that, for potential young Christians, the attraction of a belief structure that offers absolute certainty can be misleading, and in some cases even dangerous.

But many church leaders are not surprised by the enthusiasm with which youth is rediscovering its religious heritage. Many young believers, after all, had experienced the residual faith of their parents, whether it involved a visit to church at Christmas, or a trip to the mosque for Eid-ul-Adha, a key date in the Islamic calendar, or for young Jews perhaps a few hours in the synagogue for a wedding.

One of those contemplating a return to religion on a more serious level – maybe attending synagogue more regularly, studying his faith more deeply – is Neil Blair, 27, a lawyer and orthodox Jew who lives in north London. 'We're becoming much more pious than our grandfathers were,' he says. 'It's partly to do with the void left by our parents' generation, the liberalism of the 1960s and 1970s and to some extent the affluence of the 1980s, and part of it is to do with the fact that it's become acceptable, even trendy, to belong to something ethnic.

'Israel gives a focus to that, so lots more people are going there to visit, and its image has also become much better in recent years. But overall we are looking for more stability.' The south Hampstead synagogue which he attends is filled with about 500 families, of whom one third are young people. They have become a symbol of this rediscovery of roots, which previous generations had allowed to dwindle . . .

If that means that some will be overcome with piety for a few years, it is a situation that is far easier to rectify than one where there is no faith at all, says Rabbi Shlomo Levin . . .

■ ■ ■

Exercises

Write short essays on the following topics

1 Should drugs, particularly 'soft' drugs, be decriminalized?

2 Does sex education in schools work?

3 Examine the tone and content of Tony Blair's article (text 7). Should morality be a concern for government?

4 Should religious belief be gauged only by institutional observance?

5 Do you consider Britain to be a racist country? If so, how best can racism be combated?

Explain and examine the following terms

'drugs czar'	CCTV	community policing
shaming system	demography	gated communities
inclusiveness	lobby	cohabitation
solicitors	barristers	national curriculum
CRE	ethnic quotas	ethnic minorities
underclass	civil servants	institutional racism
non-traditional families	multiracial education	
political correctness	Metropolitan Police	
grievance culture	Darwinian units	

Further reading

Abrams, Mark, Gerard, David and Timms, Noel (1985) *Values and Social Change in Britain*, London: Macmillan.

Alderman, Geoffrey (1998) *Modern British Jewry*, Oxford: Clarendon Press.

Blackstone, Tessa *et al.* (ed.) (1998) *Race Relations in Britain: A Developing Agenda*, London: Routledge.

Bruce, Steve (1995) *Religion in Modern Britain*, Oxford: Oxford University Press.

Jowell, Roger, Brook, Lindsay and Prior, Gillian (1991) *British Social Attitudes Cumulative Sourcebook*, Aldershot: Gower.

Jowell, Roger, Curtice, John, Park, Alison, Brook, Lindsay and Ahrendt, Daphne (eds) (1995) *British Social Attitudes: The 12th Report*, Aldershot: Dartmouth.

Jowell, Roger, Curtice, John, Park, Alison, Brook, Lindsay and Thomson, Katrina (eds) (1996) *British Social Attitudes: The 13th Report*, Aldershot: Dartmouth.

Phillips, Mike and Philipps, Trevor (1999) *Windrush: The Irresistible Rise of Multi-racial Britain*, London: HarperCollins.

 Notes

1. Ian Murray (1999) 'A nation of prudes blamed for teenage pregnancy boom' London: *The Times* 8 February.
2. See note 1.
3. A European Commission report in 2000, *The State of Young People's Health*, reported that drug misuse among teenagers is worse in England and Wales than anywhere else in the EU. Cannabis, LSD, solvents, amphetamines and ecstacy were the most frequently used drugs. (2000) 'England's teenagers lead in drug abuse' London: *The Times* 21 March.
4. Official figures in 2000 showed that there had been a significant increase in the incidence of violent crime.
5. (1996) 'Options for Britain', Oxford: Economic and Social Research Council and Nuffield College.
6. Alexandra Frean (1999) 'More are choosing not to marry' London: *The Times* 9 January.
7. In fact, the Labour government is considering the abolition of the rule (2000) in cases where there is substantial new evidence to justify a second trial on the same charge.
8. Leader (1999) 'Race in the classroom. The right way to advance tolerance after Lawrence' London: *The Times* 26 February.
9. Edited extract from David Selbourne (1998) *Moral Evasion* London: Centre for Policy Studies 30 December.
10. See text 3. The government was forced to emphasize marriage after earlier complaints about its downgrading in schools.
11. The Church of England is still (2000) embroiled in these controversial debates.
12. The accounts of the church have now improved, but there are still many demands upon its assets and finances.
13. Sunday attendance in the Church of England has now fallen (2000) to its lowest-ever levels with only some 800,000 attending services according to *Church Statistics*.
14. See note 13.

Index

public opinion 1, 2–3, 54–7, 84–7,
   143, 147, 149, 155, 158, 164–5,
   166–7, 184–5, 193, 197, 199
public services 3, 111, 115, 185, 202
public spending 3, 6, 8, 9, 17, 25,
   111, 115, 138, 185, 188, 197

race/race relations 23–4, 31–2, 82,
   226–36
recession (economic) 3, 8, 11
referendums 126, 128, 138, 152, 165
regional assemblies 123, 127, 130,
   136, 137–8, 151
religion 39, 242–8

Scots (the)/Scotland 61–3, 65, 66, 68,
   69–73, 78–82, 83, 85, 86, 87,
   120, 127, 128, 129, 130, 131–3,
   134
Scottish Nationalists 62, 71–2, 79
service industry 8, 32
social behaviour 216–50
social change 1–2, 13, 15, 26–7, 29,
   30, 31, 34, 40–7, 51–3, 53–4,
   55–7, 103, 104, 124, 223–4, 236
social institutions 184–215
social mobility 24
social security 25, 184, 185, 186,
   188–90
sovereignty 5, 96, 106, 120, 122, 135,
   146, 147, 161
spin doctor 18, 43, 200–1
state (the) 25–7, 115, 126, 149
statutes 120

teenage pregnancies 217
Thatcher (Margaret)/Thatcherism 3,
   4, 6, 9, 16–18, 23, 30–1, 52,
   92, 93, 94, 102, 115, 157, 168,
   169
third way (the) 91, 92, 93, 94, 95–9,
   114, 155, 157
trade unions 3, 6, 168
Treasury (the) 16, 17, 18, 176

underclass 32
unemployment 9, 186, 187, 188, 190,
   191, 205
Union (the)/Unionists 63, 75, 77, 79,
   80, 83, 102, 120, 129, 130,
   131–3
United Kingdom (UK) 69, 78, 79, 87,
   120, 129, 131, 134–6, 148

Victorian values 4

welfare state (the) 7, 13, 17, 25, 26,
   50, 96, 106, 116, 184, 185–7,
   241–2
Welsh (the)/Wales 61–3, 65, 66, 67–8,
   73, 82, 85, 86, 87, 120, 128, 130,
   134
Westminster 10, 126, 127, 130, 131,
   134–6, 137–8, 142, 153, 155
Whitehall 10, 16, 17, 137–8
world role (Britain) 4–9, 64, 154–83
written constitution 18, 121, 151

yobs (hooligans) 35–40, 48, 5